The Best
Baby Food

125 Healthy & Delicious Recipes for Babies & Toddlers

Jordan Wagman & Jill Hillhouse, BPHE, CNP

Robert
ROSE

Disclaimer
The recipes in this book have been carefully tested by our kitchen and our tasters. To the best of our knowledge,
they are safe and nutritious for ordinary use and users. For those people with food or other allergies, or who
have special food requirements or health issues, please read the suggested contents of each recipe carefully and
determine whether or not they may create a problem for you. All recipes are used at the risk of the consumer.

We cannot be responsible for any hazards, loss or damage that may occur as a result of any recipe use.

For those with special needs, allergies, requirements or health problems, in the event of any doubt, please
contact your medical adviser prior to the use of any recipe.

Design and Production: Joseph Gisini/PageWave Graphics Inc.
Editor: Judith Finlayson
Copy Editor: Tracy Bordian
Proofreader: Gillian Watts
Recipe Tester: Jennifer MacKenzie
Indexer: Gillian Watts

Cover: Roasted Summer Fruit (page 132), Carrot Purée (page 48) and Potato, Parsnip and Chicken Soup (page 110).

Photo Credits
Photos on pages 43, 103, 111, 133, 167 and 213
Photography: Colin Erricson
Food Styling: Kathryn Robertson
Prop Styling: Charlene Erricson

Other photos
Cover (baby) & page 1: © iStockphoto.com/chuckcollier; page 8: © iStockphoto.com/Kativ (top left),
© iStockphoto.com/DOUGBERRY (top right), © iStockphoto.com/LOVE_LIFE (bottom left),
© iStockphoto.com/THEPALMER (bottom right); page 18: © iStockphoto.com/ wikoski; page 28:
© iStockphoto.com/miskolin (top left), © iStockphoto.com/Rinelle (top right), © iStockphoto.com/bluestocking
(bottom left), © iStockphoto.com/Dimitris66 (bottom right); page 32: © iStockphoto.com/MichaelSvoboda;
page 49: © iStockphoto.com/zia_shusha; page 59: © iStockphoto.com/ALEAIMAGE; page 64:
© iStockphoto.com/Jovanmandic; page 75: © iStockphoto.com/JMichl; page 85: © iStockphoto.com/peangdao;
page 86: © iStockphoto.com/idal; page 92: © iStockphoto.com/MarcoGovel; page 113: © iStockphoto.com/
Teleginatania; page 117: © iStockphoto.com/L_Shtandel; page 124: © iStockphoto.com/blusezhou; page 137:
© iStockphoto.com/PLBernier; page 144: © iStockphoto.com/cronopios; page 155: © iStockphoto.com/
xavierarnau; page 176: © Masterfile; page 188: © iStockphoto.com/Lizalica; page 195: © iStockphoto.com/
robynmac; page 203: © iStockphoto.com/GMVozd; page 207: © iStockphoto.com/EasyBuy4u.

The publisher gratefully acknowledges the financial support of our publishing program by the Government
of Canada through the Canada Book Fund.

Published by Robert Rose Inc.
120 Eglinton Avenue East, Suite 800, Toronto, Ontario, Canada M4P 1E2
Tel: (416) 322-6552 Fax: (416) 322-6936
www.robertrose.ca

Printed and bound in Canada

1 2 3 4 5 6 7 8 9 TCP 23 22 21 20 19 18 17 16 15

Contents

From the Chef 4

From the Nutritionist 6

The Best Food for Babies 9

Preparing Your Own Baby Food 29

Starting Solids (6 to 9 Months) 33

Establishing Preferences (9 to 12 Months) 87

Food for Toddlers (12 Months +) 125

Snacks and Desserts 177

Acknowledgments 215

Nutrient Analysis 215

Index 217

From the Chef

As the only chef in my extended family, I have learned to expect two things. The first is for friends and family to casually drop by right around dinnertime: "Hey, Jord, just came over to drop off— *Ooo*, what's for dinner?" (My family is great, but they're hardly subtle.) The second is recipe requests. Weeks or months after enjoying a particular meal, guests will inevitably ask me how to make it.

It's not as hard as it may seem to make great gourmet-inspired food for your family. In fact, I can tell you how to do it in three words: Ingredients. Ingredients. Ingredients.

It may not be breaking news, but it happens to be true. Most chefs will tell you that in order to cook great food you need to start with the best ingredients, locally grown whenever possible, and manipulate them as little as it takes. Great ingredients make the best meals.

This philosophy is one I've always abided by, not only in professional kitchens but also as "Chef Dad." Kids have educated palates, and they can be notoriously harsh critics. If adults can tell the difference between a tomato picked fresh from the vine and a tomato grown in South America and allowed to ripen en route to North America, we should assume our children can, too. So in developing the recipes for this book, I chose two very important coauthors: my 10-year-old son and executive-chef-in-training, Jonah, and my 6-year-old daughter and sous-chef-to-be, Jamie.

My approach to cooking for my children is to create meals based on the ingredients we have on hand, with a basic respect for seasonality and a few simple cooking methods. Another approach that has served me well is one my wife, who has no professional training, taught me: to vary the meals we make. Unlike my mother (no offense, Mom), Tamar doesn't serve the same dish over and over again. Most people get used to making the same five or six things and never stray too far away from them. This book will help you to break those habits. You'll see possibilities where you used to see, well, a banana.

Tamar also taught me about "changing it up." By that I mean varying the cooking methods for the same ingredients to achieve a different flavor profile. For instance, if your child doesn't like steamed sweet potato, why serve it? Instead, try roasting sweet potato, which develops the sugars. Have you ever grilled a peach or roasted a banana? It creates very different flavors.

It's amazing what happens to fruits and vegetables when they are exposed to dry heat. By roasting, you can transform an acorn squash into a piece of candy and watch your kids beg for more. You read that right: my son begs us for more acorn squash. A vegetable. And why? Because we change the cooking methods to trick our children into thinking it's a different food when, all along, it's the same vegetable they didn't enjoy steamed. We try different things.

When Jonah turned 7 months old, we were so excited because we could introduce him to new foods. We began with basic purées and progressed quickly to puréed chicken and beef recipes. It didn't take long to notice that if Jonah didn't like an ingredient (peeled and steamed butternut squash comes to mind), he would refuse to eat it. But if we changed up the cooking method (steamed versus roasted) just a little — for example, if we roasted the squash whole with the skin on — he would love it. The reason was obvious: sugar! So many of the fruits and vegetables we eat are full of healthy, natural sugars, and a smart parent will take full advantage of this asset. In this book, I'll help you understand the benefits of using alternative cooking methods with several different ingredients (in some instances I've duplicated recipes and changed only the method of cooking).

After trying a few recipes in this book, I think you'll find the following: (1) you'll be able to create great-tasting, nutritious meals for your children and yourself with only a little bit of work; and (2) you'll have learned a few simple techniques that will help you to create a variety of delicious flavors and pleasing textures using very few ingredients. For example, who would have thought the combination of pork, fresh peaches and sweet onions would emulate the flavor of authentic Southern barbecue?

I have included a fairly wide range of recipes, from basic, single-ingredient dishes to those that are more advanced. Because we introduced our children to many foods from an early age, they have learned to appreciate a wide variety of flavors. This means that on a daily basis they consume a wide range of nutrients. When we're shopping for food, I'm always amazed at their requests — "that rack of lamb" from the butcher counter or "those ogre-anic grapes" in the organics section of the store. But that's the goal, isn't it? If you introduce your kids to a variety of nutritionally balanced, good-tasting meals when they are very young, they'll develop healthy eating habits that will serve them well for the rest of their lives. That's what this book is all about.

— Jordan Wagman

From the Nutritionist

As a nutritionist, I have a passion for food — both talking about it and eating it. I believe that a nutritious diet is our most valuable tool for promoting our families' health on a daily basis. Every time we feed our children we have an opportunity not only to nourish their bodies but also to expand their world.

I am thrilled to participate in this book. As a mother first and a nutritionist second, I completely understand the time pressures on family life and the draw of ready-made foods. However, I strongly believe that as a society our biggest problem from a nutritional perspective is our increasing reliance on refined and processed foods. For decades, these foods have been displacing fresh vegetables, fruits, whole grains, good fats and proteins in our diets. As rising rates of obesity and degenerative diseases such as type 2 diabetes suggest, we have embraced convenience at the expense of our health.

Our eating habits develop early in life. Preparing your own baby food from fresh, whole ingredients will help get your baby off to the best start possible, because you are shaping her tastes and preferences in a positive direction. By using a wide variety of foods you are doing more than expanding her palate and creating new experiences with food; you are also ensuring that her diet is nutritious and her health optimal. Because children's dietary preferences are set early in life, it's important to

predispose them to having a taste for whole, healthy food rather than a preference for salty or heavily sweetened processed food. When you make your own baby food, you know exactly what your baby is eating. The added value is you can shape her taste for the better by limiting ingredients that may have potentially negative effects over the long term. Moreover, an early diet based on nutritious whole foods will help develop a healthy eater, one with a broad palate who will enjoy a wide variety of foods, while ensuring that she obtains the full range of nutrients she needs for optimal development. The recipes in this book stress the importance of whole foods and fresh ingredients. They also use a variety of foods, because variety is the foundation of a balanced, healthy diet.

Babies are social creatures who enjoy and thrive on the company of others throughout the day, including mealtime. Like most of us, they enjoy eating with other people more than eating alone. A family meal is an opportunity for you as a parent to model healthy eating habits that your baby will absorb and emulate later on. The very act of sitting down and eating with your children may also encourage them to eat what is offered and, if they see you enjoying them, to try foods they haven't had before.

In this book I have highlighted some of the nutrition issues that are important for your baby. I have also included a nutrition tip with each recipe to help you understand the inherent value of whole foods and to provide you with more detailed information about how to use them in your day-to-day life. While each tip usually focuses on a particular aspect of one of the ingredients in the recipe, I hope you will use the information to expand your knowledge of nutrition. Share it with your baby (they are never too young to start learning!). Mostly I hope it helps you to appreciate that whole foods are meant to nourish us and be enjoyed.

Feeding a baby is a wonderful experience, although at times it can be frustrating. Try to relax and enjoy the process. Remember, when you make your own baby food from natural, wholesome ingredients, you are starting your child out on a pattern of healthy eating that will have lifelong benefits.

— Jill Hillhouse
B.P.H.E., C.N.P., R.N.T.
Registered Holistic Nutritionist

The Best Food for Babies

There is a saying that variety is the spice of life. This statement is certainly true in the field of nutrition. By feeding your baby a wide variety of foods you are providing her with an extensive range of vitamins, minerals, fats, proteins, carbohydrates and phytonutrients to fuel her incredible growth.

Varying what you feed your baby is important because there is a window of opportunity for introducing tastes and textures to infants before they reach the age of 12 months. During this first year, it takes an average of 6 to 10 exposures before most babies will accept a new flavor and/or texture. After 12 months, babies may become wary of new foods and become much more difficult to feed. That's why it is so important to give your baby different types of foods during the first 12 months of her life.

In this book we have used cooked, raw and frozen foods as well as herbs and spices. All are nutrient-dense (see right). In the recipes provided, we encourage you to experiment and offer your baby new tastes. Some may seem unusual in the traditional sense of baby food, but by encouraging your baby to expand her palate from an early age, you are setting the stage for a lifetime of healthy eating.

Why Make Your Own Baby Food?

For optimal growth and development, a baby's body needs a sufficient supply of fresh water, carbohydrates, fats and proteins as well as dozens of essential vitamins and minerals. In recent years we've learned more and more about certain compounds, called phytochemicals, in fruits, vegetables and whole grains that also have health-promoting properties. The best way to provide these nutrients for your child is to serve him a balanced and varied diet based on whole foods that are minimally processed. The best way to do that is by making your own baby food using the freshest, best-quality ingredients you can find.

Nutrient Density

The term "nutrient-dense" refers to the amount of nutrients in a food compared with the calories it contains (nutrients versus calories). Naturally nutrient-rich foods have high levels of nutrients — such as vitamins, minerals, proteins, healthy fats and fiber — compared with their calorie content. "Naturally" means the food is nutrient-rich as it is; nothing, such as fortification or enrichment, has been done to alter it. For example, 1 banana and 10 potato chips have about the same number of calories. However, the banana has twice the amount of vitamin C, twice as much magnesium, 4 times the fiber, more potassium and more calcium, as well as 10 times less fat and 140 times less sodium.

Naturally nutrient-rich foods include:
- colorful vegetables and fruit
- lentils and beans
- lean meat, poultry, seafood and eggs
- nuts and seeds
- whole grains
- organic dairy products, especially from pasture-raised animals

Pesticides Are More Toxic for Babies

Babies may be more susceptible to potential carcinogens from pesticides. In part this is due to the fact that from conception through the first three or so years of his life, a baby's cells are multiplying at their peak and his vital organs and nervous system are developing. However, the key organs that assist the body in chemical detoxification — the liver and kidneys — are still immature and less able to break down and metabolize harmful substances.

So, perhaps not surprisingly, in a risk assessment forum that took place in March 2005, the United States Environmental Protection Agency concluded that, on average, carcinogens are 10 times more potent for babies than for adults. In 2012, the American Academy of Pediatrics issued a report asserting that children have unique susceptibilities to the potential toxicity of pesticide residues. The report also stated that epidemiologic evidence demonstrates associations between early-life exposure to pesticides and pediatric cancers, decreased cognitive function, and behavioral problems.

Processed Baby Food Is Less Nutritious

When ingredients such as vegetables are processed, they may lose essential nutrients. In addition, many commercially prepared baby foods contain additives that can affect the nutrient content of the food. For instance, a 1995 report by the Center for Science in the Public Interest compared fresh apricots to jarred ones from a leading baby-food manufacturer. They knew that, according to the USDA Food Database, one 4-ounce serving of fresh apricots provides about 335 mg of potassium and 2860 IU of vitamin A. By contrast, they found that one 4-ounce serving of jarred apricots contained only 139 mg of potassium and 1333 IU of vitamin A — a considerable difference. (To prepare your baby a wholesome fresh apricot purée, see our recipe on page 39.)

A 2013 study from the department of human nutrition at the University of Glasgow, published in the journal *Archives of Disease in Childhood*, found that commercial baby foods designed to be "first foods" were "more energy-dense (high in calories) than formula milk and generally less nutrient-dense than homemade foods." This means that while the commercial baby foods had more calories than formula milk, they also had fewer nutrients. In other words, your baby would need a higher volume of food to obtain the same nutrients she had been receiving in formula milk. This scenario may set the stage for a lifetime habit of eating large amounts of nutrient-poor processed food.

Another concern is that thickening agents such as modified tapioca starch and wheat, corn and potato starches, as well as added sugars and water, greatly dilute the nutrient content of prepared baby foods, making them nutritionally inferior to those made entirely from whole foods. Some commercial baby foods even contain salt and high-fructose corn syrup, which can have negative effects later in life, such as an increased risk for heart disease and obesity. To top it off, prepared baby foods are also more expensive than those you make at home.

Organic Foods Are Preferable

Organic foods are defined as those produced without conventional pesticides, herbicides, antibiotics, growth hormones, irradiation or genetic or synthetic engineering. In recent years, sales of organic foods have increased dramatically. Although people consider eating organic foods for various reasons, many people who actually purchase organic foods do so with a view toward reducing their exposure to pesticides. This is especially true for parents making decisions about the first foods to feed a baby.

Feeding your baby organically grown produce makes sense. Babies and children may be more vulnerable to pesticide residues in food and drink because, among other factors, pound for pound they eat more than adults. Moreover, because a child's diet is less varied than that of a typical adult, if one of the foods in her relatively small repertoire is high in pesticide residue, the intake will be greater in relative terms.

Pesticides in Produce

Over the past two decades, the U.S. Department of Agriculture (USDA) Pesticide Data Program has analyzed pesticides in hundreds of thousands of food samples and has found residue from one or more pesticides in almost 80 percent of the conventional produce tested. More than 90 percent of conventionally grown strawberries, peaches, pears and apples have been shown to have pesticide residues. Perhaps surprisingly, some organically grown produce also contains residues (see right).

The good news is that although organic produce is not immune to pesticide residue, it appears in much smaller quantities. USDA testing done in 2004 showed that 16 percent of the organic samples tested contained pesticide residues — less than one-quarter the incidence in conventionally grown produce. Other studies conducted by the USDA's Pesticide Data Program indicate that when chemical pesticides are present on organic produce, the average levels are substantially lower than for the same pesticide on conventionally grown produce.

Unavoidable Pesticide Residue

There are a number of reasons why pesticide residue might be found in organically grown produce. For instance, when a field is sprayed with pesticides from an aircraft, not all of the pesticide makes it to the ground. The wind can carry the spray to organic farms that may be miles away. Despite the rigorous certification programs organic farms go through to remain chemical-free, the soil may contain residues of insecticides such as DDT that still persist in the environment even though they have been banned for many years. These are called persistent organic pollutants, or POPs, and they were banned when they were found to have a devastating effect on the health of wildlife and humans.

Eat More Fruits and Vegetables

Whichever way you determine is right for you, organic or conventional, be assured that, according to the U.S. National Cancer Institute, the risk of heart disease and many cancers is greatly reduced in people who eat more fruit and vegetables — with or without pesticides — than for those who eat less. So please don't avoid the produce section of your local grocery store because it doesn't sell organic fruits and vegetables.

To Buy or Not to Buy Organic Produce

In an effort to decrease pesticide exposure to your baby even more, we have expanded the EWG's "Dirty Dozen," its original list of the 12 fruits and vegetables containing the most pesticide residue unless organically grown, to the top 20 foods found to contain the most pesticide residue, as per its expanded guidelines. Use this list to prioritize your options when you're thinking about purchasing organic produce for you and your baby. You will probably want to buy organic versions of the top 20 but may find nonorganic versions of the "Clean Fifteen" acceptable.

How Prevalent Are Pesticides?

A 2014 report from the American Academy of Pediatrics encouraged parents to consult "reliable resources on the relative pesticide content of various fruits and vegetables." It cited the Environmental Working Group (EWG), a U.S. non-profit organization, as one key resource. The EWG translates the results of tests on thousands of samples by the United States Department of Agriculture (USDA) and the Food and Drug Administration (FDA) into understandable information.

The USDA's pesticide monitoring data from 2014 included hundreds of samples of applesauce, carrots, peaches and peas packaged as baby food. Three hundred and ninety-five samples of baby food applesauce were tested for five different pesticides. Ten percent of the samples contained acetamiprid, a pesticide that the European Union has singled out for additional testing because of potential toxicity to the developing nervous system in children. Additionally, the USDA found six pesticides in apple juice. About 14 percent of the same juice samples contained diphenylamine (DPA), a growth regulator banned in Europe in 2012.

Each year the EWG puts together a "Shopper's Guide to Pesticides in Produce." The 2014 guide draws from 32,000 samples tested and monitored by the USDA and FDA. Highlights from that testing show that every sample of imported nectarines and

99 percent of apple samples tested positive for at least one pesticide residue, and the average potato had more pesticides by weight than any other food. The EWG states that you can lower your pesticide exposure substantially by following the guidelines in their shopper's guide. Similarly, the EWG's "Clean Fifteen" is a list of fruits and vegetables you may not need to buy as organic because they have much lower levels of pesticide residues.

The Top 20 Offenders

The 20 fruits and vegetables containing the most pesticide residue, from most to least, are:

1. apples
2. strawberries
3. grapes
4. celery
5. peaches
6. spinach
7. sweet bell peppers
8. nectarines, imported
9. cucumbers
10. cherry tomatoes
11. snap peas, imported
12. potatoes
13. hot peppers
14. blueberries, domestic
15. lettuce
16. kale/collard greens
17. plums
18. cherries
19. nectarines, domestic
20. pears

The "Clean Fifteen"

The 15 least contaminated fruits and vegetables, from lowest to highest pesticide load, are:

1. avocado
2. sweet corn
3. pineapple
4. cabbage
5. sweet peas (frozen)
6. onions
7. asparagus
8. mango
9. papaya
10. kiwi
11. eggplant
12. grapefruit
13. cantaloupe, domestic
14. cauliflower
15. sweet potato

Organics Are Beneficial

In 2006, a research group at the University of Washington in Seattle conducted the first dietary intervention study to examine the level of toxins in conventionally grown and organic foods. Twenty-three school-aged children were tested for organophosphate (OP) insecticides before eating a diet of organic food, while they were on the organic diet, and again after returning to a diet of conventionally produced food. All the children tested positive for OP toxins in their urine when they were eating conventionally produced food, but within 5 days of eating the all-organic diet, their OP levels virtually disappeared.

Organic Produce Is More Nutritious

Some studies have focused on the nutrient content of organic versus conventionally grown produce. One of the longest-running is the Long-Term Research on Agricultural Systems Project (LTRAS) conducted at the University of California, Davis. In June 2007, the study team reported that over a 10-year period, the level of quercetin, a phytonutrient that appears to have many healthful benefits, had increased by 79 percent in tomatoes as a result of organic management of the land. During the study, the quercetin level of the organic tomatoes increased yearly. However, the largest increase came after the land had been organically managed for 7 years, suggesting that potential long-term nutritional benefits are linked with sustainable organic farming.

In 2012, research published in the journal *Food Chemistry* reported that organic raspberries grown on a Maryland farm that had been certified as organic by the USDA were significantly higher in total antioxidant capacity than non-organic raspberries. This greater capacity was associated with greater levels of total phenols and total anthocyanins.

Some studies into organics have found little to no nutrient difference between conventional and organic produce, leading some people to question the necessity of buying organic. What is missing from these discussions is the fact that some of the health benefits of organic are due to what is *not* in the food and that the health benefits are not necessarily related to getting more nutrients from your food, but rather about getting less toxins. As noted, infants are especially vulnerable to toxic compounds. It is vital that an infant's developing brain and nervous system receive only uncontaminated, nutrient-dense foods.

Meat, Poultry, Eggs and Dairy

When purchasing meat, poultry, eggs and dairy products, there are a number of things to think about, such as whether the animals have been fed antibiotics routinely, rather than just to treat disease, or if their feed contained pesticides. Most pesticides are fat-soluble, meaning they accumulate in the fat of the animals that eat food with pesticide residue and also at the top of the food chain, in the fat of the humans eating those animals. Therefore, meat, dairy and eggs from conventionally raised livestock contain concentrated amounts of pesticides from the feed they ate over their lifespan. When we eat these products, we ingest those residues.

Antibiotic Residues

Another concern is that large meat-producing farms that raise livestock conventionally are likely to use antibiotics subtherapeutically. This means they feed their animals antibiotics to prevent disease as well as to treat it, which is problematic. Through a chain of events, this practice can lead to the creation of drug-resistant bacteria, a serious emerging problem. Regulations put in place by the FDA, the USDA and the Canadian Food Inspection Agency now require conventional farmers to stop giving their animals antibiotics for a regulated period of time before their meat, milk or eggs, in the case of poultry, are brought to market. This "withdrawal time" is specific to the antibiotic given and is designed to reduce antibiotic residues that may be present.

Growth Hormone

In the United States there is also concern around genetically engineered recombinant bovine growth hormone (rBGH), which is injected into dairy cows to increase their milk production. Milk from these cows contains substantially more of a compound called insulin-like growth factor-1 (IGF-1), a naturally occurring hormone in both cows and humans. Elevated IGF-1 levels are a known risk factor for breast, colon and prostate cancers. Approximately 20 percent of all dairy cows in the United States are injected with this hormone, although its use is banned in Canada and Europe.

Understanding Labels

In the United States, the standard definition of "grass-fed" established by the USDA states that animals must have continuous access to pasture and prohibits them from being fed grain or grain-based products at any point in their lives. The label "grass-fed" does not have a formal government approval or definition in Canada. The term "free-range" is not legally defined in the United States or in Canada and may have many interpretations, so do your best to find out all you can about where your chicken and eggs come from.

The Best Food for Babies   **15**

Free-Range Poultry

"Free-range" refers to chickens that are allowed to wander freely outdoors where they can eat whatever weeds, seeds, insects and worms they choose. This means more nutritious eggs and meat, specifically with respect to the amount of health-promoting omega-3 fats. Research conducted in 2012 at the University of Perugia in Italy shows that organically raised chickens have higher omega-3 content in their meat than conventionally raised chickens. However, when organic chickens are allowed a large outdoor space (10 square meters per bird) to roam, this omega-3 content is further enhanced by an increase in total antioxidant nutrients in the meat. The researchers in this particular study concluded that the enhanced nutrients were directly linked to the pasture activities of the birds.

Organically Raised Meat and Poultry

Organically raised animals cannot be treated with growth hormones or antibiotics and must be given feed that has been produced organically. If an animal becomes ill and requires antibiotics, it is isolated from the rest of the animals and treated, but its meat and milk (or eggs in the case of poultry) cannot be certified as organic.

Pasture-Raised Is Preferable

We recommend choosing free-range and grass-fed (pastured) meats whenever possible. There are many health benefits to using grass-fed beef. The meat is naturally leaner than grain-fed, and the omega-3 content can be as high as 7 percent of the total fat content (compared with just 1 percent in grain-fed beef). There are more minerals and vitamins and a higher level of CLA (conjugated linoleic acid), a fat that has been shown to reduce the risks of cancer, diabetes and obesity.

Genetically Modified Organisms (GMOs)

The terms "genetically modified" (GM) and "genetically engineered" (GE) mean the food's genetic material has been altered. Specifically, a gene (or genes) from one organism has been inserted into the genetic material of another organism. This process creates something altogether new that would not exist in nature.

GMO crops first came to market in 1996 and have been approved for human consumption based on company-produced science. Scientists at regulatory agencies, such as the USDA and FDA, review this data and are responsible for regulating crops. Neither these regulatory agencies nor Health Canada do their own testing, which has raised concerns among some scientists and members of the public.

Over the past few years, concerns about the long-term safety of ingesting GM foods have been increasing. The companies producing the GM foods claim they are safe, but there is ongoing debate. Increasingly, people are interested in learning more about their food, including where it comes from and what it contains. Although more than 60 nations require GM labeling, neither Canada nor the United States does so.

Avoiding GMOs

The only way to know you are not eating GMO foods is to buy food labeled "certified organic." National organic certification rules do not allow genetically engineered foods to be labeled as organic. The independent research organization Consumer Reports conducted a survey in October 2014 and found that a majority of U.S. packaged foods that were labeled "natural" actually contained a substantial level of genetically modified ingredients. Avoiding genetically engineered ingredients isn't easy, but knowing what the most common GMO foods are will help you to identify them in the ingredient listings on product labels.

According to the EWG, the four most common GE foods are:

1. field corn and corn derivatives (about 90 percent of the corn grown in the United States is genetically engineered)
2. soybeans and soybean-derived ingredients, including soybean oil, soy milk, soy sauce and tofu
3. sugar beets and, therefore, sugar
4. vegetable oils, including canola, cottonseed, soybean and corn oil

Other genetically engineered foods to be aware of include Hawaiian papayas, zucchini and yellow crookneck squash.

In this book we have pointed out the potential for genetically modified ingredients and recommend buying organic versions when these foods are called for in recipes.

Why GMO?

Genetically modified plants have been created mainly for the purpose of generating disease resistance or to reduce the need for certain pesticides. Sometimes the term "genetic modification" is used imprecisely to include older technologies, such as hybridization and plant breeding, that farmers have been using for centuries.

Raw Foods and Your Baby

Including raw fruits and vegetables in your baby's diet is an important feature of a well-rounded diet and has a number of health benefits. Raw, or "live," foods, as some people call them, contain plant compounds that function as phytochemical nutrients in our bodies, helping to maximize your growing baby's health. They are also helpful for healthy bowel function and can contain higher levels of vitamins than their cooked counterparts, depending on the particular nutrient. Water-soluble nutrients, such as vitamin C and the B vitamins, seem to be most vulnerable to degradation in processing and cooking. As a result, these nutrients are higher in raw produce.

According to a review conducted by researchers at the University of California, Davis, in 2007, depending on the method used, the loss of vitamin C during home cooking can range from 15 to 55 percent. Interestingly, though, vitamin C levels can be higher in frozen produce when compared with fresh produce, because vitamin C levels decline when fresh produce is transported and stored. This is a good reason to buy local produce when you can.

Although cooking can degrade some nutrients, it can also enhance the availability of others. Cooking breaks down the thick cell walls of many plants, releasing the nutrients stored in them. For instance, fat-soluble compounds, such as vitamins A, D, E and K and the antioxidant compounds called carotenoids, are more available to the body after cooking.

The bottom line is that no single method is superior for preserving 100 percent of the nutrients in a vegetable or fruit. The best way to get the most out of foods is to prepare and enjoy them in a variety of ways — both raw and cooked.

Take Extra Care with Raw Ingredients

Raw fruits and vegetables may harbor harmful bacteria, such as *E. coli*. So when you are preparing a recipe using raw food, make sure to be particularly careful when washing your produce.

Soy

Depending on your source, soy is either a wonder food or one that is harmful to your health. Soy has been the subject of many studies, often with conflicting results. The truth probably lies somewhere in the middle. Our perspective on soy revolves around the value of eating whole, non–genetically modified foods and the health benefits associated with eating a wide variety of foods. Based on its long history of use across a variety of cultures, we believe that soy can be a very healthful part of a well-balanced and varied diet. We like to use it as organic tofu or as an organic whole food (edamame), both of which are rich in iron, a valuable nutrient for growing bodies.

The main problem with soy is that it is likely to be genetically modified. According to the USDA, 93 percent of soybeans grown in the United States in 2012 were genetically modified. The only way to know that the food you buy is not genetically modified is to purchase organic products.

Your Baby Needs Fat

"Low fat" has been an anti-obesity mantra for almost 40 years. Whether it is valid for adults is a subject of much recent debate, but a low-fat diet is definitely not appropriate for babies. During infancy and childhood an adequate supply of fat is essential. Fat is "energy-dense," supplying 9 calories per gram compared with the 4 calories provided by the same amount of protein and carbohydrate. It is also necessary to consume fat so your body can absorb the fat-soluble vitamins A, D, E and K. And, perhaps not surprisingly, since our brains are more than 60 percent fat, a sufficient amount of this nutrient is necessary for healthy brain and nervous system development. Consuming the right kind of fat greatly affects cognitive development and performance. Be conscious about not restricting natural fats for the first three or so years of your baby's life. However, trans fats that result from the process of hydrogenation, and which are prevalent in processed foods, are not healthy fats and do not belong in anyone's diet. To identify trans fats, go beyond the nutritional panel on packaged foods you do buy and look at the ingredients listing. If hydrogenated or partially hydrogenated vegetable oils or shortening

Breast Milk

Breast milk is about 50 percent fat. It is Mother Nature's way of showing us the absolute importance of this nutrient for babies.

is listed, then the product contains trans fats, regardless of what the nutritional panel states. Be careful: there are lots of labeling loopholes.

Omega-3 Fatty Acids Are Essential

The most important fats for your baby are the omega-3 essential fatty acids. They are crucial to the healthy development of your baby's brain, central nervous system and eyes. These fats are called essential because the body can't make them. Consequently, they must be obtained from the diet.

Because omega-3 fatty acids must come from food, it is important to know where to find them. Outside of breast milk, by far the best source of these essential fats is cold-water fish, such as salmon, halibut, herring, mackerel and sardines.

There are different types of omega-3 fats. Two of the most significant, because they are the most easily used by the body, are found in cold-water fish: eicosapentaenoic acid (EPA) and docosahexaenoic acid (DHA). DHA is the primary structural component of brain tissue, and research is increasingly recognizing DHA's influence on neurotransmitters in the brain and overall cognitive function and development.

Another omega-3, alpha-linolenic acid (ALA), is found in flax seeds, flaxseed oil, unrefined organic canola oil, walnut oil and hemp oil. Most other nuts and seeds are also good sources of omega-3 fats.

Ensuring Your Baby Has Enough Omega-3s

So how do you get these crucial nutrients into your baby? Try adding $1/16$ to $1/8$ teaspoon (0.25 to 0.5 mL) of organic flax oil to your baby's favorite purée once a day for the first few days, after which time you can increase it to $1/4$ teaspoon (1 mL). If you breastfeed your baby, the fat in your breast milk will reflect the fat in your diet, so do your baby and yourself a favor and increase your consumption of omega-3 fats. Once you start venturing beyond the first purées, fish will be an important source of these crucial fats (see page 22).

Good for More Than Baby

Omega-3 fatty acids aren't crucial only for your baby. They are also beneficial for all age groups and appear to be helpful in improving a wide range of conditions, from arthritis to Alzheimer's disease. If you feed your baby formula, consider using one with high DHA (one of the omega-3 fats) content.

Omega-3s Are Easily Damaged

Omega-3 fats are unsaturated and highly unstable. That means they degrade quickly with exposure to heat, light and oxygen and, as a result, are usually removed from processed foods, such as refined grains, with a view toward increasing the shelf life of products.

Ratio Between Omega-3 and Omega-6 Fats

One important thing to know about omega-3 and omega-6 fats is that they need to be taken into the body in the proper ratio: about 2:1 of omega-6 to omega-3 fats. Unfortunately, most diets in North America are skewed to a 10:1 to 20:1 ratio of omega-6 to omega-3 fats, partially because of the processing of our foods and our increased reliance on seed oils (such as canola, sunflower and safflower oil).

Omega-3 Fats and ADHD

In recent years researchers have been looking at how omega-3 fats affect brain function, specifically in association with attention deficit hyperactivity disorder (ADHD). The results of a 2007 study published in the *Journal of Developmental and Behavioral Pediatrics* supported the link between ADHD and deficiencies in omega-3 fats. In this study, school-aged children were given capsules containing either palm oil or omega-3 fats, and their behavior was followed for 15 weeks. The children who received the omega-3 capsules showed improvement in the core symptoms of inattention, hyperactivity and impulsivity, compared with those who received palm oil.

Omega-6 Fatty Acids

The omega-6 fatty acid linoleic acid (easily confused with the alpha-linolenic acid mentioned earlier) is an essential fatty acid that must be obtained from food. While it is important, it is not in short supply in a typical North American diet. Linoleic acid is readily available in foods such as whole grains, poultry, eggs, nuts and seeds and is prevalent in certain vegetable oils. Because we tend to overconsume omega-6 fats in North America (see left) it is important to consciously add omega-3-rich foods to your diet and that of your baby. Too much omega-6 fat interferes with the absorption of omega-3 fats and may also increase harmful inflammation.

Can Your Baby Eat Fish?

For the past few decades, fish was not recommended for babies under 12 months of age because allergic reactions were a concern. However, current recommendations from both the American Academy of Pediatrics and the Canadian Pediatric Society encourage the addition of healthy protein sources, including fish, at around the 6-month mark. (As noted, fish is an important source of omega-3 fats.) They state that there is no conclusive evidence that delaying the introduction of what are considered typically allergenic foods (eggs, fish and nuts) beyond about 6 to 9 months helps to avoid food allergies (see Allergies, page 25).

Mercury Content in Fish

Mercury content is another reason people have avoided feeding their babies fish. Too much mercury is a problem for developing nervous systems. But some fish have much higher levels than others. Fish accumulate mercury in their muscle tissue primarily as a result of eating other fish. As larger predatory fish eat smaller ones, the mercury bio-magnifies up through the food chain. This means the largest predatory fish have the highest concentrations of mercury in their meat.

Fish consumption advisories vary between countries, but it is generally agreed that shark, swordfish, king mackerel and tilefish should not be consumed by anyone, because of their high mercury content. Tuna is also a large predatory fish, and consumption advisories have a recommended limit on fresh and frozen tuna as well as canned albacore (white) tuna. Canned tuna described as "light tuna" contains other species such as skipjack, yellowfin and tongol, all of which have lower mercury levels.

Improving Iron Absorption from Plant Foods

You can greatly increase the absorption of non-heme iron by ensuring that your baby (and you) consumes foods that are high in vitamin C along with plant foods containing iron. Good amounts of vitamin C can be found in apples, broccoli, Brussels sprouts, sweet potatoes, red peppers and tomatoes. During infancy and again at adolescence, the body demands more iron to fuel these times of rapid growth. Children are at higher risk for iron-deficiency anemia at these times, so care must be taken to ensure enough of this critical nutrient in the diet.

Iron

Iron is a mineral your body absolutely needs. It helps form healthy red blood cells and is the central component of hemoglobin, which carries oxygen in the blood throughout the body. During pregnancy, your baby built up the iron stores he needs to help fuel his considerable growth in the first year of life. At about the 6-month mark, these stores start to decline and your baby's food must now become the source of necessary iron. Inadequate iron intake can increase the risk of iron-deficiency anemia and affect a child's development and learning ability early in life. A low iron level can also cause the body to absorb too much lead.

There are two different types of iron that can be used by the body. One, called heme iron, is found in meat, fish, poultry (including duck) and eggs. The other type, non-heme iron, is found in plants. Plant sources rich in iron include tofu, quinoa, figs, apricots and all legumes. The iron from animal products is more easily absorbed by the body than iron from plant sources.

Gluten

Gluten is a protein composite found in a number of different grains, including barley, rye, spelt, Kamut, triticale and all types of wheat. People avoid gluten for three main reasons: celiac disease, an autoimmune disease affecting about 1 percent of the population that causes damage to the small intestine when gluten is consumed; wheat allergy, an allergic response to wheat protein that can appear as skin, respiratory and/or gastrointestinal symptoms; and non-celiac gluten sensitivity.

Non-celiac gluten sensitivity appears to be the main reason people avoid gluten. Although it does not involve the immune system, it may produce symptoms such as bloating, cramping and other gastrointestinal problems. According to the Canadian Celiac Association and the US Celiac Disease Foundation, a subgroup of people with gluten sensitivity can also experience depression, ADHD-like behavior, joint pain and headaches. The mechanism for non-celiac gluten sensitivity is not understood and is an area of much ongoing research. In my experience of treating many people with this sensitivity, there are likely a number of factors that come into play.

There is a lot of controversy around wheat and gluten today. Some practitioners, such as cardiologist Dr. William Davis, author of the book *Wheat Belly,* believe that most of the wheat we eat today has been hybridized to such an extent that it now contains novel proteins our bodies don't recognize and have trouble digesting. If so, consuming gluten can potentially increase intestinal permeability and intensify inflammation throughout the body.

Gluten is ubiquitous in the North American diet and is hidden in many products. Even if you don't serve it to your baby, he will encounter it once he is old enough for playdates and to share snacks provided by others. For health reasons and to help lower your baby's exposure to wheat and gluten, we have chosen not to include gluten-containing grains in this book.

Eating gluten-free doesn't mean you need to avoid all grains, nor does it mean you are missing out on any important nutrients. In fact, because you are not using a predominance of highly processed white or whole wheat flour, you may even be increasing the nutrition your baby receives by expanding the range of nutrients he consumes! (For instance, quinoa provides a full range of amino acids whereas wheat does not.) In this book we have included many recipes using highly nutritious healthy alternatives to gluten-containing grains as well as instructions for grinding your own gluten-free flours (see page 55). When you make your own baby food, you know all the ingredients, but I have one caution about anything you purchase — just because the label says it is gluten-free doesn't mean it is good for you!

Allergies

For decades, in order to reduce the risk of food allergies, parents were advised to delay introducing certain potentially allergenic foods to babies until after they reached 12 months (cow's milk), 24 months (eggs) or 36 months (fish, tree nuts and peanuts). In 2008, the American Academy of Pediatrics retracted these guidelines, acknowledging that there was insufficient evidence to support this practice. In fact, data are now emerging in scientific literature that suggest the delayed introduction of solid foods may actually increase the risk of eczema or food allergy and that the earlier careful introduction of allergenic foods may help prevent food allergies in infants and children. The most recent (2013) guidelines from the American Academy of Allergy, Asthma and Immunology recommend introducing babies to food earlier than in previous recommendations.

Two studies conducted in 2010 using eggs support this position. One study published in the journal *Pediatrics* reported an increased risk of sensitization to eggs at 5 years of age if egg had not been introduced to the baby until after $10^1/_2$ months. The other study, published in the *Journal of Allergy and Clinical Immunology*, determined that babies introduced to egg when they were about 6 months of age had a significantly lower risk of egg allergy than infants introduced to egg after that age.

A food allergy occurs when the baby's immune system tries to defend her body against a food it has identified as "foreign" by producing antibodies. Repeated exposure to an allergen is generally required for the body to produce enough antibodies to cause an allergic reaction. Symptoms such as skin rashes, hives, a runny nose, itching, congestion, wheezing, abdominal pain and poor weight gain can characterize an allergic reaction. The most serious allergic reaction is anaphylaxis (mouth or throat swelling, difficulty breathing), which is life-threatening and requires immediate emergency medical attention. Anaphylaxis generally happens either immediately after exposure to

One Food at a Time

When you introduce your baby to purées, it is best to try a single food at a time. Serve your baby a single purée for 3 to 5 days in a row before introducing another new food. This is especially important if there is a sibling or parent with specific food allergies. Serving just one food for a few days will help you recognize which foods, if any, your baby may not be able to tolerate or that cause an allergic reaction.

the allergen or within a number of hours. Less serious reactions may also be immediate, but they can also be delayed for up to 2 days.

Once you have determined that your child doesn't react to a certain food, you can combine it with other foods that you know won't cause a reaction. The American Academy of Allergy, Asthma and Immunology has found no conclusive evidence to support delaying typically allergenic foods, even among those at high risk of allergy (defined as having at least one first-degree relative — sibling or parent — with a documented allergic condition), and some studies are even finding a benefit in having tastes of these foods at around the 6-month mark. They also recommend that once you start offering these foods, and if your child does not have a reaction, you continue to give them to your child on a regular basis.

Filtered Water

Pure drinking water is important for all of us, but especially for pregnant women, babies and small children. Most water treatment plants in North America use chlorine as a disinfectant to reduce or eliminate bacteria and viruses, and, indeed, this has virtually eliminated life-threatening waterborne diseases. However, chlorine may have its own health implications.

Chlorine reacts with naturally occurring organic matter in water to form byproducts that may pose long-term health risks. Some of these byproducts are trihalomethanes (THMs), including carcinogenic chloroform and carbon tetrachloride. The more organic matter in the water, the greater the accumulation of THMs. The long-term risks of drinking chlorinated water include excessive free radical formation at the level of your body's cells. This increases vulnerability to genetic mutation and cancer development as well as promoting aging and atherosclerosis, or hardening of the arteries. Chorine in drinking water also destroys the protective acidophilus bacteria that live in the small intestine and promote a healthy immune system.

Filtering your water is an effective way to remove chlorine and its byproducts from municipally treated drinking water. Filtration blocks the passage of contaminants in the water through physical obstruction, chemical absorption or a combination of both processes. The most effective filters are made from carbon or a combination of carbon and other elements. Just as you want to prepare the healthiest food for your baby, be sure also to pay attention to the quality of the water she drinks or that you use when blending water into her food.

The Vegetarian Baby

Vegetarianism, which has been part of various cultures for millennia, is becoming increasingly popular in North America as a lifestyle choice. There are two basic ways of being a vegetarian: *vegans* don't eat animal products at all, including eggs, dairy and honey, while *lacto-ovo vegetarians* eat dairy products and eggs but no meat, poultry, fish or seafood. Becoming a vegetarian (or a vegan) may be a moral or ethical decision, but many adults have based their choice on the well-researched benefits of a plant-based diet and the reduction of animal fats.

Even so, being a vegetarian doesn't necessarily mean a person has a nutritious and healthful diet. You need to make sure that the foods you consume are nutrient-dense (see page 9) and well balanced in terms of the nutrients they provide. This takes careful planning. In choosing a vegetarian diet for your baby, you'll need to understand the fundamentals of carbohydrates, proteins, fats and vitamins and minerals to ensure that your baby receives optimal nutrition. It is important to know the best sources of critical nutrients such as iron, calcium, vitamin B_{12} and vitamin D, all of which are easier to find in animal foods.

If you are considering this option, please work closely with a nutrition expert to ensure proper nutrition for your baby and that you avoid any deficiency that could lead to developmental delays or illnesses.

Solid Food Before 6 Months

In this book we give the general guideline of starting solid foods around 6 months of age. You may, however, want to experiment with small quantities and little tastes of purées anytime after 4 months, with the understanding that breast milk or formula is still the best main source of nutrition for your infant at that age.

Enjoy Meals as a Family

I suspect we all know this to be true intuitively, but studies do show that regularly sharing meals together (including breakfast and lunch, as well as dinner), as a family (whatever combination makes up your family), has numerous benefits. These include improved nutritional intake, a decreased risk for unhealthy weight and better emotional health. These studies also show that children who usually join their families at mealtime do better in school and are less likely to engage in high-risk behavior such as using drugs.

Preparing Your Own Baby Food

This book is about preparing food for your baby that is extremely nutritious and tastes very, very good — so good, in fact, that it will help your baby to develop healthy eating habits that will nourish him throughout his entire life. The starting point for producing the best-tasting meals is the freshest (ideally locally produced) ingredients. Often they are very simply prepared. With the right ingredients, a little bit of planning and the recipes in this book, you can feed your baby wholesome, delicious food whenever he is hungry. And you can do it without spending hours trapped in the kitchen. We know you want to give your baby a great start by preparing your own nourishing foods, so keep the following things in mind before you start.

Keep It Clean

Because your baby's gastrointestinal tract (a key component of her immune system) isn't mature, she is more susceptible to food-borne illnesses, which are caused by ingesting foods contaminated with bacteria, viruses and chemical toxins. It's your job as a parent to minimize these risks, so before starting to prepare your baby's food, wash your hands thoroughly for at least 20 seconds with warm water and soap. Thorough hand-washing is the single most important thing you can do to prevent illness. Plain soap and water is best; you do not need any special antibacterial soap. In fact, many antibacterial soaps contain triclosan, a hormone disruptor. (As of December 2013, the FDA in the United States issued a proposed rule that would require manufacturers to provide more substantial data to demonstrate the safety and effectiveness of their antibacterial soaps.) Once your hands are clean, make sure that all your equipment, cooking utensils and work surfaces have also been thoroughly washed with hot water and soap.

Avoid Cross-Contamination

Cross-contamination refers to the transfer of harmful bacteria among foods. To avoid this possibility, keep raw meat, fish and poultry separate from produce. Use separate cutting boards and knives for these foods. Wash any utensils and cutting boards that have come into contact with them, immediately after use, in hot soapy water. After washing, sanitize them using a solution of 1 teaspoon (5 mL) chlorine bleach combined with 3 cups (750 mL) hot water. Rinse everything thoroughly to remove the bleach and then leave the equipment to air-dry.

Avoid Commercial Produce Washes

We do not recommend washing produce with detergent, antibacterial soap or bleach solutions. These products may contain chemicals that are not intended for use on foods and that porous fruits and vegetables can absorb. The Food and Drug Administration (FDA) in the United States does not recommend using commercial produce sprays or washes, because their effectiveness has not been standardized.

As many as 20 people or more may have touched the produce you're feeding to your baby, so be sure to wash it well. The best way to remove surface dirt and bacteria (and, if you're using conventionally grown produce, some of the pesticide residue) is to rub it briskly with your hands under cool or warm running water. Even if you plan to peel it, thoroughly scrub produce that has a rind, grooves or a waxy skin (such as melons, cucumber, squash, citrus, potatoes and even bananas) with a vegetable brush. Because cutting through the rind can transfer dirt and bacteria to the fleshy part inside, you want the surface to be as clean as possible. Place loose berries and bunched fruit such as blueberries and grapes in a colander and rinse under cold running water or with a spray nozzle. Even organic and prewashed vegetables need to be washed before consumption to eliminate any potential contamination caused by human handling.

Whole grains should also be washed before use. Most have been at least partially cleaned before they get to market but require a further cleansing to eliminate any dust and fine particles that may stick to the kernels. Some grains, such as quinoa, have a natural coating called saponin, which, although harmless, may impart a bitter taste to the cooked product. To wash whole grains, place them in a large bowl and add approximately three times their volume of water. Gently rub the kernels with your hands, loosening any debris. Transfer to a fine-mesh sieve and rinse under cool running water until the water runs clear.

Storing and Freezing Cooked Food

Improperly stored food can be another source of food-borne illness. If your baby does not eat all of the food you have prepared for her, transfer it to a clean container, cover and store in the refrigerator for up to 3 days. If you don't plan to use all of it within that time frame, freeze at least a portion immediately after making it.

Don't wait until the food has been in the fridge for 3 days to freeze it. To freeze, pour cooled food into a clean ice-cube tray, cover with foil and place in the freezer. Once the food is frozen solid (within 24 hours) turn out the serving-size frozen cubes into a freezer bag and label with the date and the contents. You can keep food safely frozen for up to 3 months. Freezing will preserve most of the nutrients in your homemade baby food.

Thawing

Always thaw frozen baby food in a sealed container in the fridge or in the top of a double boiler on the stove. Thawing on the countertop at room temperature can promote bacterial growth that could be unsafe for your baby. Throw away any food that has not been eaten after it has been thawed. Do not refreeze any baby food. We don't recommend using a microwave for thawing or heating baby food or bottles. There is a danger of hot spots in the food that could burn your baby's mouth or throat.

Recommended Equipment

The following is a list of the basic kitchen equipment you will need to create these delicious recipes for your baby.

- immersion blender or all-purpose blender
- potato masher
- whisk
- heatproof rubber spatula
- wooden spoon
- tongs
- colander
- fine-mesh sieve
- sharp knives
- skillet
- ovenproof skillet and saucepan
- baking dish
- rimmed baking sheet
- stock pot
- pepper grinder
- ice-cube trays
- wooden ice-pop sticks
- freezer bags
- instant-read thermometer

Starting Solids

6 to 9 Months

Introducing Solid Foods...........34

Single Fruits

Roasted Banana Purée.............36

Apple Medley....................37

Pear Purée....................38

Fresh Apricot Purée.............39

Blueberry Purée.................40

Mango Purée 41

Single Vegetables

Broccoli Purée 42

Sweet Potato Purée..............44

Roasted Sweet Potato Purée 45

Acorn Squash Purée.............46

Sweet Pea Purée 47

Carrot Purée....................48

Roasted Beet Purée 50

Caramelized Parsnip Purée.......51

Single Grains

Basic Quinoa 52

Simple Millet Cereal 53

Brown Rice Cereal 54

Grains and Fruit

Whole-Grain Oat Cereal
with Grapes.....................56

Quinoa and Banana Purée........57

Apple and Fig Brown
Rice Cereal 58

Other Combos

Tofu, Pear and Banana Purée 60

Roasted Apple, Blueberry
and Pear Purée..................61

Nectarine and Carrot Purée 62

Apricot and Acorn Squash
Purée.........................63

Green Bean Purée
with Fresh Basil 65

Honeydew, Blueberry
and Mint Purée 66

Plum and Blueberry Purée........67

Zucchini and Basil Purée..........68

Cauliflower and Parsnip Purée.....69

Cauliflower and Chickpea
Chowder........................70

Banana and Blueberry Purée 71

Carrot and Split Pea Purée 72

Red Lentil Apple Purée...........73

Raw Combos

Watermelon, Peach
and Blueberry Purée 74

Avocado, Carrot
and Cucumber Purée..............76

Peach, Chive and Basil Purée 77

Apple, Pear and Avocado Purée....78

Date and Blueberry Purée 79

Meat and Legumes

Celery Root and Chicken
Purée..........................80

Sweet Pea, Lamb and Parsnip
Purée..........................81

Chicken and Red Lentil Purée 82

Grilled Chicken and Avocado
Purée..........................83

White Navy Bean and Beef
Purée.........................84

Introducing Solid Foods

Don't Stop Breast or Bottle Feeding

Remember, while you are introducing first foods, continue breast or formula feeding, because these are still important sources of nutrition for your growing baby.

One at a Time

Be patient and take your time. Introduce single foods, one at a time, waiting 3 to 5 days before trying a new one. This way, you will be able to easily identify any foods that cause adverse reactions.

For about the first 6 months of life, your baby will get all the nutrients he or she needs from either breast milk or iron-fortified infant formula. But at around 6 months of age, when your baby's gastrointestinal tract is further developed, your baby will begin to need the additional nutrients provided by whole foods. This is the point at which the American Academy of Pediatrics and the Canadian Pediatric Society recommend introducing solid foods as a complement to breast milk or formula.

Every baby develops and progresses at his individual pace, and you know your baby best. Watch for the following signs that indicate your baby may be ready for "people food."

- Your baby is interested in the foods you are eating and may try to reach for them.

- Your baby can sit by himself or with minimal support and hold his head up well.

- Your baby opens his mouth when he sees food coming toward his face. He can close his mouth over a small spoon rather than pushing it out with his tongue.

- Your baby wants to feed more often or seems to want more after breast or bottle feeds.

- Your baby is beginning to make chewing motions with his mouth.

- Your baby can turn away or push food away with his hands.

If you recognize these signs, you and your baby are ready to embark on a very exciting journey as you explore the fascinating world of food and your baby's sense of taste expands.

Plain Foods Are Best

Plain foods that do not contain added salt or sugar are preferable at this stage of development. Herbs and spices can be added after you have tried a few plain foods. They should be encouraged for their health benefits and also because they will help to develop your baby's palate and expand his interest in a variety of flavors and foods. As with single foods, introduce herbs and spices one at a time so you can easily identify any reactions.

In this chapter we offer single fruits, vegetables and cereals to get your baby started. (Contrary to what you may have heard, starting your baby with fruit will not nurture a sweet tooth. Breast milk itself is quite sweet.) After working your way through these single foods and learning which your baby can tolerate and prefers, you can move on to various combinations you think he will enjoy.

We have developed a wide variety of single and double food purées to help you introduce your baby to a diverse assortment of nutrients and tastes. Every baby is unique and develops his own preferences for food. Just because your baby turns away the first (or tenth) time you offer a particular food doesn't mean you should stop trying. Your baby's palate will change and develop if given the opportunity. A food he once wouldn't touch may well become next month's favorite.

The preferred consistency of food will also vary from baby to baby and from month to month. If your baby prefers his food to be slightly runny, thin it with breast milk or formula or use the cooking water from recipes. This will help to maximize nutrient intake.

Introducing your baby to solid food is more of an art than a science, and a messy one at that. Allow your baby to enjoy his food and don't be too worried about exactly how much he is actually eating. At first most will end up in his hair or on the floor anyway. The important thing is to keep trying. You also want to make mealtimes enjoyable experiences for both of you.

Iron Is Important

It is important that your baby's first foods contain iron to fuel his rapid growth. Foods that contain iron include cooked egg yolk, poultry, meat, tofu and legumes. Some fruits and vegetables also contain a type of iron whose absorption is increased by the presence of vitamin C (see page 23).

Roasted Banana Purée

Your baby will love this yummy concoction! I recommend making double the quantity and using the extra to make healthy snacks for yourself or older children. With the addition of Jill's Homemade Yogurt (page 90), this makes a wonderful treat (see Roasted Banana Lassi, page 201).

(see Roasted Banana Lassi, page 201).

Makes about 1 cup (250 mL)

Chef Jordan's Tips

For the sweetest purée, use overripe bananas. This is a great way to use up any bananas you may have sitting around.

Always take care when adding hot liquids to a blender. Fill the container no more than half full or let cool before blending.

Jill's Nutrition Tip

As a first food, bananas are smooth and easy to swallow. Because they are sweet, like breast milk and formula, your baby will take to them easily. If your baby has diarrhea or vomiting, the potassium in bananas helps to replenish the mineral balance in her body. Bananas also have an astringent or drying property, which may help reduce the water loss associated with diarrhea.

- Rimmed baking sheet
- Blender
- Preheat oven to 250°F (120°C)

2	bananas, unpeeled (about 12 oz/375 g; see Tips, left)	2
½ cup	filtered water	125 mL

1. Place bananas on baking sheet and roast in preheated oven until soft, about 30 minutes. Transfer bananas to a plate and transfer cooking liquid from the baking sheet to a saucepan. Set aside and let bananas cool until they can be easily handled.

2. Peel cooled bananas, holding them over the saucepan to catch the liquid, then add to the saucepan. Add water and bring to a boil over medium heat. Remove from heat and transfer to blender or use an immersion blender in the saucepan. Purée until smooth. Let cool until warm to the touch before serving or transfer to an airtight container and refrigerate for up to 3 days or freeze for up to 1 month.

NUTRIENTS PER SERVING (¼ cup/60 mL)

Calories	53	Dietary fiber	1.5 g
Protein	0.6 g	Sodium	1.5 mg
Total fat	0.2 g	Calcium	3.9 mg
Saturated fat	0.1 g	Iron	0.2 mg
Carbohydrates	13.5 g	Vitamin C	5.1 mg

Apple Medley

In this recipe, the combination of sweet and sour apples builds a complex flavor profile. It's really worth the effort to use more than one type of apple. In my opinion, it's never too early to teach your baby to appreciate subtleties of flavor.

● ●

Makes about 2 cups (500 mL)

Chef Jordan's Tip

Pascal Olhats, a chef I once worked with in southern California, would always remind me to skim, skim, skim. "Why would you want those impurities in your sauce?" he'd ask. In this recipe, you should skim and discard the bubbles that rise to the top, which can make your purée bitter.

Jill's Nutrition Tip

Being concerned about the frequency and consistency of your infant's bowel movements is a natural state for parents of a new baby. Quite simply, all apples are great sources of both soluble and insoluble fiber, which are crucial for bowel health. The pectin in apples can help regulate both diarrhea and constipation.

Always buy organic apples.

- Blender

1 cup	filtered water	250 mL
1 cup	chopped cored organic Granny Smith or other tart apple (about 1)	250 mL
1 cup	chopped cored organic Gala or other sweet apple (about 1)	250 mL

1. In a saucepan, combine water, Granny Smith and Gala apples. Bring to a boil over medium heat. Reduce heat to low and simmer, skimming off any bubbles that rise to the top (see Tips, left), until apples are fork-tender and water has reduced by three-quarters, 12 to 15 minutes.

2. Transfer to blender or use an immersion blender in the saucepan. Purée until smooth. Let cool until warm to the touch before serving or transfer to an airtight container and refrigerate for up to 3 days or freeze for up to 1 month.

NUTRIENTS PER SERVING (¼ cup/60 mL)

Calories	16	Dietary fiber	0.7 g
Protein	0.1 g	Sodium	1.2 mg
Total fat	0.0 g	Calcium	2.7 mg
Saturated fat	0.0 g	Iron	0.1 mg
Carbohydrates	4.3 g	Vitamin C	1.6 mg

Pear Purée

This recipe brings back memories of my Gramma Jean's warm pear-apple sauce. Her recipe came all the way from Paducah, Kentucky, but it sure was a welcome treat on a cold winter's day in Toronto. Your baby will love it, too.

● ●

Makes about 2 cups (500 mL)

Chef Jordan's Tip

Often I'll choose to mix the same ingredient, cooked and raw (finely diced), before serving. I love the contrast in flavors (the cooked becomes so much sweeter) and textures. As your child is able to handle more texture, at about 8 or 9 months, try adding about ¼ cup (60 mL) peeled and diced raw pear for every 1 cup (250 mL) of purée.

Jill's Nutrition Tip

Pears are second only to bananas as a wonderful first food. They are an excellent source of fiber to help tone your baby's intestines and promote bowel health. Along with bananas, they have low allergenic potential, meaning they are not likely to cause any adverse reactions.

Always buy organic pears.

● Blender

| 2¼ cups | chopped cored organic Bosc pears (about 3) | 550 mL |
| 1 cup | filtered water | 250 mL |

1. In a saucepan, combine pears and water. Bring to a boil over medium heat. Reduce heat to low, cover, leaving a small crack to allow steam to escape, and simmer until pears are fork-tender and most of the water has evaporated, about 15 minutes.

2. Transfer to blender or use an immersion blender in the saucepan. Purée until smooth. Let cool until warm to the touch before serving or transfer to an airtight container and refrigerate for up to 3 days or freeze for up to 1 month.

NUTRIENTS PER SERVING (¼ cup/60 mL)

Calories 27		Dietary fiber . . . . 1.4 g	
Protein . . . . 0.2 g		Sodium . . . . 1.4 mg	
Total fat . . . . 0.1 g		Calcium . . . . 5.1 mg	
Saturated fat . . . . 0.0 g		Iron . . . . 0.1 mg	
Carbohydrates . . . . 7.2 g		Vitamin C . . . . 2.0 mg	

Fresh Apricot Purée

This is one of my favorite purées. Fresh apricots are a real treat for anyone — they are nutritious and delicious and a wonderful indulgence for your baby.

●●●

Makes about 1 cup (250 mL)

Chef Jordan's Tips

The quickest way to pit an apricot is to split it in half by hand and pull out the pit.

If fresh apricots aren't available, use dried apricots. They yield a more gelatinous texture but a good flavor. Use 1 cup (250 mL) dried apricots in this recipe.

Jill's Nutrition Tip

If you are using dried apricots, check the label and avoid any that contain sulfites; they will likely be bright orange. Sulfites are a common chemical preservative and are potentially toxic to developing bodies. They have been linked to allergic-type reactions and may be particularly problematic for children with asthma. Look for apricots preserved with potassium sorbate or sorbic acid; they will be more brown than orange.

Always buy organic apricots.

• Blender

1½ cups	pitted organic apricots (about 10 oz/300 g)	375 mL
½ cup	filtered water	125 mL

1. In a saucepan, combine apricots and water. Bring to a boil over medium heat. Cover, reduce heat to low and simmer until apricots are soft, about 15 minutes. Let cool to room temperature.

2. Transfer to blender or use an immersion blender in the saucepan. Purée until smooth. Serve immediately or transfer to an airtight container and refrigerate for up to 3 days or freeze for up to 1 month.

NUTRIENTS PER SERVING (¼ cup/60 mL)

Calories	34	Dietary fiber . . . . 1.4 g
Protein	1.0 g	Sodium . . . . 1.6 mg
Total fat	0.3 g	Calcium . . . . 10.1 mg
Saturated fat	0.0 g	Iron . . . . 0.3 mg
Carbohydrates	7.9 g	Vitamin C . . . . 7.1 mg

Blueberry Purée

I realized I wanted to be a chef while camping in a wilderness park. As a teenager, I used to lead children on canoe trips, and one day we made pancakes using the wild blueberries we had picked. There is no better feeling than picking food from the wild and creating something people love. Thank you, blueberries!

**Makes about
1 cup (250 mL)**

Chef Jordan's Tip

This purée tends to look thin while warm, but don't worry: it will thicken as it cools.

Jill's Nutrition Tip

Blueberries are small but mighty. They have a high ORAC (oxygen radical absorbance capacity) value, which is the measure of their antioxidant level. Even though she still has a long way to go, feeding your baby foods with high ORAC values helps decrease the risk of degenerative disease and cellular damage that comes with aging. Wild blueberries are a particularly good choice because they have an ORAC value that is almost 50 percent higher than that of farmed blueberries.

Always buy organic or wild blueberries.

• Blender

2 cups	fresh or frozen organic or wild blueberries	500 mL
1½ cups	filtered water	375 mL

1. In a saucepan, combine blueberries and water. Bring to a boil over medium heat. Boil until berries are splitting in half, about 10 minutes.
2. Transfer to blender or use an immersion blender in the saucepan. Purée until smooth. Let cool until warm to the touch before serving or transfer to an airtight container and refrigerate for up to 3 days or freeze for up to 1 month.

NUTRIENTS PER SERVING (¼ cup/60 mL)

Calories	42	Dietary fiber	1.8 g
Protein	0.6 g	Sodium	3.4 mg
Total fat	0.2 g	Calcium	7.1 mg
Saturated fat	0.0 g	Iron	0.2 mg
Carbohydrates	10.7 g	Vitamin C	7.2 mg

Mango Purée

This is a particularly sweet-tasting purée with a fresh flavor that will appeal not only to your baby but also to other family members. When mangos are in season, make a double batch and turn half into Frozen Mango Mousse (page 210) or a Mango Lassi (page 200) for a delicious dessert or snack.

• •

Makes about 1¾ cups (425 mL)

Chef Jordan's Tips

The simplest way to peel a mango is with a regular vegetable peeler. Use a paring knife to cut the flesh away from the pit.

My father-in-law introduced me to the Ataulfo mango. Golden yellow, it is the smallest of the mango varieties and is the most "buttery." If it's available, definitely choose this variety.

Jill's Nutrition Tip

Like all yellow, orange and red fruits, mangos are rich in beta-carotene, which your body makes into vitamin A. Your body requires Vitamin A in order for skin cells to reproduce correctly. This helps them reduce the mutations that can lead to cancer. Good levels of vitamin A in your baby's body can help prevent diaper rash and outbreaks of eczema.

• Blender

| 1 | large mango (or 2 small), peeled, pitted and chopped (see Tips, left) | 1 |
| 1 cup | filtered water | 250 mL |

1. In a saucepan, combine mango and water. Bring to a boil over medium heat. Reduce heat to low and simmer until mango is soft, about 5 minutes.

2. Transfer to blender or use an immersion blender in the saucepan. Purée until smooth. Let cool until warm to the touch before serving or transfer to an airtight container and refrigerate for up to 3 days or freeze for up to 1 month.

NUTRIENTS PER SERVING (¼ cup/60 mL)

Calories	20	Dietary fiber	0.3 g
Protein	0.0 g	Sodium	1.1 mg
Total fat	0.1 g	Calcium	1.1 mg
Saturated fat	0.0 g	Iron	0.0 mg
Carbohydrates	4.9 g	Vitamin C	2.6 mg

Broccoli Purée

If you and your family aren't fans of broccoli, wait until you try this purée. You want your children to acquire a taste for broccoli at an early age, because it's a cruciferous vegetable, which means its cancer-fighting abilities are well known.

**Makes about
1 cup (250 mL)**

Chef Jordan's Tips

To maintain the vibrant green color of the broccoli, cook it at a rolling boil (do not reduce to a simmer).

The term "fork-tender" means that when something is pierced with a fork and no resistance is felt, it's cooked. This is a wonderful point of reference.

Jill's Nutrition Tip

Broccoli always makes the superfood list. It is a nondairy source of calcium, an important mineral. During the rapid growth of infancy and toddlerhood, your child needs calcium in significant amounts. Calcium not only optimizes the growth of bones and teeth but also provides for healthy muscle contraction, including the heart.

• Blender

4 cups	filtered water	1 L
2 cups	broccoli florets	500 mL

1. In a saucepan, bring water to a rolling boil over high heat. Add broccoli. Cover and cook until broccoli is fork-tender (see Tips, left), about 5 minutes. Strain through a colander set over a measuring cup or bowl, reserving the cooking liquid.

2. Transfer broccoli to blender with 1 cup (250 mL) reserved liquid or return to saucepan and use an immersion blender. Purée until smooth. Let cool until warm to the touch before serving or transfer to an airtight container and refrigerate for up to 3 days or freeze for up to 1 month.

Variation

If you are feeding older children as well, add freshly grated Parmesan cheese to some of this purée to transform it into a great sauce. You can serve it over long noodles such as brown rice or quinoa spaghetti or linguine.

NUTRIENTS PER SERVING (¼ cup/60 mL)

Calories	10	Dietary fiber	1.0 g
Protein	1.1 g	Sodium	16.7 mg
Total fat	0.1 g	Calcium	24.1 mg
Saturated fat	0.0 g	Iron	0.3 mg
Carbohydrates	1.9 g	Vitamin C	33.1 mg

Also pictured: Roasted Beet Puree (page 50), Roasted Sweet Potato Puree (page 45) and Mango Purée (page 41).

Sweet Potato Purée

I'm sure that the natural sweetness of this tuber will be a huge hit with your baby — it was and continues to be one of my son Jonah's favorites.

• •

**Makes about
2 cups (500 mL)**

Chef Jordan's Tip

I never puréed sweet potatoes with their skins until my wife, Tamar, and I began to create baby food for our son, Jonah. Tamar asked me why I wasn't using the skins, and I had no good answer for her (I rarely do). I soon learned that sweet potatoes cooked with their skins have a much deeper flavor. But if you prefer, feel free to try the recipe without the skin.

Jill's Nutrition Tip

The skins of vegetables contain many important nutrients. Skins are composed of cellulose, which contributes insoluble fiber, or roughage, to the diet. Fiber is important to the way your baby's food is digested and eliminated. Sweet potatoes, particularly their skins, also contain phenolic compounds, which are antioxidants that help protect cells from oxidative damage.

• Blender

2	sweet potatoes, chopped (about 1 lb/500 g; see Tips, left)	2
1½ cups	filtered water	375 mL

1. In a saucepan, combine sweet potatoes and water. Bring to a boil over medium heat. Reduce heat to low and simmer until potatoes are fork-tender, about 15 minutes. Remove from heat.

2. Transfer potatoes and liquid to blender or use an immersion blender in the saucepan. Purée until smooth. Let cool until warm to the touch before serving or transfer to an airtight container and refrigerate for up to 3 days or freeze for up to 1 month.

Variation

Our son, Jonah, began to eat sweet potato purée with Parmesan cheese over bow-tie noodles when he was about 3 years old, and it soon became his favorite lunch. Believe it or not, at 10 years of age it continues to be one of his favorites.

NUTRIENTS PER SERVING (¼ cup/60 mL)

Calories	35	Dietary fiber	1.2 g
Protein	0.6 g	Sodium	23.8 mg
Total fat	0.0 g	Calcium	13.6 mg
Saturated fat	0.0 g	Iron	0.3 mg
Carbohydrates	8.2 g	Vitamin C	1.0 mg

Roasted Sweet Potato Purée

This recipe produces a purée that is much more candy-like than the boiled version but still has all the good nutrition.

• •

**Makes about
2 cups (500 mL)**

Chef Jordan's Tip

Steeping the sweet potato in hot liquid, then letting it cool in the liquid, softens the skin, smoothing out the purée.

Jill's Nutrition Tip

Sweet potatoes are loaded with beta-carotene, a phytochemical found in all yellow, orange, red and dark green vegetables and fruits, which your body converts to form vitamin A. Beta-carotene contains antioxidants, powerful scavengers that find and neutralize free radicals, which over time can contribute to disease. Eating richly colored fruits and vegetables on a daily basis helps minimize the long-term effects of these destructive free radicals.

• Blender
• Preheat oven to 350°F (180°C)

| 2 | sweet potatoes (about 1 lb/500 g) | 2 |
| 1 cup | filtered water | 250 mL |

1. On a baking sheet, roast sweet potatoes in preheated oven until fork-tender, about 1 hour.

2. Transfer sweet potatoes to a saucepan and add water. Bring to a boil over medium heat. Let cool to room temperature (see Tips, left).

3. Transfer to blender or use an immersion blender in the saucepan. Purée until smooth. Serve immediately or transfer to an airtight container and refrigerate for up to 3 days or freeze for up to 1 month.

Variation

If butternut squash is in season, substitute 1 small butternut squash for the sweet potato. Cook it whole and seed it after roasting. For added flavor, purée with the skin left on.

NUTRIENTS PER SERVING (¼ cup/60 mL)

Calories	35	Dietary fiber	1.2 g
Protein	0.6 g	Sodium	23.3 mg
Total fat	0.0 g	Calcium	13.1 mg
Saturated fat	0.0 g	Iron	0.3 mg
Carbohydrates	8.2 g	Vitamin C	1.0 mg

Acorn Squash Purée

This simple purée is very versatile. Babies enjoy its natural sweetness, and it is tasty enough to serve to other family members. Orange-yellow vegetables such as carrots and squash are also nutrient-dense.

● ●

Makes about 1 cup (250 mL)

Chef Jordan's Tips

The moisture content of squash can vary, so reserve the cooking liquid when straining. You may need it to thin out your purée. It's much tastier and more nutritious than water.

When shopping for acorn squash, choose one you can easily hold in your hand, 5 to 6 inches (12.5 to 15 cm) in diameter. These tend to be the sweetest.

Jill's Nutrition Tip

Darker-fleshed winter squash such as acorn and butternut and pumpkin have considerably higher amounts of beta-carotene (an antioxidant) than lighter-fleshed summer squash such as yellow zucchini and crookneck and straight-neck varieties. So while all vegetables and fruits have health benefits, as a general rule choose darkly pigmented fruits and vegetables for higher nutritional value.

● Blender

| 2½ cups | coarsely chopped peeled acorn squash (12 oz/375 g) | 625 mL |
| 2 cups | filtered water | 500 mL |

1. In a saucepan, combine squash and water. Bring to a boil over medium heat. Reduce heat to low and simmer until squash is fork-tender, about 25 minutes. In a colander set over a bowl, strain squash, reserving cooking liquid. Let cool to room temperature.

2. Transfer squash to blender or return to saucepan and use an immersion blender. Purée until smooth, adding enough of the reserved liquid to reach desired consistency (see Tips, left). Let cool until warm to the touch before serving or transfer to an airtight container and refrigerate for up to 3 days or freeze for up to 1 month.

NUTRIENTS PER SERVING (¼ cup/60 mL)

Calories	34	Dietary fiber	1.3 g
Protein	0.7 g	Sodium	6.1 mg
Total fat	0.1 g	Calcium	31.6 mg
Saturated fat	0.0 g	Iron	0.6 mg
Carbohydrates	8.9 g	Vitamin C	9.4 mg

Sweet Pea Purée

This vibrant green purée will be one of your baby's favorites. It looks great and tastes even better! Sweet green peas are a good source of protein as well as fiber, which supports digestion and elimination.

Makes about 1¼ cups (300 mL)

Chef Jordan's Tip

Generally speaking, peas in the pod can be difficult to find. Individually frozen peas, packed at their peak of freshness, are available in most grocery stores. They make a great alternative to fresh.

Jill's Nutrition Tip

Peas provide a great source of complex carbohydrates, which are slowly broken down into glucose (a simple sugar and fuel for the body) by the digestive system. Since the brain relies entirely on glucose to function, complex carbohydrates provide the perfect slow-release fuel to optimize your baby's physical and mental activities.

- **Blender**

| 1¼ cups | fresh or frozen sweet peas | 300 mL |
| 1¼ cups | filtered water | 300 mL |

1. In a saucepan, combine peas and water. Bring to a boil over medium heat. Reduce heat to low and simmer until peas are soft, about 15 minutes. Let cool until warm to the touch.

2. Transfer to blender or use an immersion blender in the saucepan. Purée until smooth. Serve immediately or transfer to an airtight container and refrigerate for up to 3 days or freeze for up to 1 month.

NUTRIENTS PER SERVING (¼ cup/60 mL)

Calories	23	Dietary fiber	1.5 g
Protein	1.5 g	Sodium	78.7 mg
Total fat	0.0 g	Calcium	1.8 mg
Saturated fat	0.0 g	Iron	0.4 mg
Carbohydrates	4.6 g	Vitamin C	2.3 mg

Carrot Purée

Carrots are a staple in our home, from yellow baby carrots to the larger everyday versions. Children love their natural sweetness.

● ●

**Makes about
1 cup (250 mL)**

Chef Jordan's Tip

I often roast carrots until caramelized, then purée them. The depth of flavor is unbelievable. Toss the chopped carrots in 1 tbsp (15 mL) extra virgin olive oil and roast in a preheated oven (300°F/150°C) until golden brown, about 30 minutes. Purée until smooth. To thin this purée, add warm filtered water until you achieve the desired consistency.

Jill's Nutrition Tip

Carrots are one of the richest vegetable sources of the antioxidant nutrient beta-carotene, which is converted to vitamin A in the liver. Your baby's developing vision relies on adequate amounts of this vitamin. Along with eye health, research suggests that eating carrots benefits cardiovascular health and helps fight against cancer.

● Blender

1½ cups	coarsely chopped peeled carrots	375 mL
1 cup	filtered water	250 mL

1. In a saucepan, combine carrots and water. Bring to a boil over medium heat. Reduce heat to low and simmer until carrots are very soft, about 25 minutes.

2. Transfer to blender or use an immersion blender in the saucepan. Purée until smooth. Let cool until warm to the touch before serving or transfer to an airtight container and refrigerate for up to 3 days or freeze for up to 1 month.

NUTRIENTS PER SERVING (¼ cup/60 mL)

Calories 20	Dietary fiber. . . . . 1.3 g
Protein. . . . . .0.5 g	Sodium. . . . . .34.9 mg
Total fat . . . . 0.1 g	Calcium . . . . .17.6 mg
Saturated fat. . . . . . . 0.0 g	Iron. . . . . 0.1 mg
Carbohydrates . . . . . . .4.6 g	Vitamin C . . . . .2.8 mg

Roasted Beet Purée

I always thought beets were a rather bland vegetable, and then I roasted them whole. Now this is one of my favorite flavors.

• •

**Makes about
1½ cups (375 mL)**

Chef Jordan's Tips

Before roasting, scrub beets with a soft brush under cool running water to remove all dirt and grit. Pat dry.

The easiest way to peel beets after roasting is to cool them in the refrigerator overnight; the skins will come off without a struggle.

Jill's Nutrition Tip

Even at this tender young age your baby's liver has more than 500 functions. One is to keep her blood clean by filtering out both internal and external toxins. Beets have a stimulating effect on the liver and its detoxification processes. Just don't be alarmed if your baby's bowel movements and urine are dyed red after enjoying this purée. Beets contain anthocyanin, a powerful antioxidant that stimulates this condition, known as beeturia.

- Blender
- Preheat oven to 350°F (180°C)

| 1½ lbs | fresh beets (3 large) | 750 g |
| 1 cup | filtered water | 250 mL |

1. On a baking sheet, roast beets in preheated oven until fork-tender, about 2½ hours. Let cool for at least 3 hours (see Tips, left).

2. Peel beets, roughly chop and transfer to a saucepan with water. Bring to a boil over medium heat.

3. Transfer to blender or use an immersion blender in the saucepan. Purée until smooth. Let cool until warm to the touch before serving or transfer to an airtight container and refrigerate for up to 3 days or freeze for up to 1 month.

NUTRIENTS PER SERVING (¼ cup/60 mL)

Calories	54	Dietary fiber	3.5 g
Protein	2.0 g	Sodium	98.8 mg
Total fat	0.2 g	Calcium	21.3 mg
Saturated fat	0.0 g	Iron	1.0 mg
Carbohydrates	12.0 g	Vitamin C	6.1 mg

Caramelized Parsnip Purée

When I was growing up, my mother rarely cooked parsnips. I learned about this very sweet tuber in culinary school. Roasting creates a delicious candy-like purée that I'm sure your baby will love.

Makes about 2 cups (500 mL)

Chef Jordan's Tip

When roasting vegetables, especially those containing a lot of sugar, drippings develop that adhere to the bottom of the cooking vessel. In professional kitchens this is called the "fond," and it is loaded with flavor that you don't want to lose. You can easily scrape the fond into the liquid by using a rubber spatula or wooden spoon.

Jill's Nutrition Tip

Parsnips look like white carrots but do not pale in the nutrients they contain. They are a good source of fiber, which helps to keep your baby's bowel healthy, and B vitamins that are used to produce energy and keep the metabolism humming. Sweet and soft, puréed parsnip is another root vegetable that works well as an introductory food.

- Blender
- Preheat oven to 350°F (180°C)

| 4 | parsnips, peeled and halved | 4 |
| 1½ cups | filtered water | 375 mL |

1. On a baking sheet, roast parsnips in preheated oven until soft and golden brown, about 1 hour.
2. Chop parsnips and transfer to a saucepan with water. Bring to a boil over medium heat. Reduce heat to low and simmer until water is reduced by about half, about 5 minutes. Transfer to blender or use an immersion blender in the saucepan. Purée until smooth. Let cool until warm to the touch before serving or transfer to an airtight container and refrigerate for up to 3 days or freeze for up to 1 month.

NUTRIENTS PER SERVING (¼ cup/60 mL)

Calories	25	Dietary fiber	1.6 g
Protein	0.4 g	Sodium	4.7 mg
Total fat	0.1 g	Calcium	13.3 mg
Saturated fat	0.0 g	Iron	0.2 mg
Carbohydrates	6.0 g	Vitamin C	5.7 mg

Basic Quinoa

Some say it's a fruit. Others argue that it's a seed. But there is no denying that this protein-packed pinhead-size "grain" is an ancient delicacy that is great for today's babies.

• •

> **Makes about
> 1¼ cups (300 mL)**

Chef Jordan's Tips

Depending upon where your baby is in terms of eating solid foods, after it's cooked, quinoa can be puréed or left whole and added to another purée to provide a nutritional boost and textural contrast.

Toasting grains in a dry pan deepens their natural flavors.

Jill's Nutrition Tip

Think of quinoa as a seed that acts like a grain. This ancient food is gluten-free, has one of the highest iron contents of any grain and is a complete protein. That means it contains all nine essential amino acids, which are the building blocks of almost everything in your baby's body. We call them essential because they must be obtained from the diet. Since most complete proteins are found in animal products, quinoa is a particularly valuable protein source for vegetarians.

½ cup	quinoa, rinsed and drained	125 mL
1 cup	filtered water	250 mL

1. Warm a saucepan over medium heat. Add quinoa and toast, stirring constantly, until golden and fragrant, about 4 minutes.

2. Add water and bring to a boil. Cover, reduce heat to low and simmer for 15 minutes. Set aside to steep until quinoa is soft and water is absorbed, about 15 minutes. Let cool to room temperature before serving or transfer to an airtight container and refrigerate for up to 3 days.

> **NUTRIENTS PER SERVING (¼ cup/60 mL)**
>
> | | |
> |---|---|
> | Calories . . . . 64 | Dietary fiber . . . . 1.0 g |
> | Protein . . . . 2.2 g | Sodium . . . . 5.0 mg |
> | Total fat . . . . 1.0 g | Calcium . . . . 11.6 mg |
> | Saturated fat . . . . 0.1 g | Iron . . . . 1.6 mg |
> | Carbohydrates . . . . 11.7 g | Vitamin C . . . . 0.0 mg |

Simple Millet Cereal

I love the nutty flavor of millet. It is quite mild and aromatic, which your baby will love. It also provides valuable nutrients, such as magnesium and the B vitamins thiamin, niacin and folate.

Makes about 2 cups (500 mL)

Chef Jordan's Tip

Millet flour stores well in an airtight container in the refrigerator.

Jill's Nutrition Tip

Millet is a wonderful grain for your baby. It is gluten-free, easily digestible and one of the least allergenic grains. It has a nice mild flavor and a protein content that is similar to wheat and rice, so it will satisfy a hungry baby's appetite. Millet is also a good source of magnesium, which has been shown to reduce the severity of asthma attacks, among other benefits.

| 3 cups | filtered water | 750 mL |
| ¾ cup | millet flour (see page 55) | 175 mL |

1. In a saucepan, bring water to a boil over medium heat. Whisk millet flour into water and continue to cook, whisking often, until mixture is thick, about 10 minutes. Remove from heat and let cool until warm to the touch. Serve immediately or transfer to an airtight container and refrigerate for up to 3 days.

NUTRIENTS PER SERVING (¼ cup/60 mL)

Calories	37	Dietary fiber	0.9 g
Protein	1.1 g	Sodium	2.7 mg
Total fat	0.4 g	Calcium	2.7 mg
Saturated fat	0.0 g	Iron	0.8 mg
Carbohydrates	7.4 g	Vitamin C	0.0 mg

Brown Rice Cereal

The difference between making your own cereal and buying something from the grocery shelves is like the difference between night and day. Finding the 10 minutes it takes to make this recipe should be the biggest chore — it's really that easy.

5 cups	filtered water	1.25 L
¾ cup	brown rice flour (see page 55)	175 mL

**Makes about
2 ¼ cups (550 mL)**

Chef Jordan's Tip

You can purchase brown rice flour in natural food stores, but I feel better about grinding my own flour (see page 55) rather than purchasing it in a bag that may have been on the shelf for many months. I get a certain pride from creating something for my children that will contribute to their long-term health.

Jill's Nutrition Tip

Chromium is found in the bran and the germ of whole grains, and a high percentage of this "ultra trace" mineral is lost when grains are refined. Chromium is important for the regulation of blood sugar, and a deficiency of this mineral is linked to the development of diabetes. Type 2 diabetes is no longer an adult disease and has been on the rise in children for the past two decades. Refined and processed grains are a large contributing factor to this problem, so making sure your baby develops a taste for whole grains from an early age positions her to maintain good health throughout her adolescent and adult life.

1. In a saucepan, bring water to a boil over medium heat. Slowly whisk rice flour into water, stirring constantly to avoid clumping. Cook, whisking constantly, until liquid turns a chocolate brown and begins to thicken, about 10 minutes. Remove from heat and set aside for at least 1 hour (the mixture will become quite thick). Continue to whisk from time to time as it cools. Serve immediately or transfer to an airtight container and refrigerate for up to 3 days.

2. To serve, reheat ½ cup (125 mL) cooked cereal with ¼ cup (60 mL) water in a saucepan over low heat, just until warm.

NUTRIENTS PER SERVING (¼ cup/60 mL)

Calories	48	Dietary fiber	0.6 g
Protein	1.0 g	Sodium	4.2 mg
Total fat	0.4 g	Calcium	4.6 mg
Saturated fat	0.1 g	Iron	0.3 mg
Carbohydrates	10.1 g	Vitamin C	0.0 mg

Fresh is Best

When you grind a whole grain, you are exposing the delicate essential oils present in the germ of the grain. These oils are very beneficial to our bodies when they are fresh but can deteriorate quickly and turn rancid with exposure to oxygen, light and heat. To preserve the freshness of these oils, try to grind just enough flour for a day or two and then store the unused portions in an airtight glass container in the fridge or freezer.

Make Your Own Flour

It takes just a few minutes to grind your own flour, and the results are worth every one of them because you produce the freshest, best-tasting flour there is. Some grains, such as millet and quinoa, benefit from a light toasting first to bring out their natural flavor. To grind flour from harder grains, such as rice and quinoa, we like to use a blender, preferably a high-powered one. If you are grinding only a very small amount, a clean coffee or spice grinder works well, too. For softer grains, such as millet and oats, an immersion blender with a small cup attachment works just fine. A clean coffee grinder or spice grinder or a home flour mill also works well for all varieties of grains. Grains can be ground and stored in an airtight container in the freezer for up to 2 months.

There is also an important health reason for making your own flour. The germ part the grain contains natural oils that have their own health benefits. When the grains are intact, these oils are protected and still pure. Heat, light and moisture cause ground grains to spoil and turn the normally healthy oils rancid. If you do purchase whole-grain flour, check the expiry date and store it in the fridge at home.

To make brown rice flour: Place long-grain brown rice in a blender, in batches if necessary, and pulse until desired consistency is achieved, about 3 minutes. Store in an airtight container in the refrigerator or freezer.

To make millet flour: In a saucepan over low heat, toast millet until aromatic, 3 to 5 minutes, stirring often to prevent burning. Remove from heat and set aside until completely cooled. Transfer to blender (or an immersion blender with a small cup attachment), in batches if necessary, and pulse until desired texture is achieved, about 3 minutes. Store in an airtight container in the refrigerator or freezer.

To make oat flour: Place steel-cut oats (our preference for nutritional reasons) or rolled oats in a blender (if you are grinding rolled oats, you can also use an immersion blender with a small cup attachment), in batches if necessary, and pulse until desired consistency is achieved, about 2 minutes. Store in an airtight container in the refrigerator or freezer.

To make quinoa flour: In a fine-mesh sieve, thoroughly rinse quinoa under cold running water, using your hand to agitate the grains, remove any bitter coating. Drain well, spread on a plate and set aside until thoroughly dry. In a saucepan over low heat, toast quinoa until it begins to pop and becomes aromatic, 3 to 5 minutes, stirring often to prevent burning. Remove from heat and set aside until completely cooled. Transfer to a blender, in batches if necessary, and pulse until desired texture is achieved, about 3 minutes. Store in an airtight container in the refrigerator or freezer.

Whole-Grain Oat Cereal with Grapes

I prefer this recipe to the packaged instant oatmeal that people often use because they think it's convenient. This version tastes better and it's healthier, too.

Chef Jordan's Tip

The grapes can be easily replaced by puréed apples, pears, peaches, plums — whatever suits you at the time.

Jill's Nutrition Tip

Whole-grain oats are a rich source of fiber and phytonutrients and they provide long-lasting energy for your baby. Often people following a gluten-free diet are advised to stay away from oats. Pure oats do not contain gluten. Rather, it is the cross-contamination with wheat, barley or rye that occurs during harvesting, milling and processing that may cause problems. If you are following a gluten-free diet, you may be able to include regular oats in your diet; if you are celiac or highly sensitive to gluten, be sure to purchase them from a source that guarantees they are gluten-free.

Always buy organic grapes.

3 cups	filtered water	750 mL
¾ cup	oat flour (see page 55)	175 mL
¼ cup	red or green organic grapes, seeded, if necessary, and puréed	60 mL

1. In a saucepan, bring water to a boil over medium heat. Whisk oat flour into water and cook, whisking constantly, until mixture is thick, about 5 minutes. Add puréed grapes and whisk thoroughly to incorporate. Remove from heat and let cool until warm to the touch. Serve immediately or transfer to an airtight container and refrigerate for up to 3 days.

Variation

For older babies who can handle chunkier food (9 to 12 months), you can add diced apples and freshly ground cinnamon or even sulfite-free dried apricots to this cereal. There are many great combinations.

NUTRIENTS PER SERVING (¼ cup/60 mL)

Calories	35	Dietary fiber	1.0 g
Protein	1.4 g	Sodium	1.6 mg
Total fat	0.6 g	Calcium	6.8 mg
Saturated fat	0.1 g	Iron	0.4 mg
Carbohydrates	6.9 g	Vitamin C	0.4 mg

Quinoa and Banana Purée

This is a great recipe for introducing quinoa to your baby. The sweetness of the bananas makes it a pleasure to eat.

• •

Makes about 1¼ cups (300 mL)

Chef Jordan's Tip

When choosing bananas for cooking, I tend to use the ripest. I'll choose from any of the sweet bananas available. Regular long yellow bananas, dwarf, finger or red bananas all work well for baby-food purées. The only variety I recommend avoiding is the plantain. While there are many delicious plantain recipes, puréeing them for baby food is not an appropriate use. Plantains are less sweet and starchier than their cousins, and they should never be eaten raw.

Jill's Nutrition Tip

Bananas have a low allergenic potential and quinoa is gluten-free. Consequently, this is a relatively safe recipe to try if you think your baby might have an allergic reaction, based on allergies you or your partner may have.

• Blender

1	banana, peeled	1
1 cup	filtered water	250 mL
½ cup	cooked quinoa (see recipe, page 52)	125 mL

1. In a saucepan, combine banana, water and quinoa. Bring to a boil over medium heat. Reduce heat to low and simmer until banana is soft, about 5 minutes.

2. Transfer to blender or use an immersion blender in the saucepan. Purée until smooth. Let cool until warm to the touch. Serve immediately or transfer to an airtight container and refrigerate for up to 3 days.

NUTRIENTS PER SERVING (¼ cup/60 mL)

Calories 46	Dietary fiber . . . . 1.0 g
Protein . . . . 1.2 g	Sodium . . . . 3.7 mg
Total fat . . . . .0.5 g	Calcium . . . . 7.8 mg
Saturated fat . . . . 0.1 g	Iron . . . . 0.7 mg
Carbohydrates . . . . . . 10.1 g	Vitamin C . . . . .2.1 mg

Apple and Fig Brown Rice Cereal

Figs add a superb, unique sweetness to the rather bland canvas provided by rice. Brown rice, which is a whole grain, is far more nutritious than white (see page 59), which has been stripped of the bran and much of the germ layers, where most of the nutrients are stored.

	Makes about 3 cups (750 mL)

Chef Jordan's Tip

Fresh figs are often available, but I also love the dried versions. Like most dried fruits, they are much sweeter and have a much more pronounced flavor than their fresh counterparts.

Jill's Nutrition Tip

Figs are entirely underrated as a superfood for babies. They are a tremendous source of fiber and minerals, such as potassium, magnesium, calcium and iron. They are also a good energy food, support blood formation and are helpful for relieving constipation.

Always buy organic apples.

5 cups	filtered water	1.25 L
¾ cup	brown rice flour (see page 55)	175 mL
2 cups	diced cored, peeled organic apples (about 2 medium)	500 mL
½ cup	chopped dried figs	125 mL

1. In a saucepan, bring water to a boil over medium heat. Slowly whisk rice flour into water, stirring constantly to avoid clumping. Cook, whisking constantly, until liquid turns a chocolate brown and begins to thicken, about 10 minutes. Add apples and figs and stir well to combine. Remove from heat and set aside for at least 1 hour or for up to 2 hours, whisking from time to time. The mixture will become quite thick as it cools. Serve immediately or transfer to an airtight container and refrigerate for up to 3 days.

2. To serve the cereal, combine with water in a ratio of ½ cup (125 mL) cooked cereal to ¼ cup (60 mL) water. Warm in a saucepan over low heat.

NUTRIENTS PER SERVING (¼ cup/60 mL)

Calories	67	Dietary fiber	1.8 g
Protein	1.0 g	Sodium	4.8 mg
Total fat	0.4 g	Calcium	18.7 mg
Saturated fat	0.1 g	Iron	0.4 mg
Carbohydrates	15.7 g	Vitamin C	1.1 mg

The Whole Story

The health benefits of grain depend entirely on its form. All grains start out as whole grains. They have three distinct parts — the endosperm (which contains the starch), the bran (where the fiber and trace minerals are) and the germ (which houses many of the good fats, B vitamins and more minerals). When a grain is processed, it loses some or all of the bran and germ, leaving only the endosperm, the part with the most carbohydrates. For instance, in the process of polishing rice to make it white, all of the bran and germ are removed, leaving only the starch component. This polishing also removes 80 percent of vitamin B_1, 67 percent of vitamin B_3, 90 percent of vitamin B_6, 60 percent of the iron, and all of the fiber and essential fatty acids. It then must be "enriched" with some of the B_1, B_3 and iron that were stripped away. Many more vitamins and minerals are removed by processing than are added back with "enrichment."

Processed and refined grains are also missing the original fiber and oils, and this changes the way the grain is digested and absorbed in the body. Processed grains cause blood sugar to rise very quickly after digestion. This rise, which is repeated multiple times over the course of a day, paves the way for unbalanced blood sugar and, ultimately, diabetes. We know that too much sugar can lead to diabetes. We've been slower to understand that processed grains act like sugar in the body and are, therefore, a large contributing factor in the progression of this epidemic lifestyle disease.

It is well known that the high fiber content of whole grains promotes digestive health. Newer studies are suggesting a wide range of benefits also associated with the exclusive use of whole grains versus processed grain. These studies show that regular consumption of whole grains reduces the risk of heart disease, some types of cancer, stroke and type 2 diabetes. People who eat whole grains have a healthier waist-to-hip ratio and lower blood serum cholesterol than people who eat processed grains. The health benefits of whole grains are a direct result of eating the entire grain, with all its original vitamins, minerals, oils and fiber, and, more important, not eating processed grains. Introducing your baby only to whole grains is a big step forward in supporting his long-term health.

Tofu, Pear and Banana Purée

This sweet purée is a great way to introduce tofu to your baby. Tofu is one of those "white canvas" foods that combine easily with other ingredients, such as fruits and vegetables.

● ●

Makes about 1 cup (250 mL)

Chef Jordan's Tip

In season, I prefer to use Bosc pears in this recipe because they have a slightly tart flavor that nicely counters the sweetness of the cooked banana, creating an excellent balance of flavors.

Jill's Nutrition Tips

Tofu, which is made from soybeans, is a complete protein from a nonanimal source (all animal foods, such as meat, poultry, eggs and fish, are complete proteins). It also provides iron, which is used for transporting oxygen throughout the body. Your baby's iron stores will begin to decline at about the 6-month mark, making iron from the diet a key nutritional consideration. Vegetable sources of iron are better absorbed when eaten with vitamin C, which in this recipe is provided by the pear.

The vast majority of soybeans grown in North America are genetically modified to withstand herbicides. Until mandatory labeling comes into use in North America, the only way to know for sure that a food is not genetically modified is to purchase its certified organic version.

Always buy organic pears and organic tofu.

● Blender

¾ cup	filtered water	175 mL
½ cup	chopped cored organic Bosc pear (see Tips, left, and Variation, below)	125 mL
½	banana	½
¼ cup	diced firm organic tofu	60 mL

1. In a saucepan, combine water, pear and banana. Bring to a boil over medium heat. Reduce heat to low and simmer until pear is fork-tender and water has reduced by about one-quarter, about 5 minutes. Remove from heat and add tofu.

2. Transfer to blender or use an immersion blender in the saucepan. Purée until smooth. Let cool until warm to the touch before serving or transfer to an airtight container and refrigerate for up to 3 days or freeze for up to 1 month.

Variation

If Bosc pears aren't available, use an equal quantity of organic Anjou or Bartlett pear.

NUTRIENTS PER SERVING (¼ cup/60 mL)

Calories	26	Dietary fiber	1.0 g
Protein	0.4 g	Sodium	1.7 mg
Total fat	0.2 g	Calcium	6.8 mg
Saturated fat	0.0 g	Iron	0.1 mg
Carbohydrates	6.6 g	Vitamin C	2.2 mg

Roasted Apple, Blueberry and Pear Purée

Blueberries add a jelly-like consistency to purées. The flavor and texture of this recipe is appealingly unique.

● ●

Makes about 3 cups (750 mL)

Chef Jordan's Tips

I prefer to use fresh berries, but frozen berries are readily available and a good option when fresh are not in season.

If you have access to wild blueberries, which have a unique flavor, use them in this recipe.

Be sure to use heatproof oven mitts to handle the skillet after it has been in the oven.

Jill's Nutrition Tip

This dynamic trio of apple, blueberry and pear is a potent source of vitamin C. The effects of this antioxidant go well beyond helping with the common cold. Vitamin C is crucial in the formation and maintenance of collagen. As the foundation of connective tissue found in skin, bones, joints and ligaments, collagen gives support and shape to your baby's body.

Always buy organic apples and pears and organic or wild blueberries.

- Ovenproof skillet
- Blender
- Preheat oven to 350°F (180°C)

3 cups	chopped cored organic apples (about 3)	750 mL
2¼ cups	finely chopped cored organic pears (about 3)	550 mL
1 cup	filtered water	250 mL
½ cup	organic or wild blueberries	125 mL

1. In ovenproof skillet, roast apples in preheated oven until skins are golden brown, about 40 minutes. Transfer skillet to the stovetop.

2. Add pears, water and blueberries. Bring to a boil over medium heat. Reduce heat and simmer, stirring occasionally, until pears are tender, about 10 minutes.

3. Transfer to blender or to a bowl if using an immersion blender. Purée until smooth. Let cool until warm to the touch before serving or transfer to an airtight container and refrigerate for up to 3 days or freeze for up to 1 month.

Variation

You can use this purée as the basis for a smoothie that will delight other members of your family. In a blender, combine 1 cup (250 mL) purée with 1 cup (250 mL) Jill's Homemade Yogurt (page 90) or plain full-fat organic yogurt.

NUTRIENTS PER SERVING (¼ cup/60 mL)

Calories 39	Dietary fiber . . . . 1.9 g
Protein . . . . .0.3 g	Sodium . . . . 1.3 mg
Total fat . . . . 0.1 g	Calcium . . . . 5.8 mg
Saturated fat . . . . 0.0 g	Iron . . . . 0.1 mg
Carbohydrates . . . . . .10.4 g	Vitamin C . . . . 3.5 mg

Nectarine and Carrot Purée

A grand recipe when nectarines are in season!

Chef Jordan's Tips

Substitute an equal amount of peaches for the nectarines.

In the absence of seasonal nectarines or peaches, use dried fruit such as apricots, pears or figs. In this recipe, use 1 cup (250 mL) dried fruit in place of the fresh.

Jill's Nutrition Tip

Nectarines and carrots both contain significant amounts of natural sugars that your baby uses as fuel for her constantly active body. Don't be afraid of trying carrots, or any vegetable for that matter, as a morning purée.

Always buy organic nectarines.

• Blender

2½ cups	quartered organic nectarines (about 3)	625 mL
1¼ cups	coarsely chopped peeled carrots	300 mL
1 cup	filtered water	250 mL

1. In a saucepan, combine nectarines, carrots and water. Bring to a boil over medium heat. Reduce heat to low and simmer until carrots are fork-tender and most of the liquid has evaporated, about 30 minutes. Let cool to room temperature.

2. Transfer to blender or use an immersion blender in the saucepan. Purée until smooth. Let cool until warm to the touch before serving or transfer to an airtight container and refrigerate for up to 3 days or freeze for up to 1 month.

Variation

For a delicious and healthy summer snack for older children, fold a touch of liquid honey and Vanilla Bean Yogurt (page 93) into some of the purée.

NUTRIENTS PER SERVING (¼ cup/60 mL)

Calories 31	Dietary fiber . . . . 1.5 g
Protein . . . . 0.7 g	Sodium . . . . 16.8 mg
Total fat . . . . 0.2 g	Calcium . . . . 11.5 mg
Saturated fat . . . . 0.0 g	Iron . . . . 0.2 mg
Carbohydrates . . . . 7.4 g	Vitamin C . . . . 4.0 mg

Apricot and Acorn Squash Purée

If your baby likes to wear her food, this is a great color. Orange vegetables such as winter squash are rich in carotenes, which are phytonutrients found in breast milk that help your baby to stay healthy.

Makes about 2 cups (500 mL)

Chef Jordan's Tips

The recommended cooking time is accurate if the acorn squash is cut to the same size as the apricots. If not, be sure to cook the squash until fork-tender.

You can substitute 3 sulfite-free dried apricots (see page 39) for the fresh apricots.

Jill's Nutrition Tip

The combination of apricot and acorn squash makes this recipe a heavy hitter for the antioxidant beta-carotene. It also provides a number of important minerals that support strong bone formation in infants, including calcium, iron, magnesium, phosphorus and potassium.

- Blender

2 cups	coarsely chopped peeled acorn squash (10 oz/300 g)	500 mL
6	apricots, pitted (about 8 oz/250 g)	6
1 cup	filtered water	250 mL

1. In a saucepan, combine squash, apricots and water. Bring to a boil over medium heat. Reduce heat to low and simmer until squash is fork-tender, about 20 minutes.

2. Transfer to blender or use an immersion blender in the saucepan. Purée until smooth. Let cool until warm to the touch before serving or transfer to an airtight container and refrigerate for up to 3 days or freeze for up to 1 month.

NUTRIENTS PER SERVING ($\frac{1}{4}$ cup/60 mL)

Calories	30	Dietary fiber	1.2 g
Protein	0.7 g	Sodium	2.3 mg
Total fat	0.2 g	Calcium	17.3 mg
Saturated fat	0.0 g	Iron	0.4 mg
Carbohydrates	7.4 g	Vitamin C	7.3 mg

Green Bean Purée with Fresh Basil

It's been said that we eat with our eyes first. If we can maintain the vibrant color of vegetables after cooking, our kids will be more likely to want to eat those vegetables (see Tips, below). Adding herbs can also help. Introducing your baby to the fresh flavors of herbs as early as possible will help him to acquire a taste for these nutrient-dense foods.

**Makes about
1 cup (250 mL)**

Chef Jordan's Tips

The best way to achieve a vibrant green for vegetables, in the absence of salt, is to keep the water at a rolling boil. When cooking larger quantities, cook in batches, being careful not to overload the water, which will lower the temperature.

Be sure to use fresh basil. In my opinion, basil is one herb that doesn't maintain its flavor when dried.

Jill's Nutrition Tip

There is more to basil than meets the nose. This fragrant herb has long been used to help relieve stomach cramps, vomiting and constipation. It is packed with nutrients such as antioxidants, acts as an immune system stimulant and also has antibacterial properties.

- Blender

1 cup	filtered water	250 mL
1½ cups	green beans, trimmed	375 mL
1 tsp	chopped fresh basil leaves (see Tips, left)	5 mL
	Ice cubes	

1. In a saucepan, bring water to a rolling boil over high heat. Add green beans. Cover, maintaining a rolling boil, and boil until beans are soft, about 10 minutes.

2. Add basil. Transfer to blender or use an immersion blender in the saucepan. Purée until smooth. Pour mixture into a bowl and place overtop of another bowl filled with ice. Stir often to stop the cooking process and ensure that the beans maintain their beautiful green color. Serve when warm to the touch or transfer to an airtight container and refrigerate for up to 3 days or freeze for up to 1 month.

NUTRIENTS PER SERVING (¼ cup/60 mL)

Calories	10	Dietary fiber	1.5 g
Protein	0.5 g	Sodium	1.8 mg
Total fat	0.0 g	Calcium	22.1 mg
Saturated fat	0.0 g	Iron	0.2 mg
Carbohydrates	2.5 g	Vitamin C	3.0 mg

Honeydew, Blueberry and Mint Purée

This recipe is so refreshing! Every summer at the cottage, I turn it into ice pops for all the kids who are there. They love them. The ice pops are a cinch to make: just freeze in ice-cube trays with wooden sticks.

Makes about 6 cups (1.5 L)

Chef Jordan's Tip

I recommend serving this purée cold, right from the refrigerator (I prefer the flavor of honeydew melon this way).

Jill's Nutrition Tip

Mint is very tummy-friendly. Its natural oils help relax the smooth muscles of the intestines, which may help relieve spasms and gas. If your baby has been struggling with gas during the day, this recipe may be a good choice to serve in the evening to reduce discomfort and help her sleep.

Always buy organic or wild blueberries.

• Blender

5 cups	coarsely chopped seeded, peeled honeydew melon (about 1 large)	1.25 L
¾ cup	organic or wild blueberries	175 mL
½	cup filtered water	125 mL
3	fresh mint leaves, chopped	3

1. In a saucepan, combine melon, blueberries and water. Bring to a boil over medium heat. (You just want to "marry" the flavors without affecting the texture of the melon.)

2. Transfer to blender or use an immersion blender in the saucepan. Add mint and purée until fully incorporated, about 1 minute. Let cool until warm to the touch before serving (see Tips, left) or transfer to an airtight container and refrigerate for up to 3 days or freeze for up to 1 month.

Variations

Although mint is a wonderful addition to this purée, you can use other herbs from your garden, if available. An equal quantity of thyme, sage or oregano works beautifully with these flavors.

This purée makes an excellent cold soup, which is a great way to cool down on a summer day. Add ½ cup (125 mL) freshly squeezed orange juice to every 1 cup (250 mL) purée.

NUTRIENTS PER SERVING (¼ cup/60 mL)

Calories	3	Dietary fiber	0.1 g
Protein	0.0 g	Sodium	0.2 mg
Total fat	0.0 g	Calcium	0.4 mg
Saturated fat	0.0 g	Iron	0.5 mg
Carbohydrates	0.7 g	Vitamin C	0.4 mg

Plum and Blueberry Purée

My son, Jonah, loved this purée with his hot cereal in the morning. Try this with Simple Millet Cereal (page 53) or Brown Rice Cereal (page 54). Your baby (and even older children) will love the combination!

• •

Makes about 2 cups (500 mL)

Chef Jordan's Tip

Once your baby has passed the 12-month mark, add 1 tsp (5 mL) liquid honey to the purée and use it as a spread. It makes a great topping for soft goat cheese. Serve to older children (over 12 months) on crackers or bread.

Jill's Nutrition Tip

It's well known that cranberries help promote urinary tract health, but did you know that blueberries do the same thing? Blueberries contain proanthocyanidins, compounds that decrease the ability of offending bacteria to stick to the lining of the bladder. Because the bacteria can't stick, they are flushed out with the urine, helping to prevent urinary tract infections, which can be common in the first year of life.

Always buy organic plums and organic or wild blueberries.

• Blender

1½ cups	sliced pitted organic plums (about 3 medium)	375 mL
1 cup	organic or wild blueberries	250 mL
½ cup	filtered water	125 mL

1. In a saucepan, combine plums, blueberries and water. Bring to a boil over medium heat. Reduce heat to low and simmer until plums are soft, about 5 minutes.

2. In a colander set over a bowl, strain fruit, reserving cooking liquid. Transfer fruit to blender or return to saucepan and use an immersion blender. Purée until smooth, adding enough of the reserved liquid to attain desired consistency. Let cool until warm to the touch before serving or transfer to an airtight container and refrigerate for up to 3 days or freeze for up to 1 month.

NUTRIENTS PER SERVING (¼ cup/60 mL)

Calories 32	Dietary fiber . . . . 1.2 g
Protein . . . . 0.5 g	Sodium . . . . 0.8 mg
Total fat . . . . 0.2 g	Calcium . . . . 4.2 mg
Saturated fat . . . . 0.0 g	Iron . . . . 0.1 mg
Carbohydrates . . . . 8.1 g	Vitamin C . . . . 6.0 mg

Zucchini and Basil Purée

Zucchini is available year-round, and this wonderfully bland-tasting vegetable is the perfect canvas for introducing your baby to deliciously perfumed fresh basil. However, zucchini that are genetically modified are entering the marketplace, so if you are not eating GMO foods, be sure to look for certified organic zucchini.

2¼ cups	coarsely chopped organic zucchini (about 3 small)	550 mL
½ cup	filtered water	125 mL
3	fresh basil leaves	3

1. In a saucepan, combine zucchini and water. Bring to a boil over medium heat. Cook until zucchini is soft and most of the liquid is absorbed, about 10 minutes. Let cool to room temperature.

2. Add basil. Transfer to blender or use an immersion blender in the saucepan. Purée until smooth. Let cool until warm to the touch before serving or transfer to an airtight container and refrigerate for up to 3 days or freeze for up to 1 month.

Makes about 1¼ cups (300 mL)

Chef Jordan's Tip

If zucchini isn't available, substitute an equal quantity of another summer squash such as crookneck squash, yellow zucchini or pattypan squash (my favorite).

Jill's Nutrition Tip

Keeping your baby well hydrated is vital to prevent constipation. Zucchini, which is 95 percent water, is a good food source of water for your baby. Zucchini also provides folic acid, or folate, which your baby needs for energy and to create red and white blood cells and keep them functioning well. Folate plays an integral role in ensuring that the blueprint of your baby's cell structure (DNA) forms correctly.

NUTRIENTS PER SERVING (¼ cup/60 mL)

Calories	8	Dietary fiber	0.6 g
Protein	0.6 g	Sodium	5.8 mg
Total fat	0.1 g	Calcium	8.8 mg
Saturated fat	0.0 g	Iron	0.2 mg
Carbohydrates	1.7 g	Vitamin C	8.7 mg

Cauliflower and Parsnip Purée

This is a wonderfully sweet purée your baby will love! Among other benefits, cooking the cauliflower makes its carotenoids more bioavailable and the parsnip adds delicious sugary notes.

● ●

Makes about 2 cups (500 mL)

Chef Jordan's Tip

Always take care when adding hot liquids to a blender. Fill the container no more than half full or let cool before blending.

Jill's Nutrition Tip

Your baby's bones are active and dynamic living things. Cauliflower contains a significant amount of vitamin K, which is vital for building and maintaining strong bones, among other benefits. This vitamin activates a protein that anchors calcium inside the bones. Other sources of vitamin K include broccoli, cabbage and leafy greens such as spinach.

● Blender

2 cups	filtered water	500 mL
2 cups	cauliflower florets	500 mL
½ cup	chopped peeled parsnip	125 mL

1. In a saucepan, combine water, cauliflower and parsnip. Bring to a boil over medium heat. Reduce heat to low and simmer until cauliflower and parsnip are fork-tender, about 20 minutes. In a colander set over a bowl, drain vegetables, reserving cooking liquid.

2. Transfer vegetables to blender or return to saucepan and use an immersion blender. Purée until smooth, adding reserved cooking liquid if necessary to achieve desired consistency. Let cool until warm to the touch before serving or transfer to an airtight container and refrigerate for up to 3 days or freeze for up to 1 month.

NUTRIENTS PER SERVING (¼ cup/60 mL)

Calories	9	Dietary fiber	0.7 g
Protein	0.3 g	Sodium	8.2 mg
Total fat	0.0 g	Calcium	9.4 mg
Saturated fat	0.0 g	Iron	0.1 mg
Carbohydrates	2.2 g	Vitamin C	7.2 mg

Cauliflower and Chickpea Chowder

This hearty purée is a wonderful addition to your baby's diet. The small amount of mint provides an enticing hint of flavor that will tease her taste buds.

● ●

Chef Jordan's Tip

You can soak and cook your own dried chickpeas or use organically grown canned chickpeas with no salt added. For this recipe, soak and cook 1 cup (250 mL) dried chickpeas. You will have about $1/3$ cup (75 mL) left over, which you can use for another purpose.

Jill's Nutrition Tip

Chickpeas (also known as garbanzo beans) are very high in fiber and are a complex carbohydrate. They are broken down slowly by the digestive system, providing sustained energy and balanced blood sugar levels. This purée will fill your baby's tummy and keep him satiated. It's a great dish to take along when the family is on the road and the time between feedings may be slightly longer than usual.

● Blender

$12/3$ cups	drained, rinsed cooked chickpeas (see page 85)	400 mL
$12/3$ cups	filtered water	400 mL
$1/3$ cup	cauliflower florets	75 mL
2	fresh mint leaves	2

1. In a saucepan, combine chickpeas, water and cauliflower. Bring to a boil over medium heat. Reduce heat to low and simmer until cauliflower is fork-tender, about 25 minutes. Add mint.

2. Transfer to blender or use an immersion blender in the saucepan. Purée until smooth. Let cool until warm to the touch before serving or transfer to an airtight container and refrigerate for up to 3 days or freeze for up to 1 month.

Variation

If you are also feeding older children, this purée makes a great dip for cut-up vegetables. Add 1 tbsp (15 mL) chopped fresh chives and $1/3$ cup (75 mL) full-fat organic sour cream to $1/2$ cup (125 mL) purée.

NUTRIENTS PER SERVING ($1/4$ cup/60 mL)

Calories	57	Dietary fiber	2.7 g
Protein	3.1 g	Sodium	4.9 mg
Total fat	0.9 g	Calcium	19.0 mg
Saturated fat	0.1 g	Iron	1.0 mg
Carbohydrates	9.6 g	Vitamin C	2.0 mg

Banana and Blueberry Purée

What could possibly be a better combination than banana and blueberry? These mouthwatering fruits are both nutritional powerhouses.

● ●

Makes about 1½ cups (375 mL)

Chef Jordan's Tip

In my house we always seem to have bananas that turn brown before someone gets the chance to eat them. These bananas are the best for cooking because they're the sweetest, so typically they get tossed into the freezer for later use. If you have bananas in the freezer, by all means use them in this recipe. Frozen bananas also make a great addition to smoothies.

Jill's Nutrition Tip

If your baby is teething, freeze some of this purée in an ice-cube tray and use it to soothe her discomfort. Some infants refuse to eat when they are experiencing teething pains, and a frozen purée may help to numb the gums. Serve a frozen purée right from the freezer, but process it just for a moment in a food processor or blender to break it down a bit.

Always buy organic or wild blueberries.

● Blender

2 cups	sliced bananas (2 medium; see Tips, left)	500 mL
1 cup	filtered water	250 mL
½ cup	organic or wild blueberries	125 mL

1. In a saucepan, combine bananas, water and blueberries. Bring to a boil over medium heat. Boil until berries are splitting in half, about 15 minutes.

2. Transfer to blender or use an immersion blender in the saucepan. Purée until smooth. Let cool until warm to the touch before serving or transfer to an airtight container and refrigerate for up to 3 days or freeze for up to 1 month.

NUTRIENTS PER SERVING (¼ cup/60 mL)

Calories	42	Dietary fiber	1.3 g
Protein	0.5 g	Sodium	1.8 mg
Total fat	0.2 g	Calcium	4.0 mg
Saturated fat	0.1 g	Iron	0.1 mg
Carbohydrates	10.8 g	Vitamin C	4.6 mg

Carrot and Split Pea Purée

This reminds me of my grandmother's split pea soup, which made her famous in Syracuse, New York. Even my picky brother Ryan loved it! So will your baby.

**Makes about
2 cups (500 mL)**

Chef Jordan's Tip

To transform this purée into a nutritious dip for older children, combine ½ cup (125 mL) purée, 2 tbsp (30 mL) plain full-fat organic yogurt and 1 tsp (5 mL) any combination of ground coriander, allspice, cumin, cardamom, paprika, nutmeg or cinnamon. It makes a wonderful Indian-inspired dip for grilled pita, naan or flatbread and veggies.

Jill's Nutrition Tip

The deeper the color of the carrot, the higher the beta-carotene content. Beta-carotene is just one member of the carotenoid family, which, among other functions, stimulate the production of T-helper immune cells to protect the body from infections and reduce inflammation. Avoid carrots that have a dark green or black rim at the top, which indicates they are old and have lost nutrients.

- Blender

3 cups	filtered water	750 mL
½ cup	coarsely chopped peeled carrot	125 mL
½ cup	dried split yellow peas, rinsed	125 mL
	Additional warm filtered water, optional	

1. In a saucepan, combine water, carrot and split peas. Bring to a boil over medium heat. Reduce heat to low and simmer, stirring occasionally, until peas are soft and water has evaporated, about 75 minutes.

2. Transfer to blender or use an immersion blender in the saucepan. Purée until smooth, adding warm water in small increments if necessary to reach desired consistency. Let cool until warm to the touch before serving or transfer to an airtight container and refrigerate for up to 3 days or freeze for up to 1 month.

NUTRIENTS PER SERVING (¼ cup/60 mL)

Calories	53	Dietary fiber	0.4 g
Protein	3.5 g	Sodium	13.6 mg
Total fat	0.0 g	Calcium	8.0 mg
Saturated fat	0.0 g	Iron	0.5 mg
Carbohydrates	10.0 g	Vitamin C	0.9 mg

Red Lentil and Apple Purée

This is an excellent recipe for introducing lentils to your baby. He will be familiar with the flavor of apples, which ensures that he will have a comfort level with the foreign texture of the lentils.

● ●

Makes about 3 cups (750 mL)

Chef Jordan's Tip

If you require more water for cooking the lentils, make sure it's hot before adding it to the pan, so you won't lower the temperature and slow the cooking.

Jill's Nutrition Tips

Steaming and especially boiling pulls some nutrients from food and into the cooking water. That's why it's a good idea to use cooking water to thin purées — it returns some of the nutrients to the meal. You can also add it, diluted with fresh water, to a sippy cup and your baby can drink it between meals.

To retain the maximum amount of nutrients, use fresh produce within a few days of purchase, cook fruits and vegetables with their skins on, and prepare baby food as close to feeding time as possible.

Always buy organic apples.

● Blender

2½ cups	filtered water, approx. (see Tips, left)	625 mL
1½ cups	red lentils, rinsed and drained	375 mL
1	organic Gala apple, cored and coarsely chopped	1

1. In a saucepan, combine water, lentils and apple. Bring to a boil over medium heat. Cover, reduce heat to low and simmer, stirring occasionally and adding more water if necessary to prevent sticking, until lentils are soft, about 25 minutes.

2. Transfer to blender or use an immersion blender in the saucepan. Purée until smooth. Let cool until warm to the touch before serving or transfer to an airtight container and refrigerate for up to 3 days or freeze for up to 1 month.

NUTRIENTS PER SERVING (¼ cup/60 mL)

Calories	35	Dietary fiber	2.2 g
Protein	2.3 g	Sodium	1.9 mg
Total fat	0.1 g	Calcium	6.6 mg
Saturated fat	0.0 g	Iron	0.8 mg
Carbohydrates	6.6 g	Vitamin C	0.9 mg

Watermelon, Peach and Blueberry Purée

This purée is definitely not for babies only. Kids of all ages will love its fresh flavors.

Makes about 4 cups (1 L)

Chef Jordan's Tip

Although seedless watermelons make your life easier when puréeing, the freshest local melons are the best, seedless or not. The best way to remove the seeds is with your best kitchen tool: your hands.

Jill's Nutrition Tip

Watermelon is not only delicious but, when it comes to the important antioxidant lycopene, it's a superstar. As the watermelon gets redder, the lycopene levels get higher, so if you are buying a quarter or half melon, look for as deep a red as you can find. This purée will be so popular that the watermelon won't last long, but rest assured that lycopene is stable for about 4 days in the fridge.

Always buy organic peaches and organic or wild blueberries.

• Blender

2¼ cups	chopped seedless watermelon (about 1½ lbs/750 g)	550 mL
2 cups	sliced pitted organic peaches (about 3)	500 mL
¼ cup	organic or wild fresh or frozen blueberries	60 mL

1. In blender, combine watermelon, peaches and blueberries. Purée until smooth. Serve immediately or transfer to an airtight container and refrigerate for up to 3 days or freeze for up to 1 month.

NUTRIENTS PER SERVING (¼ cup/60 mL)

Calories 15	Dietary fiber. . . . . .0.5 g
Protein. . . . . .0.3 g	Sodium. . . . . 0.7 mg
Total fat . . . . 0.1 g	Calcium . . . . .2.8 mg
Saturated fat. . . . . 0.0 g	Iron. . . . . 0.1 mg
Carbohydrates . . . . . . .4.3 g	Vitamin C . . . . 2.7 mg

Raw Foods for Your Baby

One of the features of a healthy diet is variety. As you introduce different foods to your baby, she learns about sweetness, temperature and texture. Initially, cooking most foods can be helpful for her developing digestive tract. But as your baby becomes more accustomed to different tastes, introducing her to the texture of raw foods, even though they are puréed, continues to expand her palate.

Foods are more than just proteins, fats and carbohydrates. Vegetables and fruit are full of beneficial phytochemicals, some of which may be degraded by processing techniques such as cooking. When fruits and vegetables are steamed or boiled, some water-soluble vitamins are lost into the water. To retain some of these displaced nutrients, we recommend that you use the cooking water to thin purées.

Fruits are the best raw foods to start your baby with because they are more easily digested. Following that, introduce raw vegetables and nut and seed butters. We don't recommend raw grains until well past the first year, when your baby's digestive system is more mature.

There is no one way to introduce foods to your baby, but providing a diet that is varied in composition and includes cooked and raw fruit and vegetables offers opportunities for exploration and learning.

Be aware, though, that raw fruits and vegetables may harbour harmful bacteria such as *E. coli*. So when you are preparing a recipe using raw food, make sure to be particularly careful when washing your produce.

Avocado, Carrot and Cucumber Purée

This recipe, which uses raw ingredients, is very refreshing. Think of it as an infant gazpacho, minus the tomatoes.

● ●

Makes about 1¾ cups (425 mL)		

Chef Jordan's Tip

Avocados tend to oxidize (turn brown) quickly. One trick, in the absence of lemon juice, is to combine all the ingredients before peeling the avocado. This gives you something to mix with the avocado, delaying the onset of oxidization. For storage, make sure the plastic wrap directly touches the purée, to prevent oxygen from reaching the mixture.

Jill's Nutrition Tip

This recipe is a smooth and creamy way to introduce raw vegetables. Carrots aren't quite as sweet when they are raw, so they balance well with the avocado and mint. Adding cucumber to your baby's diet helps to keep her hydrated while providing vitamins A and C, along with folate for healthy red blood cells.

Always buy organic cucumbers.

- Blender

¾ cup	chopped pitted, peeled avocado (see Tips, left)	175 mL
½ cup	chopped seeded, peeled organic English cucumber	125 mL
¼ cup	grated peeled carrot	60 mL
¼ cup	filtered water	60 mL
3	fresh mint leaves	3

1. In blender, combine avocado, cucumber, carrot, water and mint. Purée until smooth. Serve immediately or transfer to an airtight container and refrigerate for up to 3 days (see Tips, left).

Variation

This recipe makes an excellent dip for older children. Scoop off some for your baby and add 2 tbsp (30 mL) freshly squeezed lemon juice, a pinch of sea salt and freshly ground black pepper before serving with cut-up vegetables of your choice.

NUTRIENTS PER SERVING (¼ cup/60 mL)	
Calories 27	Dietary fiber. . . . . 1.2 g
Protein. . . . . 0.4 g	Sodium. . . . . 3.8 mg
Total fat . . . . 2.3 g	Calcium . . . . 4.6 mg
Saturated fat. . . . . 0.3 g	Iron . . . . 0.1 mg
Carbohydrates . . . . 1.8 g	Vitamin C . . . . 2.1 mg

Peach, Chive and Basil Purée

Combining fresh basil with ripe peaches is the perfect way to introduce the sweet flavor of this pungent herb to your baby. As your child grows, you can even use this as a very tasty jam to spread on her morning toast.

Makes about 2 cups (500 mL)

Chef Jordan's Tips

If fresh peaches aren't in season, substitute canned peaches packed in water.

Nectarines and apricots are a good substitute for the peaches in this recipe.

Substitute an equal quantity of fresh mint leaves for the basil.

Jill's Nutrition Tip

Chives are a nutrient-dense member of the allium family of vegetables and herbs, which also includes onions, leeks, green onions and garlic. Along with vitamins A and C, chives contain choline, a nutrient that helps with sleep, learning and memory.

Always buy organic peaches.

- Blender

2 cups	chopped pitted organic peaches (about 3 medium)	500 mL
½ cup	filtered water	125 mL
2 tbsp	roughly chopped fresh chives	30 mL
3	fresh basil leaves	3

1. In blender, blend peaches, water, chives and basil until smooth. (If you prefer, combine ingredients in a deep bowl and use an immersion blender to purée.) To thin the purée, add more water until desired consistency is achieved. Serve immediately or transfer to an airtight container and refrigerate for up to 3 days.

NUTRIENTS PER SERVING (¼ cup/60 mL)

Calories	15.3	Dietary fiber	0.6 g
Protein	0.4 g	Sodium	0.0 mg
Total fat	0.1 g	Calcium	3.4 mg
Saturated fat	0.0 g	Iron	0.1 mg
Carbohydrates	3.7 g	Vitamin C	3.0 mg

Apple, Pear and Avocado Purée

Avocado contributes perfect creaminess to the mealy texture of apple and pears.
Your baby will surprise you with requests for more of this nutritious blend.

● ●

Makes about 2 cups (500 mL)

Chef Jordan's Tip

Virtually any varieties of pears and apples can be used for this recipe.

Jill's Nutrition Tip

Avocados are a great source of monounsaturated fat, the same fat found in olive oil and the main fat supporting some of the health benefits of the Mediterranean diet. These fats help protect the heart and reduce inflammation in the body. Feeding your baby avocados on a regular basis is a heart-healthy habit.

Always buy organic apples and pears.

● Blender

1 cup	chopped pitted, peeled avocado	250 mL
½ cup	chopped cored organic apple (about ½ apple)	125 mL
½ cup	chopped cored organic pear (about ½ pear)	125 mL
¼ cup	filtered water	60 mL

1. In blender, blend avocado, apple, pear and water until smooth. (If you prefer, combine ingredients in a deep bowl and use an immersion blender to purée.) To thin the purée, add more water until desired consistency is achieved. Serve immediately or transfer to an airtight container and refrigerate for up to 3 days.

NUTRIENTS PER SERVING (¼ cup/60 mL)

Calories	39.8	Dietary fiber	1.8 g
Protein	0.4 g	Sodium	1.5 mg
Total fat	2.8 g	Calcium	3.6 mg
Saturated fat	0.4 g	Iron	0.1 mg
Carbohydrates	4.2 g	Vitamin C	2.7 mg

Date and Blueberry Purée

In addition to sweetness, dates add a unique, almost chocolaty flavor to this purée. Dates provide a wide range of nutrients and are particularly high in dietary fiber, which helps to keep your baby regular.

●●●

**Makes about
2 cups (500 mL)**

Chef Jordan's Tip

Although it's made for babies, Mom and Dad should give this purée a try as part of their next cheese platter. It's delish!

Jill's Nutrition Tip

Dates are a wonderfully sweet way to provide your baby with valuable nutrients. Your baby's iron stores from birth are declining, and food now needs to be the main source of his iron intake. Dates are high in this important mineral, which helps with the formation of hemoglobin in red blood cells.

Always buy organic or wild blueberries.

● Blender

1 cup	chopped pitted dates	250 mL
1 cup	organic or wild blueberries	250 mL
½ cup	filtered water	125 mL

1. In blender, blend dates, blueberries and water until smooth. (If you prefer, combine ingredients in a deep bowl and use an immersion blender to purée.) Serve immediately or transfer to an airtight container and refrigerate for up to 3 days.

NUTRIENTS PER SERVING (¼ cup/60 mL)

Calories 97.9	Dietary fiber. . . . . .2.7 g
Protein. . . . . .0.7 g	Sodium. . . . . 1.4 mg
Total fat. . . . . .0.2 g	Calcium . . . . .22.4 mg
Saturated fat. . . . . . . 0.0 g	Iron. . . . . .0.4 mg
Carbohydrates . . . . . .25.7 g	Vitamin C . . . . .3.4 mg

Celery Root and Chicken Purée

Your baby will love the smooth, potato-like texture of celery root, not to mention its mild celery flavor.

Makes about 1¼ cups (300 mL)

Chef Jordan's Tip

Don't be scared of celery root. Also known as celeriac, it should be firm to the touch; if there's a little bit of give, it isn't fresh. Wash the celeriac thoroughly before peeling to avoid getting dirt on the flesh. In the absence of celery root, a combination of celery and parsnip does a fabulous job of mimicking its texture and flavor. Be sure to peel your celery to ensure a smooth texture in the final product.

Jill's Nutrition Tip

Celery root provides a good range of minerals, including phosphorus, which every cell of your baby's body requires to function normally. It is also an essential mineral for strong bones and teeth (85 percent of your baby's phosphorus is found in his bones and teeth).

- Blender

1 cup	filtered water	250 mL
½ cup	diced peeled celery root	125 mL
4 oz	boneless, skinless chicken breast, cut in half	125 g

1. In a saucepan, combine water, celery root and chicken and bring to a boil over medium heat. Reduce heat to low and simmer until chicken is no longer pink inside and celery root is fork-tender, about 20 minutes.

2. Transfer to blender or use an immersion blender in the saucepan. Purée until smooth. Let cool until warm to the touch before serving or transfer to an airtight container and refrigerate for up to 3 days or freeze for up to 1 month.

Variation

Scoop off some of this purée to serve to your baby and combine the remainder with ½ cup (125 mL) organic whole milk or heavy or whipping (35%) cream. This makes a wonderful sauce for whole-grain gluten-free pasta that your older children will love.

NUTRIENTS PER SERVING (¼ cup/60 mL)

Calories 52	Dietary fiber . . . . 0.5 g
Protein . . . . 8.1 g	Sodium . . . . 44.9 mg
Total fat . . . . 1.0 g	Calcium . . . . 15.9 mg
Saturated fat . . . . 0.3 g	Iron . . . . 0.4 mg
Carbohydrates . . . . 2.3 g	Vitamin C . . . . 2.0 mg

Sweet Pea, Lamb and Parsnip Purée

The flavor of lamb can often overpower other ingredients. In this recipe, however, the sweetness of the parsnips and the earthy tone of the peas work beautifully to tame the strong taste. Among other benefits, lamb is a particularly digestible meat (see Tips, left).

Makes about 1¼ cups (300 mL)

Chef Jordan's Tip

When choosing a cut of lamb for a purée, it is important to choose a lean piece of meat. Don't use stewing lamb in this recipe: the meat isn't cooked long enough to break down the sinew.

Jill's Nutrition Tips

Lamb is a great protein source that contains significant amounts of iron. At about 6 months, infants have a greater need for both iron and protein to fuel the considerable growth that is happening at this stage in their development.

Lamb is often considered an anti-allergenic food. It may also be more easily digested than other red meats, so for many reasons it is a valuable addition to the list of first proteins for your baby. New Zealand lamb is pasture-raised (grass-fed) by law, resulting in a healthier fat content, among other nutritional benefits.

- Blender

4 oz	boneless lamb loin or leg, cubed (about ½ inch/1 cm; see Tips, left)	125 g
1 cup	filtered water	250 mL
½ cup	frozen sweet peas	125 mL
¼ cup	coarsely chopped peeled parsnip	60 mL

1. In a saucepan, combine lamb, water, peas and parsnip. Bring to a boil over medium heat. Cover, reduce heat to low and simmer until parsnip is soft, about 10 minutes.

2. Transfer to blender or use an immersion blender in the saucepan. Purée until smooth. Let cool until warm to the touch before serving or transfer to an airtight container and refrigerate for up to 3 days or freeze for up to 1 month.

NUTRIENTS PER SERVING (¼ cup/60 mL)

Calories	96	Dietary fiber	1.2 g
Protein	4.9 g	Sodium	48.6 mg
Total fat	6.7 g	Calcium	9.5 mg
Saturated fat	3.0 g	Iron	0.7 mg
Carbohydrates	4.1 g	Vitamin C	3.0 mg

Chicken and Red Lentil Purée

This Indian-inspired combination is a real hit with babies. Red lentils lose their texture when cooked, becoming purée-like on their own.

Chef Jordan's Tip

As our son, Jonah, became older, Tamar and I were able to expand the variety of foods he consumed without his realizing it. I often made "chicken wraps" filled with chicken and lentil purée, tomatoes and cheese and seared like a grilled cheese sandwich. We enjoyed them together.

Jill's Nutrition Tip

Chicken, like all meats and fish, contains all nine essential amino acids, including phenylalanine and methionine. Phenylalanine is specifically responsible for the positive brain chemicals that keep your baby's alertness levels and potential for learning at their height. Methionine's sulfur content supports detoxification pathways that help baby's body eliminate environmental toxins from the things that surround us, such as smog and exhaust fumes.

- Blender

¾ cup	red lentils	175 mL
2 oz	boneless, skinless chicken breast	60 g
1 cup	filtered water	250 mL

1. In a fine-mesh sieve, rinse lentils under cold running water until water runs clear. Drain well.
2. In a saucepan, combine lentils, chicken and water. Bring to a boil over medium heat. Reduce heat to low and simmer, stirring occasionally, until chicken is no longer pink inside, lentils are soft and most of the water has been absorbed, about 25 minutes.
3. Transfer to blender or use an immersion blender in the saucepan. Purée until smooth. Let cool until warm to the touch before serving or transfer to an airtight container and refrigerate for up to 3 days or freeze for up to 1 month.

NUTRIENTS PER SERVING (¼ cup/60 mL)

Calories	92	Dietary fiber	1.3 g
Protein	8.4 g	Sodium	51.7 mg
Total fat	0.2 g	Calcium	11.2 mg
Saturated fat	0.0 g	Iron	0.8 mg
Carbohydrates	13.6 g	Vitamin C	0.0 mg

Grilled Chicken and Avocado Purée

This is a great dish to make for baby. If you are barbecuing chicken for yourself, you can make extra and transform it into this tasty purée. I love the flavor combination of chicken and avocado and usually enjoy it at least once a week.

Makes about 2 cups (500 mL)

Chef Jordan's Tip

If timing is an issue, a store-bought rotisserie chicken is a good substitute for grilled chicken in this recipe. Remove the skin and all bones and pieces of cartilage before chopping. When buying a cooked chicken, choose one that hasn't been sitting under the heat lamp too long, as it will tend to be quite dry.

Jill's Nutrition Tip

Historically, avocados received a bad rap because they are a high-fat food. However, we now know that their fat composition is precisely what provides their unique health benefits. Avocados contain three healthy fats with wide-ranging anti-inflammatory actions that are important even in a baby's body. They are also a low-carbohydrate food that is high in fiber, to help keep your baby's energy levels even.

- Preheat barbecue to High or 500°F (260°C)
- Blender

8 oz	boneless, skinless chicken breast	250 g
1¼ cups	coarsely chopped pitted, peeled avocado (about 1)	300 mL
½ cup	filtered water	125 mL

1. On preheated barbecue, grill chicken breast until well browned, about 10 minutes. Turn and cook until no longer pink inside, 3 to 4 minutes. Let cool until warm to the touch, about 15 minutes. Cut into cubes.

2. In a saucepan, combine chicken, avocado and water. Bring to a boil over medium heat.

3. Transfer to blender or use an immersion blender in the saucepan. Purée until smooth. Let cool until warm to the touch before serving or transfer to an airtight container and refrigerate for up to 3 days or freeze for up to 1 month.

NUTRIENTS PER SERVING (¼ cup/60 mL)

Calories 89	Dietary fiber. . . . . 1.6 g
Protein . . . . 10.2 g	Sodium . . . . 25.2 mg
Total fat . . . . 4.6 g	Calcium . . . . 8.0 mg
Saturated fat. . . . . 0.8 g	Iron . . . . 0.5 mg
Carbohydrates . . . . 2.0 g	Vitamin C . . . . 2.3 mg

White Navy Bean and Beef Purée

The flavors of white beans and beef belong together — that's why this combination is a classic. From a health perspective, it is also a winner. Beef has high levels of vitamin B_{12}, which is needed for normal functioning of the brain and nervous system. However, it doesn't contain any fiber. Beans are high in fiber but don't contain any B_{12} (no plant foods contain naturally occurring B_{12}). Both provide good levels of protein for growing bodies.

• •

Makes about 2¼ cups (550 mL)

Chef Jordan's Tip

Use any dried white bean, such as navy, Great Northern or cannellini, in this recipe.

Jill's Nutrition Tip

This purée provides zinc from both the beans and the beef. Zinc is an important mineral because it is involved in more body functions than any other mineral. Adequate levels are necessary for proper immune function and to decrease the risk of infections such as cold and flu. It is also essential to help your body heal cuts and scrapes.

• Blender

3 cups	filtered water	750 mL
½ cup	dried white navy beans, soaked, drained and rinsed (see page 85)	125 mL
¾ cup	coarsely chopped peeled carrot	175 mL
4 oz	beef sirloin or thinly sliced beef short ribs	125 g

1. In a saucepan, combine water, beans, carrot and beef. Bring to a boil over medium heat. Reduce heat to low and simmer until beans are fork-tender, about 75 minutes.

2. Transfer to blender or use an immersion blender in the saucepan. Purée until smooth. Let cool until warm to the touch before serving or transfer to an airtight container and refrigerate for up to 3 days or freeze for up to 1 month.

NUTRIENTS PER SERVING (¼ cup/60 mL)

Calories	40	Dietary fiber	1.3 g
Protein	4.1 g	Sodium	18.0 mg
Total fat	1.1 g	Calcium	17.2 mg
Saturated fat	0.3 g	Iron	0.5 mg
Carbohydrates	3.6 g	Vitamin C	0.6 mg

Cook Your Own Beans

When a recipe calls for cooked beans, such as navy or cannellini beans or chickpeas, you have two options: you can cook dried beans from scratch or use canned beans, which produce a similar result. However, canned beans usually contain significant amounts of sodium. If you are using canned beans in any of our recipes, be sure to rinse them thoroughly under cold running water to remove as much of the added salt as possible, or purchase a brand with no salt added (for more on canned beans, see page 117).

While it is not difficult to prepare dried beans from scratch, you do need to plan ahead, because they need to be soaked before they are cooked. The following instructions can be adjusted to suit the quantity of beans (or chickpeas) you wish to cook — it can be halved, doubled or tripled. A good rule of thumb is that 1 cup (250 mL) dried beans makes 2 cups (500 mL) cooked. Although the sizes vary, standard cans of beans usually range from 14 oz (398 mL) to 19 oz (540 mL), each providing about 2 cups (500 mL) of cooked beans. A little more or less usually doesn't matter in a recipe.

Long soak: In a bowl, combine 1 cup (250 mL) dried beans (or chickpeas) and 3 cups (750 mL) water. Set aside for at least 6 hours or overnight. Drain and rinse thoroughly with cold water. The beans are now ready for cooking.

Quick soak: In a saucepan, combine beans (or chickpeas) and water. Cover and bring to a boil. Boil for 3 minutes. Turn off heat and soak for 1 hour. Drain and rinse thoroughly under cold water. The beans are now ready to cook.

To cook soaked beans (or chickpeas): In a saucepan, combine 1 cup (250 mL) soaked beans and 3 cups (750 mL) fresh cold water. Bring to a boil over medium-high heat. Reduce heat to low and simmer until beans are tender, 45 minutes to 1 hour, depending on the variety.

Storing
Once cooked, beans (and chickpeas) should be covered and stored in the refrigerator, where they will keep for up to 4 days. Cooked beans can be frozen in an airtight container for up to 6 months.

Establishing Preferences

9 to 12 Months

• •

Expanding Your Baby's Tastes 88

Dishes with Dairy

Jill's Homemade Yogurt 90

Vanilla Bean Yogurt 93

Stewed Leeks with Butter 94

The Best Eggplant Parmesan 95

Brussels Sprout Gratin 96

Mediterranean Fried Eggplant 97

Diced Potato Gratin 98

Poached Garlic with
Thyme and Sour Cream 99

Grains and Fruit

Summer Cherry Quinoa 100

Millet Cereal with Bananas
and Sour Cream 101

Vegetable Combos

Egg and Sweet Pepper
Fried Rice 102

Bok Choy with Ginger 104

Brussels Sprouts with Bacon 105

Oven-Roasted Cherry Tomato
Purée 106

Turnip and Parsnip Smash 107

Red Cabbage, Fennel
and Apple Purée 108

Roasted Sweet Onion
Purée 109

Potato, Parsnip and Chicken
Soup 110

Chive Parsley Pesto 112

Colorful Vegetable Medley 114

Sautéed Chard with Apples 115

Legumes

White Bean and Fennel
Purée 116

Edamame Hummus 118

Meat Combos

Oven-Roasted Chicken
with Apricots 119

Chicken with Roasted
Butternut Squash and Leeks 120

Pork with Peaches 121

Beef and Dates 122

Lamb with Parsnips and
Cranberries 123

Expanding Your Baby's Tastes

New Foods to Add

In this chapter, we have included recipes that use egg yolks, cheese and yogurt, which are appropriate for this age group. Adding these new foods to your baby's diet will help you to continue expanding your baby's palate, as well as her nutritional intake.

Throughout the 9- to 12-month period, your child's intake of breast milk or formula will decline and solid foods will replace this source of nutrients. Once your baby reaches 8 or 9 months, she may be more assertive at displaying her individuality, especially at mealtime. She is likely to be more definite about the food she likes and at times may even refuse to eat a particular food. It is common for babies of this age to tightly purse their lips, turn their heads away so the food you are offering ends up in their ear, and even throw food. This behavior can be very frustrating to parents who just want to make sure their baby gets fed.

Allowing your baby to exert some independence can go a long way toward keeping the peace at mealtime. Give your baby a small, rounded spoon to experiment with, and place some mashed food directly on her tray so she can try feeding herself. Again, every baby progresses at her own rate, so take your cues from her when determining the next step. It is your job as a parent to provide appropriate nourishing foods at each stage of your baby's life, but it is your baby who decides how much of these foods she will eat at a sitting. By respecting your baby's unspoken messages about hunger and fullness, you are helping her to establish a lifelong pattern of healthy eating.

At this age, your baby will enjoy eating slightly lumpier foods. If you make the transition to more textured food gradually, you'll provide her with time to adjust. Continue to use all the recipes from the preceding chapter, but instead of puréeing, try pulsing the food in the blender to produce a coarser texture. You can even mash it with a fork or cut it into a fine mince, depending on your baby's preferences.

Widening the Range of Foods

Using something called a baby-feeder (or a teething-feeder) can let your baby try a wide range of foods, both cooked and raw. This device is a small mesh bag that attaches tightly to an easy-to-hold handle. It allows your baby to suck, gnaw and chew the whole food through the mesh, eating just very small, manageable pieces. It works very well for frozen foods, too. Using a pacifier clip will prevent her from throwing it on the floor.

This age is also the time to introduce finger foods, as your baby's dexterity is increasing. Good options here include pieces of well-cooked (then cooled) vegetables such as turnip, squash and carrots and raw soft fruits such as peaches, pears and bananas. Make sure the pieces are soft enough to be mashed against the roof of your baby's mouth and small enough to prevent choking. Finger foods cut into ¼-inch (0.5 cm) square pieces (diced) should be small enough for her to scoop up with her fingers, but even so, you'll need to constantly supervise when your baby is eating to make sure she doesn't choke on anything. Continuing to offer her a wide variety of foods with different colors, tastes and textures will help her to accept new flavors and the new foods to come.

Your baby may show some interest in drinking from your glass and might like to try her own sippy cup. Fresh filtered water is the best thing to put in her cup. Juice, even that made from pure fruits, is still a highly concentrated sugar. It isn't necessary for a child whose diet includes puréed or mashed whole fruit. Even though she may not get too much out of the sippy cup at this point, juice can decrease her appetite for the nutrient-dense solid foods you have prepared. Now and throughout the toddler years, encourage your child to eat whole foods and drink fresh water for optimal health.

Eggs Are Very Nutritious

Introducing eggs when your baby reaches the 9-month mark adds a delicious soft food to her diet. Eggs have broad nutritional benefits for growing babies. They are an important source of protein, fat, vitamins A, D, E and B_{12}, folate, selenium, iodine and choline, which plays a central role in brain development. The World Health Organization (WHO) uses eggs as its reference standard when evaluating the protein quality of other foods. Egg protein (found in both the yolk and the white) is referred to as "HBV" (high biological value) protein, which means it contains all the essential amino acids.

Jill's Homemade Yogurt

When you make your own yogurt, you can be certain that it contains active cultures and no artificial ingredients. It is also very easy to do and cost-effective.

● ●

**Makes about
8 ½ cups (2.125 L)**

Chef Jordan's Tip

We all take pride in cooking for our families, but making a household staple, such as yogurt, from scratch is particularly satisfying. Jill's Homemade Yogurt is the perfect blank canvas for making smoothies and also to serve as an accompaniment to baby foods such as Roasted Banana Purée (page 36), Mango Purée (page 41) or Blueberry Purée (page 40) or, once your baby is old enough, topped with fresh berries.

Always buy organic milk products.

- Slow cooker
- Large saucepan with lid
- 2 large towels

8 cups	whole organic milk	2 L
½ cup	plain full-fat organic yogurt with active bacterial culture, at room temperature	125 mL

1. Set slow cooker to High and remove yogurt from fridge (see box, page 91).

2. In saucepan, heat milk over medium-high heat, stirring frequently to avoid scalding, until it begins to bubble around the edges and becomes frothy. (If you are using a kitchen thermometer, it should read 180° to 185°F/82° to 85°C.)

3. Meanwhile, fill a large basin (or the sink) with 2 to 3 inches (5 to 7.5 cm) of ice water.

4. When milk is warm, cover saucepan with lid and place in ice water (be careful not to get any water in the milk). Set aside for 10 minutes (see box, page 91).

5. When milk has cooled, turn off slow cooker. Add about 1 cup (250 mL) of the cooled milk and the yogurt to slow cooker stoneware. Whisk to combine thoroughly. Gradually add remaining milk, stirring until yogurt is thoroughly integrated.

6. Place lid on slow cooker and wrap the appliance snugly in large towels, covering both the lid and the sides. Set aside for 8 to 12 hours (the longer you let it sit, the tangier your yogurt becomes).

Jill's Nutrition Tip

We generally think of using organic products to reduce our exposure to harmful compounds such as pesticides and other toxins. While these reasons are valid when choosing organic milk, an equally compelling reason has been discovered more recently: the type of fats in the milk. A 2013 study published in the journal *PLOS One* by researchers from Washington State University revealed that organic milk contains 25 percent less omega-6 and 62 percent more omega-3 fats than conventional milk. More omega-3 fats is very beneficial for development of your baby's brain and nervous system. For more information on fats, see pages 20 to 22.

7. Remove towels and transfer slow cooker stoneware to the refrigerator. Chill for at least 2 hours, until thickened.

8. Divide yogurt among airtight glass storage containers. Refrigerate unopened containers for up to 1 month. Once opened, use within 2 weeks.

NUTRIENTS PER SERVING (¼ cup/60 mL)

Calories 37.8	Dietary fiber . . . . 0.0 g
Protein . . . . .2.2 g	Sodium . . . . 31.0 mg
Total fat . . . . .2.0 g	Calcium . . . . .69.0 mg
Saturated fat . . . . 1.3 g	Iron . . . . .0.0 mg
Carbohydrates . . . . 3.1 g	Vitamin C . . . . .0.0 mg

Just the Best Yogurt

• It's important to preheat the slow cooker and allow the stoneware to warm before starting, because the residual heat encourages the milk to culture.

• After the milk has warmed on the stovetop, it needs to sit in the ice water long enough to cool, but not so long that is no longer warm when transferred to the slow cooker.

• For the utmost convenience, place the milk in the slow cooker just before you go to bed. When you wake up in the morning, your yogurt will be ready to chill.

Vanilla Bean Yogurt

When it comes to vanilla, nothing beats the bean. Your baby will love this, not only plain and simple but also added to fruit purées or hot cereals.

● ●

Makes about 2 cups (500 mL)

Chef Jordan's Tip

Vanilla beans can be purchased in well-stocked supermarkets and specialty shops. Using a vanilla bean is preferable because it is the most natural form of this spice. However, for convenience you can use dried vanilla beans ($1/2$ tsp/ 2 mL) or alcohol-free organic vanilla extract (1 tsp/5 mL). Be aware that some alcohol-free vanilla extract may contain unwanted additives. Read the label carefully.

Jill's Nutrition Tip

When purchasing yogurt, check the label to make sure it contains active bacteria culture, including the friendly bacterium *Lactobacillus acidophilus*, which is found in large amounts in your baby's intestines. These probiotics are fierce protectors of your baby's immune system and should be replaced constantly, especially if she has recently been prescribed antibiotics.

Always buy organic milk products.

1	vanilla bean or 1 tsp (5 mL) pure vanilla extract (see Tips, left)	1
2 cups	Jill's Homemade Yogurt (page 90) or plain full-fat organic yogurt	500 mL

1. Using a paring knife, cut vanilla bean in half lengthwise, exposing the seeds. Scrape seeds into a bowl. Add yogurt and mix well. Serve immediately or transfer to an airtight container and refrigerate for up to 3 days.

Variation

Reserve the vanilla pod to flavor sugar or salt. Simply place it in an airtight container along with the sugar or salt, cover and set aside for 1 to 2 weeks before using. Vanilla salt makes a great substitute for unflavored salt in most baking recipes.

NUTRIENTS PER SERVING ($1/4$ cup/60 mL)

Calories	39	Dietary fiber	0.0 g
Protein	2.1 g	Sodium	28.2 mg
Total fat	2.0 g	Calcium	74.2 mg
Saturated fat	1.3 g	Iron	0.0 mg
Carbohydrates	2.9 g	Vitamin C	0.3 mg

Stewed Leeks with Butter

If you and your family have never enjoyed leeks, try this simple recipe. Leeks have a very mild flavor, unlike their pungent relatives, onions. Their pleasing, delicate flavor is impossible to duplicate!

Makes about 1 cup (250 mL)

Chef Jordan's Tip

Leeks can be sandy but are easy to clean. Cut them in half lengthwise, rinse thoroughly under cold running water and pat dry.

Jill's Nutrition Tip

A member of the allium family, leeks are cousins of onions and garlic. This family of vegetables contains sulfur compounds that have a very positive effect on your health. Among other benefits, these compounds support the normal function of the liver, helping this organ to detoxify your baby's body of possible contaminants.

- Blender

| 1 tbsp | organic unsalted butter | 15 mL |
| 2¼ cups | chopped leeks, white part only (see Tips, left) | 550 mL |

1. In a saucepan, melt butter over low heat. Add leeks, cover and cook, stirring often, until very soft, about 30 minutes.

2. Transfer to blender or use an immersion blender in the saucepan. Purée to your baby's preferred consistency, pulsing for a chunkier consistency. Let cool until warm to the touch before serving or transfer to an airtight container and refrigerate for up to 3 days.

Variations

I'm fortunate to live in a region where, in the spring, I can find wild leeks, also known as ramps. Ramps have a delicate onion flavor with a slight hint of garlic, and an equal quantity would work beautifully in this recipe.

If your family is having a pizza night at home, share some of baby's leeks. They work well as a topping. Just spread on top after you take the pizza out of the oven.

NUTRIENTS PER SERVING (¼ cup/60 mL)	
Calories 52	Dietary fiber . . . . 0.9 g
Protein . . . . 1.8 g	Sodium . . . . 0.4 mg
Total fat . . . . 2.9 g	Calcium . . . . 36.2 mg
Saturated fat . . . . 1.8 g	Iron . . . . 2.4 mg
Carbohydrates . . . . 5.3 g	Vitamin C . . . . 23.8 mg

The Best Eggplant Parmesan

This versatile purée, embellished with roasted tomatoes and basil, is a hit with babies, but older children will love it, too!

● ●

Makes about 3 cups (750 mL)

Chef Jordan's Tip

From time to time, I'll come across an eggplant that is a little bitter and that needs to be "sweated." Slice the eggplant, sprinkle with kosher salt and let it stand in a colander for an hour or so, which draws out quite a bit of liquid. After a thorough rinsing under cold running water, pat the eggplant dry with a paper towel.

Jill's Nutrition Tip

Eggplant purée has a gelatinous and velvety mouthfeel. Introducing food that has an unusual texture, like eggplant, to your baby at this point may increase the chances that he will accept new and more exotic foods as he grows older. Expanding your baby's palate now will predispose him to enjoy a wide variety of foods as an adult, providing the nutritional benefit that comes from a varied diet.

- Ovenproof skillet
- Blender
- Preheat oven to 350°F (180°C)

2 tbsp	extra virgin olive oil (approx.)	30 mL
8 cups	coarsely chopped eggplant (about 1 medium, 2 lbs/1 kg)	2 L
1½ cups	Oven-Roasted Cherry Tomato Purée (see page 106)	375 mL
⅓ cup	freshly grated organic Parmesan cheese	75 mL
2	fresh basil leaves	2

1. In ovenproof skillet, heat oil over medium-high heat. Add eggplant, in batches, and cook, stirring constantly, until golden brown, adding more oil as necessary, about 5 minutes per batch. Return all eggplant to the skillet. Stir in tomato purée and cheese. Bake in preheated oven until eggplant is very soft and sauce is boiling, about 35 minutes.

2. Add basil. Transfer to blender or to a bowl if using an immersion blender. Purée to your baby's preferred texture, pulsing for a chunkier consistency. Let cool until warm to the touch before serving or transfer to an airtight container and refrigerate for up to 3 days.

NUTRIENTS PER SERVING (¼ cup/60 mL)	
Calories 60	Dietary fiber. . . . . 3.1 g
Protein. . . . . .2.0 g	Sodium. . . . . 35.9 mg
Total fat . . . . .3.6 g	Calcium . . . . 35.2 mg
Saturated fat. . . . . . . .0.8 g	Iron . . . . .0.3 mg
Carbohydrates . . . . 6.1 g	Vitamin C . . . . 7.2 mg

Brussels Sprout Gratin

You won't believe these are the same Brussels sprouts your mom used to serve! Adding Parmesan cheese creates a match made in heaven.

●●

Makes about 1 cup (250 mL)

Chef Jordan's Tip

Typically found in late fall and winter, these tiny members of the cabbage family should be bright green and firm to the touch.

Jill's Nutrition Tip

Brussels sprouts are a cruciferous vegetable and part of the brassica family, which also includes their big brothers cabbage, broccoli, cauliflower and kale. These vegetables are known for their cancer-fighting ability. Sulforaphane, a phytonutrient found in Brussels sprouts, enhances the activity of your baby's natural defense systems, protecting against many diseases.

Always buy organic milk products.

- Casserole dish with lid
- Preheat oven to 350°F (180°C)
- Blender

2 cups	coarsely chopped Brussels sprouts (about 6 oz/175 g)	500 mL
⅓ cup	freshly grated organic Parmesan cheese	75 mL
¼ cup	filtered water	60 mL
2 tbsp	full-fat organic sour cream	30 mL

1. In casserole dish, combine sprouts, cheese, water and sour cream. Stir well, cover and bake in preheated oven until sprouts are soft, about 1 hour.

2. Transfer to blender or use an immersion blender in the dish. Purée to your baby's preferred consistency, pulsing for a chunkier texture. Let cool until warm to the touch before serving or transfer to an airtight container and refrigerate for up to 3 days.

NUTRIENTS PER SERVING (¼ cup/60 mL)

Calories 61	Dietary fiber . . . . 1.6 g
Protein . . . . 3.7 g	Sodium . . . . .112.5 mg
Total fat . . . . 3.1 g	Calcium . . . . .85.3 mg
Saturated fat . . . . .1.8 g	Iron . . . . 0.1 mg
Carbohydrates . . . . . . .3.6 g	Vitamin C . . . . 37.5 mg

Mediterranean Fried Eggplant

While living in Israel, I would frequently visit Tamar's cousins, who had twin daughters. They often served this purée to their babies and they loved it. I'm sure your baby will enjoy it, too.

• •

Makes about 2 cups (500 mL)

Chef Jordan's Tips

Cooking in batches helps maintain pan temperature. Overloading tends to lower the temperature, which in this case can result in eggplant with a soggy texture.

Substitute other fresh herbs, such as oregano, parsley, chervil, tarragon or dill, for the basil.

Jill's Nutrition Tip

When selecting eggplant, choose those that are heavy for their size and have smooth, shiny skins free of scars and bruising, which can indicate that the flesh inside is damaged. Keep the eggplant unwashed and whole until you are ready to use it, because it deteriorates quickly when cut. A fresh eggplant will last for up to 1 week in the crisper of the refrigerator or for just a few days at room temperature. While eggplant contains many nutrients, it is especially rich in antioxidants, which help keep your baby's immune system healthy.

• Blender

1/2 cup	extra virgin olive oil, divided	125 mL
1	medium eggplant, cut into 1-inch (2.5 cm) thick round slices (about 2 lbs/1 kg)	1
1/3 cup	freshly grated organic Parmesan cheese	75 mL
2 tbsp	thinly sliced fresh basil leaves	30 mL

1. In a large skillet, heat 2 tbsp (30 mL) of the oil over medium-high heat. Add eggplant in batches (see Tips, left) and cook, turning once, until golden brown on both sides, about 4 minutes per side. Transfer to a plate lined with paper towels. Add more oil and reheat pan between batches as necessary.

2. Add cheese and basil. Transfer to blender or to a bowl or cup if using an immersion blender. Purée to your baby's preferred consistency, pulsing for a chunkier texture. Let cool until warm to the touch before serving or transfer to an airtight container and refrigerate for up to 3 days.

Variation

You can also use this purée as a spread. Serve it to older children on toast to create a bruschetta of sorts. If you have leftover Oven-Roasted Cherry Tomato Purée (page 106), stir it in, to taste, for an impromptu version of caponata. To really gild the lily, add a smattering of chopped fresh herbs.

NUTRIENTS PER SERVING (1/4 cup/60 mL)

Calories	174	Dietary fiber	3.9 g
Protein	2.4 g	Sodium	50.8 mg
Total fat	15.9 g	Calcium	46.4 mg
Saturated fat	2.7 g	Iron	0.3 mg
Carbohydrates	6.6 g	Vitamin C	2.6 mg

Diced Potato Gratin

I'll never forget the time the legendary chef Paul Bocuse came to Pascal, the restaurant in Newport Beach, California, where I was chef. He taught me this very simple potato recipe. It is so easy to make and encapsulates the essence of French cuisine: simple ingredients, made with lots of love. Your baby will love it, and the recipe makes enough for the rest of the family to enjoy as well.

● ●

> **Makes about
> 4 cups (1 L)**

Chef Jordan's Tips

Cooks are taught to store cut potatoes in water to avoid oxidization, but this process also draws out the starch. In this case starch is good because it helps the milk to thicken. So when making this recipe, dice the potatoes and use them immediately.

Try Yukon Gold, russet or fingerling potatoes.

Jill's Nutrition Tip

The beneficial nutrients in potatoes are found in both the flesh and the skin. These nutrients include flavonoids, which may help to protect your baby from respiratory problems such as asthma, and a compound called kukoamine, which appears to keep blood pressure in check.

Always buy organic milk products and potatoes.

● Potato masher

2½ cups	organic whole milk	625 mL
1 tbsp	organic unsalted butter	15 mL
2 cups	finely diced organic baking potatoes, unpeeled (see Tips, left)	500 mL
⅔ cup	freshly grated organic Parmesan cheese	150 mL

1. In a saucepan, combine milk and butter. Bring to a simmer over medium heat. Stir in potatoes. Reduce heat to low and simmer until potatoes are fork-tender, about 20 minutes.

2. Stir in cheese. Using potato masher, mash to your baby's preferred consistency. Let cool until warm to the touch before serving or transfer to an airtight container and refrigerate for up to 3 days.

NUTRIENTS PER SERVING (¼ cup/60 mL)

Calories	66	Dietary fiber	0.6 g
Protein	3.1 g	Sodium	66.4 mg
Total fat	3.0 g	Calcium	84.3 mg
Saturated fat	1.8 g	Iron	0.3 mg
Carbohydrates	6.9 g	Vitamin C	5.6 mg

Poached Garlic with Thyme and Sour Cream

I understand that you may be reluctant to serve your baby a purée of garlic. However, when garlic is poached with aromatics such as fresh thyme, it becomes sweet and quite mild. When combined with sour cream, the texture and flavor are similar to mashed potatoes. And the health benefits of garlic are legendary. It is never too early to start your baby on the path to healthy living.

- -

**Makes about
¾ cup (175 mL)**

Chef Jordan's Tip

If you want to use whole raw garlic cloves for another purpose, here's a useful tip: The skins come off easily after the cloves are poached whole. Bring water to a boil and blanch the garlic cloves for 3 to 5 minutes. The skins will come off easily and the garlic will remain raw.

Jill's Nutrition Tip

One of garlic's most studied roles is that of infection fighter, a result of its allicin content. Numerous studies have shown that allicin acts as a broad-spectrum antibacterial that can battle a wide range of pathogens, such as *E. coli* and salmonella, that can be brought into the home environment on food products. Always consult your doctor if you think your baby is sick, but add some garlic to her diet, too, for good measure.

Always buy organic milk products.

1¼ cups	garlic cloves, unpeeled (see Tips, left)	300 mL
1 cup	filtered water	250 mL
1	sprig fresh thyme	1
2 tbsp	organic full-fat sour cream	30 mL

1. In a saucepan, combine garlic, water and thyme. Bring to a boil over medium heat. Reduce heat to low and simmer until garlic is fork-tender, about 15 minutes. Set aside until cool enough to handle.

2. Squeeze each clove of garlic to remove skin and round "stem" at one end of clove (both should come off quite easily) and place in a bowl. Add sour cream and mash to desired consistency. Serve immediately or transfer to an airtight container and refrigerate for up to 3 days or freeze for up to 1 month.

NUTRIENTS PER SERVING (¼ cup/60 mL)

Calories	105	Dietary fiber	1.2 g
Protein	4.0 g	Sodium	15.4 mg
Total fat	2.0 g	Calcium	112.7 mg
Saturated fat	1.2 g	Iron	1.0 mg
Carbohydrates	19.1 g	Vitamin C	18.1 mg

Summer Cherry Quinoa

I wish there was a secret to pitting cherries, but there isn't! It's messy and time-consuming but well worth the fuss. The fresh cherries complement the quinoa beautifully in this recipe.

● ●

**Makes about
1½ cups (375 mL)**

Chef Jordan's Tips

Bing cherries, which are available in spring and throughout summer, are my favorite cherry. This dark purple, firm fruit has unique contrasting flavors of sweet and sour.

With a slight nutty flavor, quinoa, which is naturally gluten-free, can easily substitute for couscous or rice in most recipes.

Jill's Nutrition Tip

Cherries contain flavonoids, compounds that are very high in antioxidant activity. Among their many benefits, flavonoids appear to have anti-inflammatory properties and may help your baby to fight an allergic response.

Always buy organic cherries.

● Blender

1 cup	pitted organic Bing or other sweet cherries	250 mL
1 cup	filtered water	250 mL
¾ cup	cooked quinoa (see page 52)	175 mL

1. In a saucepan, combine cherries and water. Bring to a boil over medium heat and cook, stirring often, until almost falling apart, about 5 minutes.

2. Transfer to blender or use an immersion blender in the saucepan. Purée until smooth. Return to the saucepan, if necessary, and add quinoa. Place over low heat and simmer, stirring occasionally, until thick, about 20 minutes. Let cool until warm to the touch before serving or transfer to an airtight container and refrigerate for up to 3 days.

NUTRIENTS PER SERVING (¼ cup/60 mL)

Calories	20	Dietary fiber	0.6 g
Protein	0.4 g	Sodium	1.7 mg
Total fat	0.3 g	Calcium	5.6 mg
Saturated fat	0.0 g	Iron	0.1 mg
Carbohydrates	4.8 g	Vitamin C	0.8 mg

Millet Cereal with Bananas and Sour Cream

This is a cereal for both baby and family. The Wagman family often substitutes millet cereal for porridge in the morning, adding a drizzle of pure maple syrup.

	Makes about
	3¼ cups (800 mL)

Chef Jordan's Tips

Sour cream adds a unique citrus undertone to this cereal. Alternatively, an equal quantity of creamy goat cheese would have a similar effect.

In this recipe I prefer to use alcohol-free organic vanilla extract. However, be aware that some alcohol-free vanilla extract may contain unwanted additives. Read the label carefully.

Jill's Nutrition Tip

Millet is a wonderful grain for your baby. It is gluten-free and hypoallergenic and has a nice mild flavor. Millet contains two important minerals for optimal growth and development: manganese helps keep calcium in place for strong bone formation, while magnesium has many protective properties for your baby's heart.

Always buy organic milk products.

3½ cups	filtered water	875 mL
¾ cup	millet flour (see page 55)	175 mL
1 cup	coarsely chopped bananas (about 2)	250 mL
2 tbsp	organic full-fat sour cream	30 mL
1 tsp	pure vanilla extract (see Tips, left)	5 mL

1. In a saucepan, bring water to a boil over medium heat. Slowly add millet flour, whisking constantly to avoid lumps. Add bananas and cook, whisking, until thick (almost porridge-like), about 10 minutes. Remove from heat and set aside, covered, until very thick, about 20 minutes.

2. Stir in sour cream and vanilla until thoroughly combined. Serve immediately or transfer to an airtight container and refrigerate for up to 3 days. To serve, reheat ½ cup (125 mL) cooked cereal with ¼ cup (60 mL) water in a saucepan over low heat, just until warm.

NUTRIENTS PER SERVING (¼ cup/60 mL)

Calories	21	Dietary fiber	0.5 g
Protein	0.3 g	Sodium	2.9 mg
Total fat	0.5 g	Calcium	4.4 mg
Saturated fat	0.3 g	Iron	0.1 mg
Carbohydrates	4.1 g	Vitamin C	1.5 mg

Egg and Sweet Pepper Fried Rice

This is a great way to introduce your baby to the wonders of Chinese food.

● ●

**Makes about
2½ cups (625 mL)**

Chef Jordan's Tip

We have made this recipe using brown basmati rice because it is far more nutritious than the white variety. If you are in a hurry and prefer to use white basmati rice, reduce the simmering time to 5 minutes before setting the rice aside. Also, reduce the quantity of water to 1¼ cups (300 mL).

Jill's Nutrition Tip

Ounce for ounce, red peppers have even more vitamin C than oranges. Since you and your baby can't make or store vitamin C, it is important to get it from food on a regular basis. Vitamin C is essential for the formation of collagen, used in the development of tendons, bones, teeth and healthy skin.

Always buy organic bell peppers.

2 tbsp	extra virgin olive oil, divided	30 mL
½ cup	finely diced organic red bell pepper	125 mL
½ cup	finely diced sweet onion, such as Vidalia	125 mL
1 tsp	minced peeled gingerroot	5 mL
¾ cup	brown basmati rice, rinsed and drained	175 mL
1½ cups	filtered water	375 mL
2	egg yolks, whisked	2

1. In a saucepan, heat half of the oil over medium heat. Add pepper, onion and ginger, and sauté until onion is translucent. Stir in rice. Add water and bring to a rapid boil. Cover, reduce heat to low and simmer for 20 minutes. Remove from heat and set aside, covered, until liquid is absorbed, about 25 minutes.

2. In a large skillet, heat remaining oil over high heat. Add egg yolks, swirl and cook until they form a thin "omelet." Stir in rice mixture. Cook, without stirring, for 3 minutes. Stir well and cook until mixture is warm throughout, about 5 minutes. Purée to your baby's preferred consistency, pulsing for a chunkier texture. Let cool until warm to the touch before serving or transfer to an airtight container and refrigerate for up to 2 days.

NUTRIENTS PER SERVING (¼ cup/60 mL)

Calories 92.5	Dietary fiber. . . . . .0.8 g
Protein. . . . . .1.8 g	Sodium. . . . . 3.9 mg
Total fat . . . . 4.0 g	Calcium . . . . 10.6 mg
Saturated fat. . . . . . . .0.8 g	Iron. . . . . .0.4 mg
Carbohydrates . . . . . . 12.3 g	Vitamin C . . . . 6.5 mg

Bok Choy with Ginger

Bok choy and ginger is a classic Chinese flavor combination that your baby will love. Introducing him to healthy leafy greens at an early age will serve him well throughout life.

Makes about
1¾ cups (425 mL)

Chef Jordan's Tip

Older children will enjoy this purée served over cooked brown rice, possibly with a dash of soy sauce. When it comes to soy sauce, my preference is tamari. Tamari is usually wheat-free (check the label) and is typically made just from soybeans, as opposed to many soy sauces that are frequently made with grains, including wheat.

Jill's Nutrition Tip

Trains, planes and automobiles! Ginger has the amazing property of calming motion sickness and nausea in sensitive tummies. When you travel, pack this soothing purée to lessen these unpleasant effects.

- Blender

¼ cup	filtered water	60 mL
1 lb	bok choy, chopped (about 4 cups/1 L)	500 g
2 tsp	minced peeled gingerroot	10 mL

1. In a saucepan, bring water to a boil over high heat. Stir in bok choy and gingerroot. Cover, reduce heat to low and cook until bok choy is soft, about 20 minutes.

2. Transfer to blender or use an immersion blender in the saucepan. Purée to your baby's preferred consistency, pulsing for a chunkier texture. Let cool until warm to the touch before serving or transfer to an airtight container and refrigerate for up to 3 days.

Variation

One of my favorite vegetables is gai-lan, or Chinese broccoli. With a very thin, tender stalk (much more tender than traditional broccoli) and luscious green leaves, it's another leafy green vegetable that your kids will easily take to. Give it a try in place of the bok choy. It's a winner here!

NUTRIENTS PER SERVING (¼ cup/60 mL)

Calories	10	Dietary fiber	0.7 g
Protein	1.1 g	Sodium	46.7 mg
Total fat	0.2 g	Calcium	75.3 mg
Saturated fat	0.0 g	Iron	0.6 mg
Carbohydrates	1.7 g	Vitamin C	32.2 mg

Brussels Sprouts with Bacon

Just because you didn't like these mini-cabbages when you were growing up doesn't mean they won't be one of your baby's favorites. Your parents just didn't know how to make them taste great! A little bit of bacon makes a big difference.

**Makes about
1 cup (250 mL)**

Chef Jordan's Tip

Nitrates, which are found in most processed meats, are added as a preservative. Concerns were raised about their long-term safety because it appeared they might have carcinogenic effects. Perhaps I'm being overly cautious, but to be safe, I use bacon that is nitrate-free.

Jill's Nutrition Tip

For decades we have heard about the potential health consequences associated with the nitrates in our prepared meats. Researchers are now taking a second look, suggesting that there may not be as close an association as they once thought.
To add to the confusion, "nitrate-free" meat generally contains celery extract, which contains naturally occurring nitrates. Until we hear otherwise, the healthiest bet may be to use bacon from pasture-raised and organically fed pigs, regardless of whether it has been preserved with nitrates or celery extract.

- Blender

1 oz	nitrate-free bacon, minced (about 1 slice)	30 g
2 cups	coarsely chopped Brussels sprouts (about 6 oz/175 g)	500 mL
¼ cup	filtered water	60 mL

1. In a saucepan, over medium heat, sauté bacon until crispy and brown, about 3 minutes. Stir in Brussels sprouts. Reduce heat to low and cook, stirring frequently to avoid browning, until sprouts are soft, about 10 minutes. Add water and simmer until water has evaporated, about 5 minutes.

2. Transfer to blender or use an immersion blender in the saucepan. Purée to your baby's preferred consistency, pulsing for a chunkier texture. Let cool until warm to the touch before serving or transfer to an airtight container and refrigerate for up to 3 days.

NUTRIENTS PER SERVING (¼ cup/60 mL)

Calories 58	Dietary fiber. . . . . .1.6 g
Protein. . . . . .3.4 g	Sodium. . . . . .168.4 mg
Total fat . . . . .3.4 g	Calcium . . . . 12.0 mg
Saturated fat. . . . . .1.1 g	Iron. . . . . 0.1 mg
Carbohydrates . . . . . . .3.2 g	Vitamin C . . . . 37.5 mg

Oven-Roasted Cherry Tomato Purée

You'll want to make this your new staple tomato sauce and get rid of store-bought imposters. For baby, add to cooked quinoa or rice to create an excellent meal. This should become a staple in your home for everyday use. It makes a great substitute for store-bought ketchups, which contain so much unnecessary sugar, or a delicious spread for sandwiches.

● ●

**Makes about
1½ cups (375 mL)**

Chef Jordan's Tip

This recipe works particularly well with cherry, currant or grape tomatoes, but plum tomatoes will work, too. Cut plum tomatoes in half and roast until wilted but still retaining moisture, about 1 hour, then complete Step 2.

Jill's Nutrition Tip

Tomatoes are an excellent source of lycopene, a phytonutrient that has anti-cancer properties. Lycopene is a strong antioxidant that helps prevent cell damage, even in babies. It is highly concentrated in breast milk but cannot be synthesized by humans, so your baby must get it in her diet from foods such as tomatoes, watermelon and papayas. Cooking heightens lycopene absorption, as does the addition of olive oil. The combination of fat and heat maximizes the free-radical-hunting ability of this nutrient.

- Preheat oven to 350°F (180°C)
- Ovenproof saucepan
- Blender

1 lb	organic cherry tomatoes (about 2 cups/500 mL)	500 g
1 tsp	extra virgin olive oil	5 mL
2	sprigs fresh thyme	2
1 tsp	chopped fresh basil leaves	5 mL

1. In ovenproof saucepan, combine tomatoes, oil and thyme. Roast in preheated oven until tomatoes are soft and golden brown, about 30 minutes.

2. Add basil. Transfer to blender or use an immersion blender in the saucepan. Purée until smooth. Let cool until warm to the touch before serving or transfer to an airtight container and refrigerate for up to 3 days or freeze for up to 1 month.

NUTRIENTS PER SERVING (¼ cup/60 mL)

Calories 22	Dietary fiber. . . . . 1.0 g
Protein. . . . . .0.8 g	Sodium. . . . . .4.2 mg
Total fat . . . . 1.0 g	Calcium . . . . 9.6 mg
Saturated fat. . . . . 0.1 g	Iron. . . . . .0.3 mg
Carbohydrates . . . . . . .3.3 g	Vitamin C . . . . .11.0 mg

Turnip and Parsnip Smash

This is a wonderful, mild-tasting introduction to the flavor of turnips, and your baby will love it.

**Makes about
1 cup (250 mL)**

Chef Jordan's Tip

When buying turnips to feed to babies, choose those that are relatively small. Turnips can develop a rather strong taste as they grow. Don't confuse turnips with rutabaga, a larger vegetable with yellowish flesh that is quite a bit more pungent.

Jill's Nutrition Tip

While the turnip root is a rich source of many nutrients, including fiber, turnip greens are actually more nutritious. Store the greens separately from the roots but combine them when cooking this purée, for a bigger nutritional boost. Cut off and discard the tough stems and wash well. Add the leaves, whole or sliced, to the turnip pan for the last 10 minutes of cooking.

• Blender

2 cups	filtered water	500 mL
2 cups	coarsely chopped peeled parsnips	250 mL
1 cup	coarsely chopped peeled white turnip	250 mL

1. In a saucepan, combine water, parsnips and turnip. Bring to a boil over medium heat. Reduce heat to low and simmer until vegetables are soft and most of the water has evaporated, about 20 minutes.

2. Transfer to blender or use an immersion blender in the saucepan. Purée to your baby's preferred consistency, pulsing for a chunkier texture. Let cool until warm to the touch before serving or transfer to an airtight container and refrigerate for up to 3 days.

NUTRIENTS PER SERVING (¼ cup/60 mL)

Calories	56	Dietary fiber	3.6 g
Protein	1.0 g	Sodium	29.0 mg
Total fat	0.2 g	Calcium	33.4 mg
Saturated fat	0.0 g	Iron	0.5 mg
Carbohydrates	13.3 g	Vitamin C	17.2 mg

Red Cabbage, Fennel and Apple Purée

The combination of cabbage and fennel creates an extraordinary flavor. Give your baby every opportunity to acquire a taste for these vegetables, because it will likely have long-term benefits for her health (see Tips, below).

Chef Jordan's Tips

Red cabbage can stain your clothes (a cautionary word to the wise), so wear an apron when making this recipe.

Gala apples, which are sweet and juicy and well suited to cooking, are a perfect choice for this recipe.

Jill's Nutrition Tip

There is more documented research on the anti-cancer properties of the cabbage family, which includes broccoli, cauliflower, kale and Brussels sprouts, than for any other vegetable group. The American Cancer Institute recommends including these cruciferous vegetables in your diet on a regular basis as a powerful natural weapon against cancer. We say cancer prevention starts with nutritious homemade baby food!

Always buy organic apples.

- Blender

2 cups	filtered water	500 mL
1 cup	thinly sliced red cabbage	250 mL
¾ cup	coarsely chopped cored organic apple (about 1)	175 mL
⅓ cup	thinly sliced fresh fennel	75 mL

1. In a saucepan, combine water, cabbage, apple and fennel. Bring to a boil over medium heat. Reduce heat to low and simmer until fennel and cabbage are soft, about 40 minutes.

2. Transfer to blender or use an immersion blender in the saucepan. Purée to your baby's preferred consistency, pulsing for a chunkier texture. Let cool until warm to the touch before serving or transfer to an airtight container and refrigerate for up to 3 days or freeze for up to 1 month.

NUTRIENTS PER SERVING (¼ cup/60 mL)

Calories 20	Dietary fiber . . . . 1.5 g
Protein . . . . 0.5 g	Sodium . . . . 12.0 mg
Total fat . . . . 0.1 g	Calcium . . . . 18.8 mg
Saturated fat . . . . 0.0 g	Iron . . . . 0.2 mg
Carbohydrates . . . . 5.0 g	Vitamin C . . . . 12.3 mg

Roasted Sweet Onion Purée

Aside from sugary desserts, this purée has the sweetest flavor you'll ever taste! The onions are also very nutritious. Their sulfur-containing compounds are active cancer fighters, and the flavonoid quercetin helps prevent bacterial infections.

● ●

**Makes about
2 cups (500 mL)**

Chef Jordan's Tip

If you're buying the best onions, roasting them should make them taste like heaven. For extra flavor, make this dish using Roasted Chicken Stock (page 152) instead of water. Beef or vegetable stocks that don't contain salt would also work nicely.

Jill's Nutrition Tip

Onions are a terrific source of the prebiotic inulin. Prebiotics are a type of soluble fiber that is indigestible by humans but stimulates the growth of beneficial gut bacteria. A healthy intestine supports your baby's immune system and helps prevent both constipation and diarrhea.

- Preheat oven to 350°F (180°C)
- Baking sheet
- Blender

| 4 | sweet onions, such as Vidalia, unpeeled (about 2 large, 1½ lbs/750 g) | 4 |
| ½ cup | filtered water | 125 mL |

1. Place onions on baking sheet and roast in preheated oven until soft, about 2 hours. Transfer to a plate and let cool until they can be easily handled. Peel off skins and roughly chop.

2. In a saucepan, combine peeled onions and water. Bring to a boil over medium heat and boil for 5 minutes.

3. Transfer to blender or use an immersion blender in the saucepan. Purée until smooth. Let cool until warm to the touch before serving or transfer to an airtight container and refrigerate for up to 3 days or freeze up to 1 month.

NUTRIENTS PER SERVING (¼ cup/60 mL)

Calories	53	Dietary fiber	1.5 g
Protein	1.3 g	Sodium	13.7 mg
Total fat	0.1 g	Calcium	33.6 mg
Saturated fat	0.0 g	Iron	0.4 mg
Carbohydrates	12.5 g	Vitamin C	7.9 mg

Potato, Parsnip and Chicken Soup

This is one of my favorite and tastiest ways to use up leftover chicken. Not only are the potatoes a great thickener, they are loaded with nutrition. For instance, potatoes with their skin are one of the best food sources of potassium, ounce for ounce rivaling bananas.

Makes about 3½ cups (875 mL)

Chef Jordan's Tip

Although it's a bit of extra work, the Chive Parsley Pesto adds an incredible burst of flavor to this soup. It is also wonderful to have on hand for adding flavor and nutrients to a wide variety of basic recipes, such as cooked grains.

Jill's Nutrition Tip

This is an all-in-one meal. You have complete protein from the chicken, complex carbohydrates from the potato and easily digestible fat from the butter. There is an assortment of vitamins and minerals from the parsnips and garlic and, if you add the pesto, you have the added benefit of concentrated health-promoting phytochemicals from the herbs.

Always buy organic potatoes.

- Blender

1 tbsp	organic unsalted butter	15 mL
1 cup	finely diced organic baking potato (russet)	250 mL
¾ cup	chopped boneless, skinless cooked chicken	175 mL
½ cup	finely diced peeled parsnip	125 mL
2	cloves garlic, minced	2
3 cups	filtered water (see Variation, below)	750 mL
2 tbsp	Chive Parsley Pesto (page 112), optional	30 mL

1. In a saucepan, melt butter over medium heat. Add potato, chicken, parsnip and garlic and cook until potato begins to soften, about 5 minutes. Add water and bring to a boil. Reduce heat and simmer until vegetables are falling apart, about 10 minutes. Remove from heat and stir in pesto, if using.

2. Transfer to blender or use an immersion blender in the saucepan. Purée to your baby's preferred consistency, pulsing for a chunkier texture. Let cool until warm to the touch before serving or transfer to an airtight container and refrigerate for up to 3 days.

Variation

This really is a great way to use up leftover chicken. For added flavor, leave the potato unpeeled and substitute Vegetable Stock (page 154) or Roasted Chicken Stock (page 152) for the water.

NUTRIENTS PER SERVING (¼ cup/60 mL)	
Calories 35	Dietary fiber . . . . 0.4 g
Protein . . . . 1.3 g	Sodium . . . . 39.1 mg
Total fat . . . . 2.1 g	Calcium . . . . 5.9 mg
Saturated fat . . . . 0.7 g	Iron . . . . 0.1 mg
Carbohydrates . . . . 2.7 g	Vitamin C . . . . 1.9 mg

Chive Parsley Pesto

This is a spin on a classic Italian basil pesto, which would normally contain pine nuts. This version, which is more French (in France the basil-based version is called pistou*), contains only the clean flavors of parsley, chives, garlic and olive oil. It is wonderful over cooked grains (pages 52 to 54) or, as your baby gets older (past 12 months), with noodles or pasta and Parmesan cheese. In other words, it's a great all-purpose condiment/sauce. You can freeze leftovers for future use.*

• •

Makes about
½ cup (125 mL)

Chef Jordan's Tip

Fresh herbs are loaded with nutrition. Introducing their robust flavors to children at a young age helps to ensure that they will enjoy their benefits for years to come.

Jill's Nutrition Tip

All green plants contain some amount of chlorophyll, but the greener the vegetable, the more chlorophyll it contains. Parsley's rich green color indicates that it is loaded with this nutrient. Chlorophyll fights infections and stimulates new cell growth, two functions that are important for your growing baby.

• Blender

¾ cup	fresh flat-leaf (Italian) or curly parsley, chopped	175 mL
½ cup	extra virgin olive oil	125 mL
¼ cup	fresh chives, chopped	60 mL
2	cloves garlic, minced	2

1. In blender, combine parsley, oil, chives and garlic. Purée until smooth. Use immediately or transfer to an airtight container and refrigerate for up to 3 days.

NUTRIENTS PER SERVING (¼ cup/60 mL)

Calories 547	Dietary fiber. . . . . .0.9 g
Protein. . . . . .1.0 g	Sodium. . . . . .13.1 mg
Total fat . . . . .59.4 g	Calcium . . . . .40.7 mg
Saturated fat. . . . . . . .8.3 g	Iron. . . . . 1.5 mg
Carbohydrates . . . . . . .2.6 g	Vitamin C . . . . .33.4 mg

Healing Herbs and Spices

Herbs and spices have long been used as flavor enhancer, but recent research shows many health benefits. In fact, the USDA reports that, ounce for ounce, some have more antioxidant activity than many fruits and vegetables.

Take basil, for instance. Basil is a very good source of beta-carotene, a powerful antioxidant that protects against free-radical damage, which is a contributing factor in asthma.

Oregano has both antibacterial and antiviral properties that make it effective against food-borne illnesses. It is also helpful for treating yeast-based infections such as oral thrush, which many babies experience.

Thyme has long been used in natural medicine to help with respiratory problems such as coughs, chest congestion and bronchitis. Researchers have now discovered that its volatile oils are responsible for these healing qualities.

The volatile oil in sage, called rosmarinic acid, encourages cells to make substances called prostacyclins, which help keep airways open for easier breathing.

And, last but not least, parsley. Compounds in parsley qualify it as a "chemoprotective" food that can help neutralize certain carcinogens in the everyday environment to which both you and your baby are exposed.

On a sweeter note, mint and ginger have historically been used to calm an upset tummy and relieve uncomfortable muscle spasms in the colon. Mint extracts have also been shown to help relieve the stuffy nose of colds and allergies.

Herbs are the green leaves of some plants. To maximize their healthful properties, it is generally better to use them in their fresh form. Spices are usually the dried bark, stem, root or seeds of a plant that has aromatic properties. Cinnamon is a wonderfully aromatic spice that gives a warming, sweet taste without sugar. Interestingly, much current research into cinnamon indicates that it is helpful for regulating blood sugar, an important step in reducing childhood obesity. Curcumin, a component of turmeric, has well-documented anti-inflammatory properties. Moreover, there is reason to believe these substances work synergistically. When researchers in India studied the antioxidant ability of individual spices such as cinnamon, pepper and ginger alone and then together, they found the combination produced greater health benefits.

Colorful Vegetable Medley

This recipe offers the colors and textures of ratatouille, a vegetable dish that is traditionally French. The robust colors of the vegetables will draw your baby in, but it's their magnificent flavor that will make her want seconds. You don't need to tell her that it's good for her, too!

• •

Makes about 1¼ cups (300 mL)

Chef Jordan's Tip

Eggplant skin is easily removed by cutting the eggplant into large discs and laying them flat on a cutting board. Trim away the skin using a knife, not a peeler.

Jill's Nutrition Tip

What a great way to give your baby the benefit of a whole bunch of vegetables and a smattering of fresh herbs! A recipe like this provides a wide range of vitamins, minerals and phytonutrients that are unlikely to be found in just one vegetable. Ensuring that your baby has a varied diet can help prevent a deficiency in any one nutrient while expanding his taste experience.

Always buy organic peppers and zucchini.

• Blender

1 tbsp	organic unsalted butter	15 mL
¾ cup	finely diced peeled eggplant	175 mL
½ cup	finely diced organic red bell pepper	125 mL
½ cup	finely diced organic yellow bell pepper	125 mL
¼ cup	finely diced organic zucchini	60 mL
¼ cup	finely diced red onion	60 mL
1	sprig fresh thyme	1
⅓ cup	filtered water	75 mL
2	fresh basil leaves, chopped	2

1. In a saucepan, melt butter over medium-low heat. Add eggplant, red and yellow peppers, zucchini, onion and thyme and sauté until vegetables are soft, about 10 minutes. Add water and basil and cook, stirring frequently, until liquid has evaporated, 3 to 5 minutes. Discard thyme.

2. Transfer to blender or use an immersion blender in the saucepan. Purée to your baby's preferred consistency, pulsing for a chunkier texture. Let cool until warm to the touch before serving or transfer to an airtight container and refrigerate for up to 3 days.

NUTRIENTS PER SERVING (¼ cup/60 mL)

Calories	41	Dietary fiber	1.3 g
Protein	0.8 g	Sodium	3.9 mg
Total fat	2.5 g	Calcium	11.7 mg
Saturated fat	1.5 g	Iron	0.3 mg
Carbohydrates	4.7 g	Vitamin C	52.8 mg

Sautéed Chard with Apples

These days, as their health benefits become increasingly obvious, we're all trying to eat more greens. The addition of apples makes it much easier to introduce Swiss chard to your baby and to help him develop a taste for nutrient-dense leafy greens. The fruit's inherent sweetness complements the flavor very well.

Makes about 1¼ cups (300 mL)

Chef Jordan's Tips

To prepare the chard for this recipe, trim and discard the base of each stem. Separate the leaves from the stems, including the thick center rib. Chop stems and ribs into similar-sized pieces to ensure even cooking. Wash and rinse thoroughly, as leafy greens tend to be gritty.

Always take care when adding hot liquids to a blender. Fill the container no more than half full or let cool before blending.

Jill's Nutrition Tip

Chard's combination of phytochemicals (particularly anthocyanins), vitamins, minerals, fiber and chlorophyll makes it an incredibly potent anti-cancer food. By starting your baby on Swiss chard early, you are providing him with lifelong health benefits.

Always buy organic apples and Swiss chard.

- Blender

1 tbsp	organic unsalted butter	15 mL
½ cup	finely diced cored, peeled organic apple	125 mL
⅓ cup	finely diced sweet onion, such as Vidalia	75 mL
3 cups	chopped organic Swiss chard	750 mL
¾ cup	filtered water	175 mL

1. In a saucepan, melt butter over medium heat. Add apple and onion and sauté until onion is translucent, about 3 minutes. Add chard and sauté until wilted, 3 to 4 minutes. Add water and bring to a boil. Reduce heat to low and simmer until most of the liquid has evaporated, about 15 minutes.

2. Transfer to blender or use an immersion blender in the saucepan. Purée to your baby's preferred consistency, pulsing for a chunkier texture. Let cool until warm to the touch before serving or transfer to an airtight container and refrigerate for up to 3 days.

NUTRIENTS PER SERVING (¼ cup/60 mL)

Calories 34	Dietary fiber . . . . 0.7 g
Protein . . . . 0.6 g	Sodium . . . . 47.8 mg
Total fat . . . . 2.4 g	Calcium . . . . 15.7 mg
Saturated fat . . . . 1.5 g	Iron . . . . 0.4 mg
Carbohydrates . . . . . . 3.2 g	Vitamin C . . . . 7.7 mg

White Bean and Fennel Purée

In addition to being an awesome baby food, this purée can be used as a dip for vegetables that older children will also enjoy. Although fennel is often overlooked, it is a nutritious vegetable that provides a variety of nutrients, including valuable antioxidants such as quercetin.

• •

Makes about 1¾ cups (425 mL)

Chef Jordan's Tip

When cooking fennel, be sure to save the fronds, which make a wonderful garnish if you are serving this purée to older children as a dip. They can also be added to salads.

Jill's Nutrition Tip

One of the challenges of a vegetarian diet is ensuring that it contains enough protein. Legumes (dried beans and lentils) are one of the best vegetarian sources of protein, even though they don't contain all eight essential amino acids. However, this purée can be combined with one of our grain recipes, such as brown rice or quinoa, to provide your baby with the complete range of amino acids.

• Blender

1 cup	soaked dried white beans, such as navy or cannellini (see page 85)	250 mL
4 cups	filtered water	1 L
1¼ cups	coarsely chopped fresh fennel	300 mL

1. In a saucepan, combine beans, water and fennel. Bring to a boil over medium heat. Reduce heat to low and simmer until beans are soft, about 1¼ hours.
2. Transfer to blender or use an immersion blender in the saucepan. Purée to your baby's preferred consistency, pulsing for a chunkier texture. Let cool until warm to the touch before serving or transfer to an airtight container and refrigerate for up to 3 days or freeze for up to 1 month.

Variation

Substitute 2 cups (500 mL) rinsed, drained canned beans for the dried beans (see page 117). Add to saucepan in step 1 and reduce cooking time to about 20 minutes, until fennel is tender. Add filtered water to blend, if necessary to achieve desired consistency.

NUTRIENTS PER SERVING (¼ cup/60 mL)

Calories 44	Dietary fiber . . . . .3.5 g
Protein . . . . .2.5 g	Sodium . . . . .17.1 mg
Total fat . . . . .0.2 g	Calcium . . . . .34.3 mg
Saturated fat . . . . 0.0 g	Iron . . . . .0.8 mg
Carbohydrates . . . . . . .8.6 g	Vitamin C . . . . .3.2 mg

Using Canned Beans

Although canned beans are more convenient, most are problematic, even for adults, because they are loaded with sodium. If you are using canned beans, be sure to rinse them very well under cold running water to remove as much of the added salt as possible, or to purchase brands with no salt added.

Sodium is a mineral necessary in the body and is found in many foods, including vegetables and breast milk, but no one needs the excessive amounts of sodium usually added to canned and many other kinds of prepared foods. A few companies are producing canned beans, usually organic, with no salt added. These may be seasoned with seaweed, which is fine for your baby to have.

Seaweed does contain sodium, but in acceptable amounts. It also contains beneficial minerals such as iodine. Your thyroid gland, which regulates your body's metabolism, won't function at its best without an adequate supply of iodine.

Whether you are using canned beans or cooking your own (see page 85), beans (and other legumes, such as lentils) are an important part of a healthful diet. We recommend eating them at least three times a week. Legumes are a good source of protein, fiber and minerals such as calcium and iron. Eating them regularly can help protect against type 2 diabetes, among other diseases. They are also one of our best sources of fiber to help promote good bowel health.

Edamame Hummus

This is a particularly nutritious variation on one of my favorite purées. Hummus is my spread of choice. I love it on everything, from chicken breasts to bread. Your family will, too.

**Makes about
2 cups (500 mL)**

Chef Jordan's Tip

Fresh or frozen soybeans are widely available in grocery chains, typically in the health/organic freezer section. In their absence, green peas are an excellent substitute.

Jill's Nutrition Tip

Soybeans have numerous health-promoting benefits: they are a complete protein source, are high in fiber and contain essential fatty acids as well as phytonutrients such as phytosterols and isoflavones. Essential fats are crucial for good brain development.

Be sure to purchase organically grown soybeans to avoid genetically modified products.

• Blender

2 cups	cooked chickpeas, drained and rinsed (see page 85)	500 mL
1 cup	filtered water	250 mL
1/2 cup	fresh or frozen (thawed) shelled organic edamame	125 mL
2	cloves garlic	2

1. In a saucepan, combine chickpeas, water, soybeans and garlic. Bring to a boil over medium heat, cover and simmer until soybeans are soft, about 3 minutes.

2. Transfer to blender or use an immersion blender in the saucepan. Purée until smooth. Let cool to room temperature before serving or transfer to an airtight container and refrigerate for up to 3 days.

Variation

Serve this purée to older children, too. It makes an excellent snack with flatbread or freshly cut vegetables.

NUTRIENTS PER SERVING (1/4 cup/60 mL)

Calories	76	Dietary fiber	2.7 g
Protein	5.2 g	Sodium	173.6 mg
Total fat	1.9 g	Calcium	55.6 mg
Saturated fat	0.1 g	Iron	1.3 mg
Carbohydrates	10.1 g	Vitamin C	5.1 mg

Oven-Roasted Chicken with Apricots

My mother-in-law introduced me to this flavor combination. She's not the greatest cook in the world (I will be removing this page from her copy of this book), so she will be surprised to hear that I learned something culinary from her. Thank you, Lee!

Makes about 1½ cups (375 mL)

Chef Jordan's Tip

People are always staring at me in the grocery store because they see me smelling every last piece of fruit I purchase, to ensure that my family has the best and freshest available. I've always chosen fruit with my nose first because if it smells like a great apricot, it should taste like one, too. After the fruit passes the smell test, try to choose an apricot that is neither too firm nor too soft. The flesh should spring back if poked lightly with your finger.

Jill's Nutrition Tip

Apricots contain the carotenoid lutein, which protects the retina of the eye from the damage caused by blue light. If she hasn't already, your baby will be exposed to and playing with computers and other devices that emit blue light from their screens. Over time, this light can damage the retina, the part of the eye that actually picks up the visual image from the environment. Other lutein-rich foods to enjoy are carrots, squash, spinach and kale.

Always buy organic apricots.

- Ovenproof skillet
- Preheat oven to 350°F (180°C)
- Blender

8 oz	bone-in, skin-on chicken thighs (2 thighs)	250 g
5	fresh organic apricots, pitted (about 6 oz/175 g; see Tips, left)	5
½ cup	filtered water	125 mL

1. In ovenproof skillet, combine chicken, apricots and water. Roast in preheated oven until chicken is golden brown and juices run clear when pierced, 35 to 40 minutes. Let cool until chicken can be easily handled. Remove skin and remove meat from the bone, discarding skin and bones.

2. Transfer chicken and apricots to blender or to a cup or bowl if using an immersion blender. Purée to your baby's preferred consistency, pulsing for a chunkier texture. Serve immediately or transfer to an airtight container and refrigerate for up to 3 days.

Variation

Fresh apricots are extremely perishable and only available seasonally in North America in June and July. Although fresh apricots are best, dried can be substituted in this recipe. Use about 10 dried apricots to replace this quantity of fresh. Be sure to purchase sulfite-free organic dried apricots.

NUTRIENTS PER SERVING (¼ cup/60 mL)

Calories 71		Dietary fiber . . . . .0.6 g	
Protein . . . . .5.9 g		Sodium . . . . .25.0 mg	
Total fat . . . . .3.8 g		Calcium . . . . 7.5 mg	
Saturated fat . . . . .1.1 g		Iron . . . . .0.4 mg	
Carbohydrates . . . . . . .3.2 g		Vitamin C . . . . 3.7 mg	

Chicken with Roasted Butternut Squash and Leeks

I love how the sweetness of the leeks complements the chicken and squash. The squash in this recipe is an excellent source of vitamin A, along with a variety of other valuable nutrients, including vitamin C and fiber.

Makes about 1½ cups (375 mL)

Chef Jordan's Tip

I prefer dark meat when cooking for babies because of its higher fat content, but in a pinch I wouldn't hesitate to use a chicken breast.

Jill's Nutrition Tip

When your baby is this age, you can offer her poultry or other protein sources such as legumes, egg yolks, organic tofu or grass-fed meat a couple of times a day. The vegetables in this recipe add a variety of vitamins, minerals, phytonutrients and filling fiber, making it a well-rounded meal that will promote growth and development.

• Blender

1 tbsp	organic unsalted butter	15 mL
¾ cup	diced and peeled butternut squash	175 mL
1	diced boneless, skinless chicken thigh (about 4 oz/125 g)	1
½ cup	chopped leeks, white part only	125 mL
1 cup	filtered water	250 mL

1. In a saucepan, over medium heat, melt butter. Add squash and sauté until golden, about 5 minutes. Add chicken and leeks and sauté until leeks are wilted, about 2 minutes. Add water and bring to a boil. Reduce heat to low and simmer until chicken is cooked through, about 5 minutes.

2. Transfer to blender or use an immersion blender in the saucepan. Purée to your baby's preferred consistency, pulsing for a chunkier texture. Let cool until warm to the touch before serving or transfer to an airtight container and refrigerate for up to 3 days.

NUTRIENTS PER SERVING (¼ cup/60 mL)

Calories 48	Dietary fiber . . . . 0.7 g
Protein . . . . 2.7 g	Sodium . . . . 14.0 mg
Total fat . . . . 2.4 g	Calcium . . . . 21.7 mg
Saturated fat . . . . 1.3 g	Iron . . . . 0.5 mg
Carbohydrates . . . . . . .4.5 g	Vitamin C . . . . 7.2 mg

Pork with Peaches

If you enjoy barbecue, try this recipe. You'll think you're in the deep South!

• •

**Makes about
1¼ cups (300 mL)**

Chef Jordan's Tips

Use any cut of pork to make this recipe: part of a tenderloin, pork chop or butt.

Brown butter is a versatile ingredient used in French cooking. In this case, browning the butter and searing the pork develop a crisp, golden brown outside that creates a delicious flavor profile.

If peaches aren't in season, use canned peaches packed in water (no sugar added).

Jill's Nutrition Tip

Pork is the highest meat source of thiamin (vitamin B_3), which is one of the many B-complex vitamins necessary for the optimal use of all foods in your baby's body. It is also essential for the growth and repair of nerve and muscle tissue.

Always buy organic peaches.

• Blender

1 tsp	organic unsalted butter	5 mL
1 cup	coarsely chopped sweet onions, such as Vidalia	250 mL
1	organic peach, pitted and sliced (see Tips, left)	1
4 oz	pork, diced (see Tips, left)	125 g
1 cup	filtered water	250 mL

1. In a saucepan, melt butter over high heat until it turns a slight hazelnut-brown color, about 1 minute (see Tips, left). Add onions, peach and pork and sauté until pork is golden brown, about 5 minutes. Add water and bring to a boil. Reduce heat and simmer until water has reduced by half, about 7 minutes.

2. Transfer to blender or use an immersion blender in the saucepan. Purée to your baby's preferred consistency, pulsing for a chunkier texture. Let cool until warm to the touch before serving or transfer to an airtight container and refrigerate for up to 3 days.

NUTRIENTS PER SERVING (¼ cup/60 mL)

Calories 62	Dietary fiber . . . . .0.6 g
Protein . . . . .5.8 g	Sodium . . . . 14.5 mg
Total fat . . . . .2.4 g	Calcium . . . . 6.9 mg
Saturated fat . . . . 1.0 g	Iron . . . . .0.4 mg
Carbohydrates . . . . . . 4.4 g	Vitamin C . . . . 2.9 mg

Beef and Dates

This is a slightly sweet and very enjoyable meat purée. Babies will love it!

Makes about 1¼ cups (300 mL)

Chef Jordan's Tip

When making this recipe, avoid chewy cuts of beef such as flank. My choices include rib, strip and tenderloin.

Jill's Nutrition Tip

Dates contain easily digestible carbohydrates along with considerable amounts of important energy-promoting B vitamins. Combined with the protein in the beef, this recipe provides long-lasting energy to fuel your active baby.

- Blender

1 tsp	organic unsalted butter	5 mL
⅓ cup	diced beef (see Tips, left)	75 mL
1¼ cups	filtered water	300 mL
¼ cup	dates, pitted	60 mL

1. In a saucepan, over medium heat, melt butter. Add beef and cook, stirring constantly, until browned, about 3 minutes. Add water and dates and bring to a boil. Cook until liquid is reduced by half, 5 to 6 minutes.

2. Transfer to blender or use an immersion blender in the saucepan. Purée to your baby's preferred consistency, pulsing for a chunkier texture. Let cool until warm to the touch before serving or transfer to an airtight container and refrigerate for up to 3 days or freeze for up to 1 month.

Variation

Dates are quite easy to find in grocery stores. In this recipe, they impart a unique flavor profile but could easily be replaced by an equal quantity of prunes, dried apricots or dried peaches.

NUTRIENTS PER SERVING (¼ cup/60 mL)

Calories 46	Dietary fiber . . . . 0.6 g
Protein . . . . 3.0 g	Sodium . . . . 9.0 mg
Total fat . . . . 1.3 g	Calcium . . . . 6.0 mg
Saturated fat . . . . 0.7 g	Iron . . . . 0.4 mg
Carbohydrates . . . . 6.4 g	Vitamin C . . . . 0.0 mg

Lamb with Parsnips and Cranberries

Your baby will love the flavor combination of cranberries and lamb, balanced by the sweetness of parsnips. Lamb is often recommended for hypoallergenic diets, so it makes a great introduction to healthy grass-fed red meat for your baby. Look for 100 percent pasture-raised lamb.

Makes about 1¼ cups (300 mL)

Chef Jordan's Tip

As this recipe cooks quite quickly, I suggest using a leaner cut of meat such as the loin, leg or even shoulder.

Jill's Nutrition Tip

We often think of fish when talking about omega-3 fats, but 100 percent grass-fed lamb is a significant source of these fats, whose benefits range from healthy brain development to heart health. Grass-fed lamb also contains conjugated linoleic acid (CLA), another valuable fat associated with reduced body fat.

- Blender

1 tsp	organic unsalted butter	5 mL
½ cup	finely diced parsnip	125 mL
¼ cup	finely diced lamb (about 2 oz/60 g; see Tips, left)	60 mL
2 tbsp	unsweetened dried cranberries	30 mL
1 cup	filtered water	250 mL

1. In a saucepan, over medium heat, melt butter. Add parsnip, lamb and cranberries and sauté until meat begins to brown, about 3 minutes. Add water and bring to a boil. Reduce heat to low and simmer until parsnip is soft, about 8 minutes.

2. Transfer to blender or use an immersion blender in the saucepan. Purée to your baby's preferred consistency, pulsing for a chunkier texture. Let cool until warm to the touch before serving or transfer to an airtight container and refrigerate for up to 3 days or freeze for up to 1 month.

NUTRIENTS PER SERVING (¼ cup/60 mL)

Calories 41	Dietary fiber . . . . 0.8 g
Protein . . . . 2.4 g	Sodium . . . . 10.1 mg
Total fat . . . . 1.4 g	Calcium . . . . 7.5 mg
Saturated fat . . . . 0.7 g	Iron . . . . 0.3 mg
Carbohydrates . . . . 4.9 g	Vitamin C . . . . 2.3 mg

Food for Toddlers

12 Months +

Feeding Toddlers 126

Fruit

Strawberries with Apple. 127

Nectarine and Orange
Compote 128

Apple and Strawberry
Compote 129

Pineapple with Cottage Cheese. . . 130

Citrus Fruit Salad with
Fresh Basil. 131

Roasted Summer Fruit 132

Papaya and Coconut Milk
Purée. 134

Vegetables

Oven-Roasted Artichokes 135

Asparagus and Roasted
Tomato Purée. 136

Fennel and Orange Sauté. 138

Smashed New Potatoes. 139

Crispy Potato Galette 140

Broccoli, Potato and
Spinach Pie 141

Grilled Asparagus with
Three Cheeses. 142

Potato Salad with Cheddar
Cheese and Boiled Eggs. 143

Oven-Roasted Cauliflower
with Fresh Herbs. 145

Soups

Quick Mushroom Soup. 146

Corn and Chickpea Chowder 147

Quinoa Minestrone 148

Asparagus Basil Soup 149

Carrot and Sweet Potato Soup 150

Onion Soup with Chicken 151

Roasted Chicken Stock. 152

Vegetable Stock. 154

Grains

Jonah's "Mac and Cheese" 156

Pasta with Fresh Herbs
and Parmesan Cheese. 157

Millet and Cauliflower
with Fresh Oregano 158

Millet with Cheddar Cheese
and Apple 159

Savory Rice Pudding
with Basil. 160

Soft Polenta with
Cheddar Cheese and Broccoli 161

Jasmine Rice with Butternut
Squash and Saffron. 162

Oat Crêpes with Warm
Bananas 163

Fish

Halibut in a Wrapper. 164

Best-Ever Salmon Cakes. 166

Salmon, Potato and Cauliflower. . . 168

World's Best Fish Sticks 169

Meat

Beef Stew. 170

Pork with Red Cabbage. 171

Chicken with Caramelized
Apples. 172

Oven-Roasted Duck
with Red Cabbage. 173

Gramma Jean's Turkey Meatloaf. . 174

Feeding Toddlers

Try, Try Again . . . and Again

Feeding a toddler has its challenges, especially when he makes it clear he is not going to eat a particular food today. It is important to stick with the habits you have already established — continue to offer a variety of vegetables, fruit, protein and real whole grains. It may take a dozen or two attempts to get your child to try something new, but when he does, he may discover a new favorite. Food dislikes are often learned behavior, so be aware of your own food habits, too. Just because you don't like something doesn't mean you shouldn't prepare it for your child. Who knows, maybe it will even taste better to you this time around.

The changes that happen around the time your baby celebrates his first birthday are quite exciting. All the crawling, "scooting" and walking he is likely doing increase his need for energy in the form of nutrient-dense calories. The problem is, toddlers are so busy exploring they may not want to sit still long enough to eat. You may need to feed your toddler more frequently — from four to six times a day, in addition to his breast milk or formula intake. Appropriate finger foods, including vegetable- or protein-based snacks, should help to meet this increased demand.

When first introducing finger foods, steamed vegetables or soft fruits, such as tiny broccoli trees or bits of ripe banana, are a good choice because he is familiar with the tastes from the purées he enjoyed as early foods. Also, these foods are easy to pick up and eat. As his dexterity increases and he progresses to being able to tolerate and enjoy foods with more texture, he will be able to expand his range and enjoy foods such as thin strips of raw cucumber and red pepper or grated carrots and thin slices of apple. The recipes in this chapter offer exciting new tastes, many of which can be enjoyed by the whole family. They can be mashed or cut to suit your child's preferences.

At this stage, sticking to a regular meal pattern remains important. Toddlers need routine. A regular schedule encourages good eating habits and predisposes your toddler to enjoy the socializing that takes place when sharing a nutritious meal with his family.

Instead of being too focused on the amount of food your toddler is eating at one sitting, look at his food intake over several days. Children's appetites vary depending on their rate of growth, their surroundings and whether they are tired. It is important for you to remain patient and flexible. You need to be ready to address your child's changing preferences while continuing to offer a variety of nutritious foods and at the same time not overfeeding him.

Strawberries with Apple

This recipe is unlike most foods for baby, as the apple is left raw, lending unique flavor and texture. Your baby will love this for breakfast, or as a dessert or afternoon snack. And your mother was right: an apple a day keeps the doctor away.

● ●

**Makes about
1 cup (250 mL)**

Chef Jordan's Tip

I prefer to use Granny Smith apples in this recipe because of their wonderfully tart flavor, but any apple will work well.

Jill's Nutrition Tips

Apples are on almost every list of superfoods. They are loaded with nutrients, including quercetin, a powerful antioxidant that has many health benefits. Quercetin appears to have anti-inflammatory properties and is also being studied as a natural antihistamine that could be helpful with both asthma and allergies.

After his first birthday, your baby will start eating bits and pieces of cut-up apple. To reduce the amount of "rusting" (when the apple turns brown, or oxidizes), dip the pieces in a solution of lemon juice and water. For one apple, use about 3 cups (750 mL) water and ¼ cup (60 mL) freshly squeezed lemon juice.

Always buy organic apples and strawberries.

¾ cup	whole organic strawberries, stems removed	175 mL
¾ cup	filtered water	175 mL
⅔ cup	finely chopped cored organic apples	150 mL

1. In a saucepan, combine strawberries and water. Bring to a boil over high heat. Reduce heat to low and simmer until berries are soft and water has reduced by half, about 8 minutes. Remove from heat, add apple and mash or cut up to desired consistency.

2. Let cool until warm to the touch before serving or transfer to an airtight container and refrigerate for up to 3 days or freeze for up to 1 month.

Variation

In season, substitute any berry you like. If using raspberries or blackberries, cook them for about 10 minutes, then strain to get rid of the bitter seeds. Then add the apples and mash.

NUTRIENTS PER SERVING (½ cup/125 mL)

Calories 61	Dietary fiber . . . . 3.2 g
Protein . . . . 0.8 g	Sodium . . . . 4.3 mg
Total fat . . . . 0.3 g	Calcium . . . . 20.4 mg
Saturated fat . . . . 0.0 g	Iron . . . . 0.5 mg
Carbohydrates . . . . . . 16.0 g	Vitamin C . . . . 55.2 mg

Nectarine and Orange Compote

This sweet compote can be used to top hot cereal or on its own as a dessert. Oranges are rich in phytonutrients such as polyphenols, which help to fight inflammation.

Makes about 1¼ cups (300 mL)

Chef Jordan's Tip

Although I suggest creating this dish with citrus fruit segments, I prefer the slightly more labor-intensive version of "supremes," which means removing the peel, pith and membranes of a citrus fruit and separating its wedges. Supremes are much more delicate and easier for children to eat.

Jill's Nutrition Tip

The orange and nectarine in this recipe provide healthy doses of vitamin C and enough sweetness that the compote can be used as a dessert. Vitamin C strengthens your child's blood vessels, helping to minimize bruising from the many bumps and falls experienced at this age.

Always buy organic nectarines.

1 tsp	organic unsalted butter	5 mL
1½ cups	diced pitted organic nectarines	375 mL
½ cup	orange segments (see Tips, left)	250 mL
1	2-inch (5 cm) stick cinnamon	1

1. In a saucepan, melt butter over medium-low heat. Add nectarines, orange segments and cinnamon stick and sauté until nectarines are soft but still maintain their shape, about 5 minutes. Let cool until warm to the touch before serving or transfer to an airtight container and refrigerate for up to 3 days. Discard cinnamon stick before serving.

Variation

If nectarines aren't available, substitute an equal quantity of apricots, peaches or even canned peaches that have not been packed with sugar. The recipe will be wonderful no matter which fruit you use.

NUTRIENTS PER SERVING (½ cup/125 mL)

Calories	112	Dietary fiber	3.4 g
Protein	2.1 g	Sodium	22.3 mg
Total fat	3.1 g	Calcium	37.4 mg
Saturated fat	1.2 g	Iron	0.5 mg
Carbohydrates	21.2 g	Vitamin C	45.2 mg

Apple and Strawberry Compote

When Jonah and Jamie started attending junior kindergarten, instead of packing store-bought packaged fruit mixes, which are loaded with unwanted sugar, I sent them to school with this, and guess what? All the other kids wanted to trade. Can you blame them? Like all berries, strawberries are a wonderful source of antioxidants and health-promoting polyphenols. Unfortunately these compounds decline with time spent in the fridge, so be sure to purchase deep red strawberries and use them within a few days.

Makes about 1¼ cups (300 mL)

Chef Jordan's Tip

I encourage you to experiment with vinegars as often as you can. They can be used to season dishes other than salad dressings, such as this delicious compote.

Jill's Nutrition Tip

Eating is as much about the social circumstances in which food is consumed as it is about the food itself. Being rushed, stressed and not fully present at family meals can actually impair the enzymes needed for healthy digestion. Create an environment where an easy pace, laughter and gentle discussion are the guests that join you and your little one at the table.

Always buy organic apples and strawberries.

1 tsp	organic unsalted butter	5 mL
2 cups	diced cored, peeled organic apples	500 mL
½ cup	diced organic strawberries	125 mL
½ tsp	white wine vinegar	2 mL

1. In a saucepan, melt butter over medium-low heat. Add apples and strawberries and sauté until strawberries have virtually disintegrated, about 10 minutes. Remove from heat and stir in vinegar. Let cool until warm to the touch before serving or transfer to an airtight container and refrigerate for up to 3 days.

NUTRIENTS PER SERVING (½ cup/125 mL)

Calories 68	Dietary fiber. . . . . 1.8 g
Protein. . . . . .0.5 g	Sodium. . . . . .0.5 mg
Total fat . . . . .1.8 g	Calcium . . . . 10.0 mg
Saturated fat. . . . . . . .1.0 g	Iron. . . . . .0.2 mg
Carbohydrates . . . . . .14.2 g	Vitamin C . . . . 21.6 mg

Pineapple with Cottage Cheese

I have fond memories of eating cottage cheese and pineapple with my parents and siblings for breakfast, lunch or dinner. It was the go-to meal whenever one of us was rushing off to something like hockey practice or dance lessons. My mother made hers using canned pineapple. Really, Mom, there's nothing like the taste of warm fresh pineapple. The addition of basil or parsley adds a slight bitterness that is important for stimulating digestive juices.

Makes about 3½ cups (875 mL)

Chef Jordan's Tip

Many stores sell sliced peeled pineapple. You can use it here for convenience if you don't feel like cutting up a pineapple yourself.

Jill's Nutrition Tips

Pineapple contains a unique extract called bromelain that is a protein-digesting enzyme. This means it is an excellent digestive aid. The pineapple in this recipe will help your baby digest the protein-rich cottage cheese.

Herbs such as basil and parsley are often in our fridge but we tend to use them only as a decorative garnish. It's time to think of these greens as valuable health-promoting additions to our meals. Not only can dark green herbs help form strong bones and teeth with their high levels of vitamin K, but incorporating them regularly into baby's meals will ease her into the stronger tastes of nutrient-dense greens.

½ cup	filtered water	125 mL
2 cups	diced pineapple (about 12 oz/375 g)	500 mL
1 tsp	chopped fresh basil or parsley leaves	5 mL
2 cups	organic full-fat cottage cheese	500 mL

1. In a saucepan, bring water to a boil over high heat. Add pineapple. Reduce heat to medium-low and simmer until water has fully evaporated and pineapple is caramelized, about 15 minutes. Stir in basil. Mash or cut up to desired consistency. Let cool to room temperature or transfer to an airtight container and refrigerate for up to 3 days.

2. Serve over cottage cheese.

NUTRIENTS PER SERVING (½ cup/125 mL)

Calories 90	Dietary fiber . . . . .0.6 g
Protein . . . . 7.7 g	Sodium . . . . .246.7 mg
Total fat . . . . .2.9 g	Calcium . . . . .63.6 mg
Saturated fat . . . . 1.7 g	Iron . . . . 0.1 mg
Carbohydrates . . . . . . .8.5 g	Vitamin C . . . . .16.1 mg

Citrus Fruit Salad with Fresh Basil

This is a very refreshing fruit salad not only for baby but also for the rest of the family. My family loves eating this right from the fridge on hot summer days. The combination of citrus fruits makes this salad a standout for vitamin C (for strong ligaments and tendons) and the electrolyte potassium (so important for nerves and the heart).

● ●

**Makes about
2 ½ cups (625 mL)**

Chef Jordan's Tips

Serve this on its own, with breakfast muesli or over plain full-fat organic yogurt.

Although citrus fruit segments will work in this dish, I prefer to use "supremes," which are much more delicate and easier for children to eat. To make supremes, separate citrus fruit into wedges and remove the peel, pith and membrane.

Jill's Nutrition Tip

Citrus fruits and their skins are loaded with antioxidants that work from the inside out, protecting your baby's delicate skin from premature development of skin damage. The rind contains hyaluronic acid (a component of connective tissue), which is important in the body for tissue repair. The vitamin C in oranges and lemons supports the production of hyaluronic acid, which has been called "the key to the fountain of youth."

1 ²⁄₃ cups	grapefruit segments (see Tips, left)	400 mL
1 tsp	freshly grated orange zest	5 mL
1 cup	orange segments	250 mL
½ cup	clementine segments	125 mL
¼ cup	freshly squeezed lemon juice	60 mL
1 tbsp	pure maple syrup	15 mL
1 tsp	chopped fresh basil or parsley leaves	5 mL

1. In a bowl, combine grapefruit segments, orange zest and segments, clementine segments, lemon juice, maple syrup and basil. Cover and refrigerate overnight or for up to 3 days before serving.

NUTRIENTS PER SERVING (½ cup/125 mL)

Calories	65	Dietary fiber	2.2 g
Protein	1.0 g	Sodium	0.9 mg
Total fat	0.2 g	Calcium	35.2 mg
Saturated fat	0.0 g	Iron	0.2 mg
Carbohydrates	16.8 g	Vitamin C	56.1 mg

Roasted Summer Fruit

This recipe works for virtually any fruit and can be served with breakfast, lunch or dinner. Although roasting fruit does demand a wee bit of work, the return is worth it. The caramelization of natural sugars created by roasting is tough to duplicate. Try it once and I promise you'll do it over and over again.

• •

	Makes about 4 cups (1 L)

Chef Jordan's Tips

The combination of the natural sugars in the fruit with sugar results in a very rich caramel. The key to caramelization is patience, but it's really worth the wait!

You can also serve this with pancakes or on toast.

Don't be worried about the quantity. You can transform any leftovers into a mouthwatering smoothie (see page 202) — in fact, you may want to make extra to keep on hand for this purpose.

Jill's Nutrition Tip

The combination of fruits in this recipe makes for a powerhouse of nutrition. The plums bring a phytonutrient called chlorogenic acid, while the berries bring resveratrol and ellagic acid — all of which provide protection from oxidative stress and inflammation for your baby, deep down at a cellular level where damage can start.

Always buy organic plums, peaches, raspberries and blueberries, unless they are wild.

• Baking dish, lightly greased
• Potato masher, optional
• Preheat oven to 300°F (150°C)

2	organic peaches, pitted	2
1½ cups	raspberries	375 mL
1½ cups	organic or wild blueberries	375 mL
1½ cups	whole organic strawberries, stems removed	375 mL
2	organic plums, pitted	2
2 tbsp	evaporated cane juice sugar or coconut sugar	30 mL

1. In prepared baking dish, combine peaches, raspberries, blueberries, strawberries, plums and sugar, stirring until fruit is evenly coated with sugar.

2. Roast in preheated oven until fruit is soft and nicely caramelized (see Tips, left), about 1 hour. Mash or cut to desired consistency. Let cool until warm to the touch before serving or transfer to an airtight container and refrigerate for up to 3 days or freeze for up to 1 month.

Variations

In winter substitute apples for the peaches or cranberries or frozen berries for the berries.

NUTRIENTS PER SERVING (½ cup/125 mL)

Calories 65	Dietary fiber . . . . 2.1 g
Protein . . . . 1.0 g	Sodium . . . . 0.6 mg
Total fat . . . . 0.2 g	Calcium . . . . 10.5 mg
Saturated fat . . . . 0.0 g	Iron . . . . 0.3 mg
Carbohydrates . . . . . . 17.3 g	Vitamin C . . . . 27.6 mg

Papaya and Coconut Milk Purée

Both you and your baby will love this delicious blend of tropical papaya, creamy coconut and warm ginger.

● ●

Makes about 2 ½ cups (625 mL)

Chef Jordan's Tip

When tomatoes are in season, they make an excellent alternative or complement to some of the papaya in the recipe. Peel before using.

Jill's Nutrition Tip

Coconut milk, not to be confused with coconut water (found sitting inside the fruit) is made from soaked grated coconut flesh. The fat content of coconut is very high but most of it is a medium-chain fatty acid called lauric acid. Not only can the body easily use this fat for energy (as opposed to storing it as fat), lauric acid has antiviral, antibacterial and antiprotazoa properties, making it very helpful against infections.

Most of the papaya grown in Hawaii is genetically modified, so we suggest buying this fruit from another region.

● Blender

2 cups	chopped peeled papaya (see Tips, left)	500 mL
1 cup	filtered water	250 mL
½ cup	unsweetened coconut milk (see Tips, left)	125 mL
½ tsp	minced peeled gingerroot	2 mL

1. In a saucepan, combine papaya, water, coconut milk and ginger. Bring to a boil over medium heat. Reduce heat to low and simmer until papaya is soft, 5 to 7 minutes.

2. Transfer to blender or use an immersion blender in the saucepan. Purée until smooth. Let cool until warm to the touch before serving or transfer to an airtight container and refrigerate for up to 3 days.

NUTRIENTS PER SERVING (½ cup/125 mL)

Calories	80	Dietary fiber	1.6 g
Protein	0.9 g	Sodium	7.0 mg
Total fat	6.1 g	Calcium	19.0 mg
Saturated fat	5.4 g	Iron	0.5 mg
Carbohydrates	6.9 g	Vitamin C	35.3 mg

Oven-Roasted Artichokes

Artichokes are chock-full of important minerals for your baby's developing organs and tissues, as well as fiber for good bowel function and nicely balanced energy.

Makes about 2 cups (500 mL)

Chef Jordan's Tip

If turkey bacon doesn't appeal to you, smoked turkey breast or thigh works just as well. Break up the turkey into small pieces and follow the recipe as written. If you are concerned about nitrates (see page 105), make sure your bacon or turkey is nitrate-free.

Jill's Nutrition Tip

Artichokes are a nutrient-dense food, packed with fiber, minerals, vitamin C and folate. They also contain powerful antioxidants called cynarin and silymarin, which support detoxification and protect the liver from the chemical and environmental toxins that, unfortunately, your baby is exposed to right from the start.

- Preheat oven to 400°F (200°C)
- Ovenproof skillet

2	artichokes (about 1½ lbs/750 g)	2
1 tbsp	extra virgin olive oil	15 mL
¼ cup	finely diced turkey bacon	60 mL
¼ cup	finely diced sweet onion, such as Vidalia	60 mL
2	cloves garlic, minced	2
1	sprig fresh thyme	1
¼ cup	freshly grated organic Parmesan cheese	60 mL
2 tbsp	filtered water	30 mL

1. Remove artichoke stems and set aside. Trim off the top two-thirds of each artichoke and remove the bright green leaves, exposing the whitish leaves. Plunge a spoon into the middle of the choke, removing the thorny middle leaves and exposing the heart. Cut each artichoke into 4 slices.

2. Peel the outer portion of the stems, leaving the tender white core in the middle. Slice the stems.

3. In ovenproof skillet, heat oil over medium heat. Add bacon, onion, garlic and thyme and sauté until onion is soft, 3 to 4 minutes.

4. Stir in artichoke slices and stems and transfer skillet to preheated oven. Roast, stirring often to prevent bacon from burning, until artichokes are fork-tender, about 25 minutes. Remove from oven and stir in cheese and water. Cut pieces to desired size. Let cool until warm to the touch before serving or transfer to an airtight container and refrigerate for up to 3 days.

NUTRIENTS PER SERVING (½ cup/125 mL)

Calories	156	Dietary fiber	10.2 g
Protein	9.8 g	Sodium	399.3 mg
Total fat	6.0 g	Calcium	53.0 mg
Saturated fat	1.6 g	Iron	0.2 mg
Carbohydrates	21.7 g	Vitamin C	1.3 mg

Asparagus and Roasted Tomato Purée

Tomatoes are nutrient-dense but in their raw state may be difficult for your toddler to digest. Roasting the tomatoes for this soup brings out their natural sweetness and helps to improve their digestibility. Combining them with asparagus creates fabulous flavor.

Chef Jordan's Tips

Peel your asparagus for the best result. As tender as asparagus can be, it may still be fibrous, making it tough for children to chew.

To peel asparagus, use a vegetable peeler. Peel from under the tip all the way down the stalk, rotating until all of the whitish flesh is exposed.

Jill's Nutrition Tip

When we think of potassium, we often think of bananas, but tomatoes are also a significant source of this important mineral. Potassium is one of the body's main electrolytes, which means it generates electrical impulses that keep your nervous system working. This function can become unbalanced when your baby suffers from vomiting or diarrhea.

- Preheat oven to 350°F (180°C)
- Rimmed baking sheet
- Blender

½ cup	cherry tomatoes	125 mL
8 oz	asparagus, trimmed and cut in half	250 g
2 cups	water or Roasted Chicken Stock (page 152) or Vegetable Stock (page 154)	500 mL
2	fresh basil leaves	2

1. On baking sheet, roast tomatoes in preheated oven until soft and skins begin to split, about 20 minutes. Transfer to a saucepan and add asparagus and water. Bring to a boil over medium heat. Reduce heat to low and simmer until asparagus is tender and liquid has reduced by one-quarter, about 8 minutes.

2. Add basil. Transfer to blender or use an immersion blender in the saucepan. Pulse to desired consistency. Let cool until warm to the touch before serving or transfer to an airtight container and refrigerate for up to 3 days.

Variation

Try serving this as a cold soup. Add about ½ cup (125 mL) chicken or vegetable stock to 1 cup (250 mL) purée. Top with shredded organic Cheddar cheese.

NUTRIENTS PER SERVING (½ cup/125 mL)

Calories	23	Dietary fiber	1.7 g
Protein	1.6 g	Sodium	5.3 mg
Total fat	0.1 g	Calcium	20.7 mg
Saturated fat	0.0 g	Iron	0.3 mg
Carbohydrates	3.9 g	Vitamin C	10.1 mg

Celebrate Spring

For a farmer, spring means the ground has thawed and is soft enough to plant. For a gardener, it's the first lovely blooms on previously bare trees. For me, it means the arrival of certain foods, such as the first locally grown asparagus, which is my favorite springtime delicacy. I love the tender stalks and sweet flavor of this beautiful vegetable. Used in combination with tomato and basil, as it is in the recipe opposite, asparagus creates a fabulous contrast in textures. Asparagus is as versatile a food as they come. It can be served on its own, as a simple side or in salads, and it combines beautifully with many other ingredients — not only those featured opposite but also those in my recipe for halibut (page 164).

Fennel and Orange Sauté

In this recipe, the sweet-and-sour flavor of the orange complements the fennel beautifully. Although it's a relatively sophisticated pairing, your baby will love the mild licorice flavor of the fennel, which is moderated by the orange. Fennel provides a wide range of nutrients: vitamin C and various B vitamins as well as minerals such as calcium, iron and magnesium.

Makes about ¾ cup (175 mL)

Chef Jordan's Tip

When available, substitute clementine zest and juice for the orange in this recipe. Clementines have a unique flavor that is slightly different from oranges, and it is awesome in this pairing.

Jill's Nutrition Tip

Because you are using the peel, we strongly recommend choosing organic oranges for this recipe. The chemical residue of dyes, waxes and pesticides is concentrated in the skin of most conventionally grown fruit. Your baby is exposed to environmental and chemical toxins every day; this is one small step you can take to limit his exposure.

- Potato masher, optional

1 tsp	organic unsalted butter	5 mL
1¾ cups	finely diced fennel	425 mL
1 tbsp	freshly grated orange zest (see Tips, left)	15 mL
⅓ cup	freshly squeezed orange juice	75 mL

1. In a saucepan, melt butter over medium heat. Add fennel and sauté until soft, about 10 minutes. Stir in orange zest and juice. Reduce heat to low and simmer until liquid has evaporated, about 5 minutes. Mash or cut to desired consistency. Let cool until warm to the touch before serving or transfer to an airtight container and refrigerate for up to 3 days.

NUTRIENTS PER SERVING (½ cup/125 mL)

Calories	82	Dietary fiber	3.7 g
Protein	1.7 g	Sodium	53.8 mg
Total fat	2.8 g	Calcium	61.8 mg
Saturated fat	1.6 g	Iron	0.8 mg
Carbohydrates	14.1 g	Vitamin C	38.2 mg

Smashed New Potatoes

I first made this for Jonah when he was a toddler. His response was "They tastes like french fries, Daddy." And no frying necessary. Potatoes are a good source of the important vitamin B$_6$, which is involved in dozens of enzymes in the body and the formation of virtually every cell!

**Makes
8 to 10 servings**

Chef Jordan's Tip

We've made a large quantity of this dish because it is one you'll enjoy every bit as much as your baby. *Bon appétit.*

Jill's Nutrition Tip

It is important to consider the type of oil you use when cooking at high temperatures, because when oils are overheated, free radicals and other unhealthy products form. Butter and coconut oils, for example, have a sturdy structure and do not change substantially when heated to below their smoking point. Seed and nut oils such as flax, pumpkin and walnut are extremely sensitive to heat and easily oxidize, so heating is not recommended. Oxidized fats represent considerable health risks in cardiovascular disease.

Always buy organic potatoes.

- 2 baking sheets

2 lbs	small new organic potatoes	1 kg
12 cups	filtered water	3 L
2 tbsp	extra virgin olive oil or coconut oil	30 mL

1. In a large pot, combine potatoes and water. Bring to a boil over medium heat. Reduce heat and simmer until fork-tender, about 20 minutes. Drain and transfer to one baking sheet.

2. Preheat oven to 350°F (180°C).

3. Using second baking sheet, cover the potatoes and press down to crush, essentially flattening them into a thick, chunky pancake. Drizzle half the olive oil on the potatoes, turn them over, and drizzle with the remainder.

4. Roast in preheated oven until crispy, about 20 minutes. Transfer to a plate and let cool until warm to the touch before serving or transfer to an airtight container and refrigerate for up to 3 days.

NUTRIENTS PER SERVING

Calories	106	Dietary fiber	1.9 g
Protein	2.1 g	Sodium	18.1 mg
Total fat	3.1 g	Calcium	22.6 mg
Saturated fat	0.5 g	Iron	0.8 mg
Carbohydrates	18.0 g	Vitamin C	9.8 mg

Crispy Potato Galette

Potato galette makes an excellent snack in place of store-bought potato chips, and it's much tastier, too.

● ●

**Makes about
4 servings**

Chef Jordan's Tips

To shred the potato for this recipe, use the large holes of a box grater.

Believe it or not, this galette stores well in the refrigerator, so it is excellent to keep on hand for those times when your toddler is feeling peckish. To reheat, bake in a preheated 350°F (180°C) oven until crisp, about 5 minutes.

Jill's Nutrition Tip

Scrub your potatoes well and leave the skins on. That's where the nutrients are concentrated, especially potassium, which every cell of your baby's body requires. Don't use potatoes that are the least bit green or have any sprouts. Both indicate the presence of solanine, which can detrimentally affect collagen repair, important for your baby's bones and joints.

Always buy organic potatoes.

2 tbsp	coconut oil	30 mL
1 cup	shredded organic baking potato, skin on	250 mL

1. In a small nonstick skillet, heat coconut oil over high heat. Add potato, spreading evenly over the entire surface of the pan to create what looks like a small pizza crust. Reduce heat to low and cook until bottom is golden brown, about 10 minutes. Flip and cook until other side is golden brown and potato is tender, about 10 minutes.

2. Transfer to a plate and let cool until warm to the touch before serving or wrap in plastic wrap and refrigerate for up to 3 days. To serve, cut into wedges.

NUTRIENTS PER SERVING

Calories	87.5	Dietary fiber	0.8 g
Protein	0.8 g	Sodium	2.3 mg
Total fat	6.8 g	Calcium	4.5 mg
Saturated fat	5.9 g	Iron	0.3 mg
Carbohydrates	6.6 g	Vitamin C	7.4 mg

Broccoli, Potato and Spinach Pie

This "crustless" pie is a huge hit in my family; we all enjoy it. It is a great way to help your baby develop a taste for healthful leafy greens. Broccoli has long been identified as a superfood. In combination with spinach, it helps to establish this recipe as a nutritional powerhouse.

Makes about 8 servings

Chef Jordan's Tips

If you prefer, substitute $\frac{1}{2}$ cup (125 mL) organic whole milk for the cream in this recipe.

If your toddler is a budding gourmand, garnish the pie with soft organic goat cheese and thin strands of fresh basil or finely chopped parsley leaves.

Jill's Nutrition Tip

You can get calcium from vegetables, too! Spinach is second only to kale as the highest vegetable source of this mineral. It also contains a significant amount of iron, which is needed for red blood cells to transport oxygen throughout the body to keep your toddler's energy up.

Always buy organic potatoes and spinach.

- 9-inch (23 cm) pie plate
- Preheat oven to 300°F (150°C)

1 lb	new organic red potatoes (about 4 small), thinly sliced	500 g
2 tsp	melted organic unsalted butter	10 mL
4 cups	organic baby spinach	1 L
1 cup	chopped broccoli florets	250 mL
¾ cup	organic heavy or whipping (35%) cream	175 mL
¾ cup	freshly grated organic Parmesan cheese	175 mL

1. In a bowl, combine potatoes and butter, tossing until well coated. Transfer to pie plate, overlapping slices as necessary. Bake in preheated oven until potatoes are soft, about 25 minutes.

2. In another bowl, combine spinach, broccoli, cream and cheese. Pour over potatoes. Bake in preheated oven until liquid is thick and potatoes are fork-tender, about 20 minutes.

3. Cut pie or mash to desired consistency. Let cool until warm to the touch before serving or wrap in plastic wrap and refrigerate for up to 3 days.

NUTRIENTS PER SERVING

Calories	185	Dietary fiber	1.6 g
Protein	5.0 g	Sodium	149.5 mg
Total fat	12.8 g	Calcium	111.9 mg
Saturated fat	7.9 g	Iron	0.9 mg
Carbohydrates	13.1 g	Vitamin C	9.0 mg

Grilled Asparagus with Three Cheeses

I love how the cheese melts together to cover the asparagus, and now that they are older, my children love that they can eat the spears with their hands. When making this dish, mash some for your toddler and serve the remainder as finger food to older children. Although in culinary terms asparagus is often perceived as a special treat, this vegetable is loaded with valuable nutrients such as potassium, folate and vitamin K, which among other benefits helps to build strong bones.

● ●

Makes about 2½ cups (625 mL), diced

Chef Jordan's Tip

So many of my friends cook their asparagus directly on the barbecue without blanching (boiling) it first. My spears are beautifully green and crunchy and theirs are gray-black and quite woody. There is really no comparison.

Jill's Nutrition Tip

In addition to the nutrients mentioned above, asparagus contains inulin, a carbohydrate that helps to promote the growth of friendly bacteria in your baby's gut. Inulin is resistant to digestion in the small intestine, so it reaches the large intestine, or colon, largely intact. Here it is fermented by and provides fuel for the friendly healthy intestinal bacteria that are a key component of your baby's immune system. Garlic and leeks are other good sources of inulin.

Always buy organic milk products.

- Potato masher, optional
- Preheat barbecue to High (500°F/260°C)

8 cups	filtered water	2 L
1 lb	asparagus, peeled (see Tips, page 136)	500 g
¼ cup	freshly grated organic Parmesan cheese	60 mL
¼ cup	shredded organic Cheddar cheese	60 mL
1 tbsp	finely diced organic Brie cheese	15 mL

1. In a saucepan, bring water to a rolling boil over medium heat. Add asparagus and cook until vibrant green and soft, about 3 minutes. Drain well.

2. Cook asparagus on preheated barbecue until grill marks appear, about 2 minutes.

3. In a bowl, combine grilled asparagus and Parmesan, Cheddar and Brie cheeses. Cut or mash to desired consistency. Let cool until warm to the touch before serving or transfer to an airtight container and refrigerate for up to 3 days.

NUTRIENTS PER SERVING (½ cup/125 mL)

Calories 70	Dietary fiber . . . . 2.0 g
Protein . . . . 5.0 g	Sodium . . . . 122.7 mg
Total fat . . . . 3.5 g	Calcium . . . . 123.6 mg
Saturated fat . . . . 2.2 g	Iron . . . . 0.4 mg
Carbohydrates . . . . 4.3 g	Vitamin C . . . . 8.8 mg

Potato Salad with Cheddar Cheese and Boiled Eggs

Most of the potato salads I remember from my childhood were full of mayonnaise or oil. Here the combination of chopped boiled egg with shredded carrots creates wonderful texture. The mixture of protein (eggs and cheese) and complex carbohydrates (potatoes and carrots) provides long-lasting steady energy for your toddler.

Makes about 2 cups (500 mL)

Chef Jordan's Tip

To shred the carrots for this recipe, use the medium holes on a box grater.

Jill's Nutrition Tips

Which came first, the chicken or the egg? In this case, it's the feed the chicken eats. You can increase your baby's consumption of omega-3 fats by buying eggs that are richer in this nutrient. When chickens are fed flax seeds, their eggs contain more of these beneficial fats. Look for them in the supermarket.

Although pre-shredded cheese may feel like a time-saver, a closer look might make you change your mind. Generally potato starch and cellulose have been added to prevent the cheese from clumping. Cellulose is derived from wood pulp and is a white powder. It is combined with potato starch (which is translucent) so the "real" color of the cheese is maintained. Because of this coating, these products don't melt the way uncoated cheese does — and they are considerably more expensive.

Always buy organic potatoes and milk products.

1¾ cups	cubed organic red potatoes	425 mL
2	hard-cooked eggs, chopped	2
½ cup	shredded peeled carrots	125 mL
⅓ cup	shredded organic Cheddar cheese	75 mL

1. In a saucepan, cover potatoes with cold water. Bring to a boil over medium heat. Reduce heat to low and simmer until fork-tender, about 20 minutes. Drain well. Let cool to room temperature.

2. In a bowl, combine eggs, carrots and cheese. Stir in potatoes. Cover and refrigerate overnight or for up to 3 days.

NUTRIENTS PER SERVING (½ cup/125 mL)

Calories	137	Dietary fiber	1.3 g
Protein	6.7 g	Sodium	105.3 mg
Total fat	5.2 g	Calcium	83.1 mg
Saturated fat	2.7 g	Iron	1.1 mg
Carbohydrates	15.4 g	Vitamin C	17.0 mg

Oven-Roasted Cauliflower with Fresh Herbs

Cauliflower, broccoli and Brussels sprouts are cruciferous vegetables, which are cancer protective, especially when eaten multiple times per week. Make this in season when cauliflower is fresh. Break the florets into toddler-friendly pieces either before or after roasting.

• •

Makes about 5 cups (1.25 L)

Chef Jordan's Tip

This recipe yields a large quantity because other family members will enjoy it, too. If you are making it just for baby, halve the recipe.

Jill's Nutrition Tip

When cruciferous vegetables such as cauliflower, broccoli, cabbage and Brussels sprouts are chopped or chewed, a compound called sulforaphane is formed. Research cited by the American Cancer Society shows that this compound triggers the liver to produce enzymes that detoxify cancer-causing chemicals. Human population studies show that diets high in cruciferous vegetables are associated with reduced incidence of certain cancers. It is never too early to establish eating habits that will help to keep your baby healthy throughout her life.

• Rimmed baking sheet
• Preheat oven to 350°F (180°C)

2	heads cauliflower, cut into florets (about 4 lbs/2 kg)	2
1/4 cup	extra virgin olive oil	60 mL
2 tbsp	chopped fresh parsley leaves	30 mL
1 tbsp	chopped fresh thyme leaves	15 mL

1. In a bowl, combine cauliflower and oil, mixing thoroughly to coat well. Spread evenly on baking sheet and roast in preheated oven until golden brown, about 30 minutes.

2. Add parsley and thyme and toss to coat. Let cool until warm to the touch before serving or transfer to an airtight container and refrigerate for up to 3 days.

Variation

Fresh goat cheese is a nice addition to this recipe. In a bowl, toss the roasted cauliflower, right from the oven, with 1/4 cup (60 mL) soft organic goat cheese, then add the herbs.

NUTRIENTS PER SERVING (1/2 cup/125 mL)

Calories	89	Dietary fiber	4.6 g
Protein	3.6 g	Sodium	54.9 mg
Total fat	4.9 g	Calcium	41.9 mg
Saturated fat	0.7 g	Iron	0.9 mg
Carbohydrates	9.7 g	Vitamin C	85.6 mg

Quick Mushroom Soup

This recipe epitomizes what I call "simple elegance" — basic in method and refined in taste. Since mushrooms are very well known as immune-system boosters, it makes sense to help your child acquire a taste for these tasty fungi early in life. This recipe makes a large quantity. The theory is that other members of the family will enjoy it, too.

**Makes about
5 cups (1.25 L)**

Chef Jordan's Tip

For years only the common button mushroom was available at our local grocery stores. Today, a number of varieties can be found, such as portobello, shiitake and oyster mushrooms. Each has its own unique flavor and texture. Feel free to experiment with one or a combination of mushrooms. This recipe will taste great no matter which ones you choose.

Jill's Nutrition Tip

Mushrooms are a delicious way to ensure there is enough folate in your baby's diet. All types of mushrooms contain folate, a B vitamin that is important for your baby's healthy growth and development. Among other functions, folate is essential for the formation of red and white blood cells in the bone marrow.

Always buy organic milk products.

- Blender

1 tbsp	organic unsalted butter	15 mL
5 cups	sliced mushrooms (see Tips, left)	1.25 L
1 cup	diced white onions	250 mL
¾ cup	finely diced peeled carrots	175 mL
3	cloves garlic, minced	3
2	fresh sage leaves	2
3 cups	Roasted Chicken Stock (page 152)	750 mL
1 cup	organic whole milk	250 mL
1 tsp	extra virgin olive oil	5 mL

1. In a large pot, melt butter over high heat. Add mushrooms, onions, carrots, garlic and sage and sauté until carrots are soft, about 10 minutes. Add chicken stock and milk and bring to a boil. Reduce heat to low and simmer until carrots are falling apart, about 30 minutes. Add olive oil.

2. Transfer to blender or use an immersion blender in the pot. Purée until smooth. Let cool until warm to the touch before serving or transfer to an airtight container and refrigerate for up to 3 days.

NUTRIENTS PER SERVING (½ cup/125 mL)

Calories	54.7	Dietary fiber	1.0 g
Protein	2.9 g	Sodium	64.9 mg
Total fat	2.8 g	Calcium	37.4 mg
Saturated fat	1.3 g	Iron	0.3 mg
Carbohydrates	5.1 g	Vitamin C	2.8 mg

Corn and Chickpea Chowder

Although it's a bit of extra work to roast the corn for this chowder, it creates a distinctly out-of-the-ordinary flavor. It's definitely worth the effort, but if you are pressed for time, substitute any cooked corn, including frozen kernels. Corn contains different types of fiber that support healthy populations of friendly bacteria in your toddler's intestines that in turn support a healthy immune system.

● ●

Makes about 4½ cups (1.125 L)

Chef Jordan's Tips

This makes a large quantity of soup to feed to baby, but other family members will enjoy it, too.

To roast corn, place 4 ears on a preheated barbecue (500°F/260°C). Cook, rotating often, until the husk is dark brown, about 20 minutes. (The corn will not be fully cooked.) Let cool for at least 5 minutes. Remove husks and silks by hand and, using a sharp knife and working over a container, trim off the kernels. Scrape the cob, which releases the milky juices that will develop the flavor in your chowder.

Jill's Nutrition Tip

When putting together a meal for your toddler, it is important to make sure it is balanced. The chickpeas in this chowder provide protein for building muscle, and the corn provides carbohydrates to fuel physical activity. To round out the meal, add a green vegetable such as Sautéed Chard with Apples (page 115).

Always buy organic bell peppers, corn and milk products.

● Blender

1 tbsp	organic unsalted butter	15 mL
1½ cups	roasted organic corn kernels (see Tips, left)	375 mL
1½ cups	cooked chickpeas, drained and rinsed (see page 85)	375 mL
1	roasted organic red bell pepper, peeled, seeded and diced	1
1 tbsp	diced lean bacon, optional (see Tips, page 105)	15 mL
1 tbsp	minced garlic	15 mL
3¼ cups	filtered water or Roasted Chicken Stock (page 152) or Vegetable Stock (page 154)	800 mL

1. In a saucepan, melt butter over medium heat. Add corn, chickpeas, red pepper, bacon (if using) and garlic and cook, stirring often, for 5 minutes. Add water and bring to a boil. Reduce heat to low and simmer until chickpeas are very soft, about 35 minutes.

2. Transfer to blender or use an immersion blender in the saucepan. Pulse to desired consistency. Let cool until warm to the touch before serving or transfer to an airtight container and refrigerate for up to 3 days or freeze for up to 3 months.

NUTRIENTS PER SERVING (½ cup/125 mL)

Calories	40.7	Dietary fiber	0.8 g
Protein	1.0 g	Sodium	0.8 mg
Total fat	1.6 g	Calcium	4.2 mg
Saturated fat	0.8 g	Iron	0.2 mg
Carbohydrates	6.5 g	Vitamin C	27.5 mg

Quinoa Minestrone

This very simple tomato-based soup is certain to become one of your toddler's favorites. Among other benefits, the addition of nutrient-dense quinoa provides complete protein.

• •

**Makes
4 ½ cups (1.125 L)**

Chef Jordan's Tip

Store-bought tomato sauce works wonderfully in this recipe, but when tomatoes are in season, consider puréeing garden-fresh tomatoes to create your own sauce.

Jill's Nutrition Tip

Although tomatoes are extremely nutritious, they can also trigger reactions in sensitive individuals. They contain a high amount of histamine, a chemical that performs many useful functions in your baby's body but which some people have difficulty breaking down. Tomatoes are also high in salicylates, chemicals that are found in many foods, drugs and personal care products, which can also evoke an allergic response that may present as hives, hyperactivity or asthma. If you find that your baby is reacting to tomatoes, seek help from a health professional to pin down the real cause.

• Blender

1 tbsp	organic unsalted butter	15 mL
2	cloves garlic, minced	2
¼ cup	quinoa, rinsed and drained	60 mL
¼ cup	finely diced white onion	60 mL
¼ cup	finely diced peeled carrot	60 mL
2 cups	Roasted Chicken Stock (page 152), Vegetable Stock (page 154) or filtered water	500 mL
2 cups	tomato sauce (see Tips, left)	500 mL

1. In a large saucepan, melt butter over medium heat. Add garlic, quinoa, onion and carrot and cook until quinoa is light brown and toasted, about 5 minutes. Add chicken stock and tomato sauce and bring to a boil. Reduce heat and simmer until quinoa is tender, about 15 minutes. (You will know when it's cooked because there will be a white "tail" around the seeds. That's the germ, which bursts out of the seed.)

2. Let cool until warm to the touch before serving or transfer to an airtight container and refrigerate for up to 3 days.

NUTRIENTS PER SERVING (½ cup/125 mL)

Calories 59.9	Dietary fiber. . . . . 1.4 g
Protein. . . . . 2.0 g	Sodium. . . . . 42.4 mg
Total fat . . . . 1.7 g	Calcium . . . . 13.6 mg
Saturated fat. . . . . 0.9 g	Iron. . . . . 0.7 mg
Carbohydrates . . . . . . .8.8 g	Vitamin C . . . . 7.9 mg

Asparagus Basil Soup

This very fresh and colorful soup is an easy way to introduce your toddler to the virtues of asparagus. Not only is it delicious, asparagus is an excellent source of folate, a B vitamin, which among other benefits helps to reduce the risk of cancer.

Makes
4 ½ cups (1.125 L)

Chef Jordan's Tip

Roasted Chicken Stock adds a wonderful depth of flavor to this recipe, but it is not absolutely necessary. You can substitute an equal quantity of water or vegetable stock, which also makes this dish vegetarian.

Jill's Nutrition Tip

Asparagus contains a good amount of fiber and is relatively high in protein for a vegetable. It also contains sulfur, which helps the liver with its detoxification jobs, and folate to help with heart health. Some people notice that their urine has a particular smell after eating asparagus. It comes from the amino acid asparagine, which is named after this vegetable.

● **Blender**

1 tbsp	organic unsalted butter	15 mL
2	cloves garlic, minced	2
⅓ cup	finely diced onion	75 mL
4 cups	Roasted Chicken Stock (page 152), Vegetable Stock (page 154) or filtered water	1 L
2 cups	finely chopped asparagus	500 mL
¼ cup	fresh basil leaves	60 mL

1. In a large saucepan, melt butter over medium heat. Add garlic and onion and cook, stirring often, until onion is translucent, 3 to 5 minutes. Add chicken stock and bring to a boil. Add asparagus and cook until it turns bright green, 2 to 3 minutes.

2. Add basil and, using an immersion blender, purée soup. (You can also do this in a food processor, in batches.) Let cool until warm to the touch before serving or transfer to an airtight container and refrigerate for up to 3 days.

NUTRIENTS PER SERVING (½ cup/125 mL)

Calories 30.3	Dietary fiber . . . . .0.8 g
Protein . . . . 1.9 g	Sodium . . . . 67.7 mg
Total fat . . . . 1.8 g	Calcium . . . . .11.3 mg
Saturated fat . . . . .0.9 g	Iron . . . . 0.7 mg
Carbohydrates . . . . 2.1 g	Vitamin C . . . . .2.4 mg

Carrot and Sweet Potato Soup

This soup is so sweet and flavorful your children will think you've gone crazy and replaced their meal with candy. Softening the carrots in butter helps to ensure that their valuable beta-carotene is absorbed by your baby's body.

● ●

Makes
4 1/2 cups (1.125 L)

Chef Jordan's Tip

I prefer to cook my sweet potatoes with their skin on, as I find it provides a wonderfully deep flavor profile. Feel free to try the recipe using peeled sweet potatoes, if desired.

Jill's Nutrition Tip

This soup is an anti-inflammatory and antioxidant powerhouse, providing overall support for your baby's metabolic processes. The carrots and sweet potato provide an abundance of beta-carotene; the onion provides quercitin; and the cumin rounds it out with its anticancer properties.

● Blender

1 tbsp	organic unsalted butter	15 mL
2	cloves garlic, minced	2
1/2 tsp	ground cumin	2 mL
1/4 cup	finely diced onion	60 mL
3/4 cup	finely diced sweet potato (see Tips, left)	175 mL
1 cup	finely diced peeled carrot	250 mL
4 cups	Roasted Chicken Stock (page 152), Vegetable Stock (page 154) or filtered water	1 L

1. In a large saucepan, melt butter over medium heat. Add garlic, cumin, onion, sweet potato and carrot and cook, stirring often, until onion is translucent, 3 to 5 minutes. Add chicken stock and bring to a boil. Reduce heat and simmer until sweet potato and carrots are soft, 5 to 7 minutes.

2. Using an immersion blender, purée soup. (You can also do this in a food processor, in batches.) Let cool until warm to the touch before serving or transfer to an airtight container and refrigerate up to 3 days.

NUTRIENTS PER SERVING (1/2 cup/125 mL)

Calories	40.7	Dietary fiber	0.9 g
Protein	1.5 g	Sodium	85.1 mg
Total fat	1.7 g	Calcium	11.8 mg
Saturated fat	0.9 g	Iron	0.3 mg
Carbohydrates	4.8 g	Vitamin C	1.4 mg

Onion Soup with Chicken

This twist on classic French onion soup is very simple and delicious. This recipe makes a relatively large quantity because older children and adults can enjoy it, too. As part of the allium family, onions are very rich in sulfur-containing nutrients, which studies repeatedly show to have anticancer benefits. Cooking with onions many times a week will help to ensure more protection.

● ●

Makes about 5 cups (1.25 L)

Chef Jordan's Tip

There are times, as parents, when we struggle against the clock to make a nutritious meal. Why not set yourself up to deal with those times of need by having frozen portions of this hearty soup on hand? Reheat from frozen in a covered saucepan over low heat.

Jill's Nutrition Tip

When your baby is about 12 months of age, you will be starting to establish a food routine as you discover when he is hungriest and when he needs to snack. It is normal to be concerned about how much your baby does or doesn't eat, but try to look at the bigger picture of his overall growth and weight rather than being too concerned with the volume eaten in a particular day.

1 tbsp	organic unsalted butter	15 mL
3 cups	sliced white onions	750 mL
2	sprigs fresh thyme	2
2	cloves garlic, minced	2
4 cups	Roasted Chicken Stock (page 152)	1 L
1 cup	shredded cooked chicken (see Tips, page 83)	250 mL

1. In a saucepan, melt butter over medium heat. Add onions, thyme and garlic and sauté until onions are soft, about 10 minutes.

2. Add chicken stock and chicken and bring to a boil. Reduce heat to low and simmer until soup has reduced by one-quarter, about 10 minutes. Cut or mash your baby's portion to desired consistency. Let cool until warm to the touch before serving or transfer to an airtight container and refrigerate for up to 3 days.

NUTRIENTS PER SERVING ($\frac{1}{2}$ cup/125 mL)

Calories	57.7	Dietary fiber	0.6 g
Protein	5.8 g	Sodium	72.5 mg
Total fat	2.2 g	Calcium	11.7 mg
Saturated fat	1.0 g	Iron	0.3 mg
Carbohydrates	3.6 g	Vitamin C	2.9 mg

Roasted Chicken Stock

This is the mother of all stocks. It can be used to enhance the flavor of just about everything, from soups and grains to poached chicken and beef.

● ●

Makes about 14 cups (3.5 L)

Chef Jordan's Tips

Try shredding the reserved cooked chicken and using it in tacos.

When adding the chicken to the stockpot, be sure to scrape up and include all the appetizing brown bits from the bottom of the skillet. They will make your stock more flavorful.

After straining the stock, reserve the chicken for another use and discard the vegetables.

Jill's Nutrition Tip

Rich chicken stock has always been a valued remedy for the flu, and for good reason. In order to fight infection, the body needs many resources, including the easily absorbable minerals from the bones, marrow and cartilage that go into a good stock. Fish bones and heads can be used in the same way to make a fish stock high in iodine, a mineral in short supply in North American diets.

Always buy organic celery.

- Large ovenproof skillet and stock pot
- Fine-mesh sieve
- Preheat oven to 450°F (230°C)

1 tbsp	extra virgin olive oil	15 mL
1	whole chicken, cut into quarters (about 3 lbs/1.5 kg)	1
16 cups	filtered water	4 L
2 cups	chopped organic celery	500 mL
2 cups	chopped peeled parsnips	500 mL
1½ cups	chopped peeled carrots	375 mL
1½ cups	chopped onions	375 mL
6	cloves garlic	6
½ cup	fresh parsley sprigs	125 mL
1 tsp	whole black peppercorns	5 mL
2	bay leaves	2

1. In ovenproof skillet, heat oil over medium heat. Add chicken pieces, skin side down, and transfer skillet to preheated oven. Roast until chicken is golden brown, about 35 minutes.

2. Transfer chicken to stock pot. Add remaining ingredients. Bring to a boil over high heat. Reduce heat and simmer, using a slotted spoon to skim off the impurities that rise to the surface, until liquid is flavorful and chicken is cooked, about 40 minutes.

3. Using fine-mesh sieve set over a bowl, strain the stock. Let cool to room temperature. Transfer to airtight containers and refrigerate for up to 3 days or freeze for up to 3 months.

NUTRIENTS PER SERVING (1 cup/250 mL)

Calories 22	Dietary fiber . . . . 0.1 g
Protein . . . . 2.6 g	Sodium . . . . 150 mg
Total fat . . . . 1.1 g	Calcium . . . . 7.0 mg
Saturated fat . . . . 0.3 g	Iron . . . . 0.5 mg
Carbohydrates . . . . . . 0.4 g	Vitamin C . . . . 0.5 mg

Bone Broth

Bone broth is a traditional food that has recently become popular for its numerous health benefits. In fact, purveyors of fresh bone broth are springing up across North America. Bone broth takes a step beyond regular stock. It is simmered for a longer time and an acid, such as lemon juice or cider vinegar, is added to increase the broth's nutritional content. The acid draws compounds that have significant health benefits from the bones, marrow and ligaments. These include collagen (for healthy skin, hair and joints), and the amino acids proline (for tissue repair and collagen formation) and glycine (for healthy functioning of the central nervous system). Bone broth also contains a range of minerals, including calcium, magnesium, phosphorus and silicon in forms that the body can easily absorb.

Bone broth is a staple of some special diets. It is, for instance, often used to heal the lining of the digestive tract and is thought to improve immunity. A study of chicken broth conducted by the University of Nebraska Medical Center found that its amino acids reduced inflammation in the respiratory system and improved digestion.

When making bone broth, it is important to use bones from organically-raised, pastured or grass-fed animals. The flavor will be enhanced if you roast the bones first in a 350°F (180°C) oven for about 30 minutes (You can also use the bones from leftover roasted chicken).

Use about 3 lbs (750 g) of bones to make 3 quarts (2.8 L) of broth. Place the roasted bones in a large saucepan and cover with cool filtered water. Add 2 tbsp (30 mL) freshly squeezed lemon juice or apple cider vinegar and let stand for 30 to 60 minutes. (This jump-starts the process of leaching the minerals out of the bones.) Add vegetables of your choice; those from the Roasted Chicken Stock recipe (page 152) work well but avoid vegetables from the brassica family (such as broccoli or cabbage), which will make your broth bitter). Bring to a boil and boil rapidly for 5 minutes, skimming off any scum from the top and discarding. Transfer bones, vegetables and liquid to a large slow cooker. Add about 8 cups (2 L) cool filtered water Cover and cook on Low for 12 to 24 hours. Let cool and strain. Store in glass containers in the refrigerator for up to 5 days or in the freezer for up to 6 months. Do not skim off the fat.

Bone broth is a good way to make sure your baby gets important minerals he needs for growth and development. You can use it as a base for soups and sauces and for the vegetable, meat and legume purées in this book. Any dishes that call for stock or broth provide an opportunity to introduce the entire family to the health benefits of bone broth. On its own, it makes a delicious drink for a sippy cup. If you are using it as a drink, reheat gently on the stovetop (not in the microwave, please). For convenience, pour cooled broth into ice cube trays and freeze. Transfer the cubes to a freezer bag, label with the date and store in the freezer for up to 6 months.

Vegetable Stock

I like to use vegetable stock as a cooking liquid in many dishes because it adds flavor. Use this stock in place of water to cook vegetables or, once all the ingredients it contains have been introduced to your child, to make or thin (if you're freezing them in ice-cube trays) purées. You can also use this stock instead of water to cook grains such as rice, barley, millet or quinoa for added flavor. Making your own stock ensures that it doesn't contain any preservatives or added salt, unlike prepared stocks.

● ●

Makes about 8 cups (2 L)

Chef Jordan's Tip

When making stock, be sure not to overboil it. After 45 minutes, all of the flavor will have been leached from the vegetables; continuing to cook them will not enhance the stock.

Jill's Nutrition Tip

Other than its superior taste, the major benefits of homemade stock are that you control the ingredients as well as the amount of added salt. A serving-size portion of a commercial stock can contain up to one-third of the recommended daily intake of sodium for adults. Commercial products may also contain other flavor enhancers, such as monosodium glutamate (MSG), which may not be noted on the label. MSG is listed only if it appears in its pure form, not if it is part of another ingredient such as hydrolyzed vegetable protein. Homemade is always best.

Always buy organic celery.

- Large stock pot
- Fine-mesh sieve

10 cups	filtered water	2.5 L
2 cups	coarsely chopped peeled carrots	500 mL
2 cups	chopped onions	500 mL
1 cup	coarsely chopped organic celery	250 mL
1 cup	coarsely chopped parsnips	250 mL
1 cup	garlic cloves	250 mL

1. In stock pot, combine water, carrots, onions, celery, parsnips and garlic. Bring to a boil over medium heat. Reduce heat to low and simmer until broth is flavorful, about 45 minutes.

2. Using fine-mesh strainer set over a pot or bowl, strain out solids and discard. Cover and refrigerate for up to 3 days or freeze in airtight containers for up to 3 months.

NUTRIENTS PER SERVING

We have not provided a nutrient analysis for Vegetable Stock because it contains such a minute quantity of nutrients. One serving provides just 1 calorie. However, it is more flavorful than water as a base for soup and, as noted above, you can control the amount of sodium.

The Vegetarian Baby

A vegetarian or vegan diet can be a healthy choice for your baby as long as it is well planned. The more restricted it is, the more carefully you'll need to plan to ensure your baby gets the full range of nutrients she needs to grow and develop properly. Because many of the nutrients your baby needs are easier to obtain from animal products — for example, protein, iron, vitamin B_{12} and vitamin D — you will want to pay particular attention to ensuring that her diet includes foods that are rich in these nutrients.

For the first year or so of your baby's life, breast milk and formula will provide vitamin B_{12}. If you are nursing and are a strict vegetarian or vegan, you will need to make sure you are getting enough supplemental B_{12} to ensure there is a sufficient supply in your breast milk. Subsequently, your baby may be able to obtain an adequate supply of this nutrient from milk and dairy products, but you should still be careful that she is getting enough. After weaning, vegans may need to look specifically for foods fortified with B_{12}, such as fortified soy products and fortified plant milks (rice or almond milk).

Good sources of protein are eggs, plain yogurt, cheese, soy products such as tofu, and beans and lentils. While whole nuts should not be given to toddlers because of the risk of choking, nut and seed butters and ground nuts and seeds are balanced sources of protein, carbohydrates and good fats. Serious allergies to some nuts and seeds affect less than 1 percent of the population, but if your baby's father, brothers or sisters have nut allergies, consult your pediatrician. For further information about allergies, see page 25.

Iron is found in whole grains (such as millet and quinoa), dark green vegetables (such as broccoli and spinach), lentils, beans and soy products, and dried apricots. Plant iron (non–heme iron) is much harder for the body to absorb than the iron from animal products (heme iron). Including foods rich in vitamin C (such as red pepper, broccoli and papaya) at the same meal will help the body absorb the plant iron and is highly recommended.

Vitamin D is found mostly in fortified milk and fatty fish (such as salmon, mackerel and sardines), but the best source is unprotected (meaning no sunscreen) but safe exposure to the sun. Consult your pediatrician for appropriate guidelines.

Jonah's "Mac and Cheese"

This is the only version of macaroni and cheese my son, Jonah, knew for the first four years of his life, and he couldn't get enough of it. Nowadays we are fortunate that so many gluten-free whole-grain pastas are widely available, making the combination of ingredients in this recipe particularly delicious and nutritious.

Makes about 2¼ cups (550 mL)

Chef Jordan's Tip

Feel free to use your pasta of choice. Other gluten-free whole-grain options include organic corn noodles and brown rice noodles.

Jill's Nutrition Tips

Whole-grain gluten-free pasta is a great alternative to wheat pasta. Emerging science is alerting us to the idea that non-celiac gluten sensitivity can manifest itself in many ways other than stomachaches and cramping, including depression, cognitive issues and ADD-ADHD symptoms (see page 24).

Like the rest of your baby's diet, variety is key for developing healthy eating habits. Experiment with a number of gluten-free pastas — different grains offer different levels of nutrients. If you want to try corn pasta and are eating GMO-free, make sure you use organic pasta.

Always buy organic milk products.

5 cups	filtered water	1.25 L
1 cup	dried quinoa penne pasta	250 mL
½ cup	Roasted Sweet Potato Purée (page 45)	125 mL
¼ cup	freshly grated organic Parmesan cheese	60 mL
2 tbsp	organic full-fat sour cream	30 mL

1. In a large pot, bring water to a boil over high heat. Add pasta and cook, stirring often, until soft, about 20 minutes. Reserving 1 cup (250 mL) of the cooking water, drain pasta.

2. Return pasta and reserved water to the pot over low heat. Stir in sweet potato purée, cheese and sour cream. Cook, stirring, until mixture is thick and noodles are evenly coated, 2 to 3 minutes. Cut up to desired consistency. Let cool until warm to the touch before serving or transfer to an airtight container and refrigerate for up to 3 days.

NUTRIENTS PER SERVING (½ cup/125 mL)*

Calories	27.4	Dietary fiber	0.3 g
Protein	1.0 g	Sodium	46.2 mg
Total fat	1.1 g	Calcium	24.1 mg
Saturated fat	0.6 g	Iron	0.3 mg
Carbohydrates	3.47 g	Vitamin C	0.2 mg

* Based on pasta containing rice and quinoa.

Pasta with Fresh Herbs and Parmesan Cheese

If your children love the taste of macaroni and cheese, just wait until they try this!

Chef Jordan's Tip

I use fresh herbs a lot because they impart a unique flavor to dishes. When you introduce this recipe to your baby, start with equal amounts of fresh flat-leaf (Italian) parsley and basil, which will produce a mildly flavored result. After a while, add some stronger-tasting herbs, such as tarragon or oregano.

Jill's Nutrition Tip

All pasta is moderate on the glycemic index, which is a scale that ranks carbohydrates by the rate at which they are digested and converted into glucose (your body's energy source). Moderate and low-glycemic foods help balance blood sugar and provide a prolonged release of energy. Whole-grain pastas have the same glycemic values as those made from refined flour but contain a full range of nutrients, unlike their processed counterparts, and are much higher in fiber.

Always buy organic milk products.

1 tbsp	organic unsalted butter	15 mL
2 cups	cooked gluten-free penne, such as quinoa pasta	500 mL
1/3 cup	freshly grated organic Parmesan cheese	75 mL
1/4 cup	chopped fresh herbs (see Tips, left)	60 mL

1. In a saucepan, melt butter over medium heat. Add pasta and cook, stirring, until warm, about 3 minutes. Stir in Parmesan cheese and herbs. Let cool until warm to the touch before serving or transfer to an airtight container and refrigerate for up to 3 days.

NUTRIENTS PER SERVING (1/2 cup/125 mL)*

Calories	97.8	Dietary fiber	0.3 g
Protein	3.2 g	Sodium	137.6 mg
Total fat	5.1 g	Calcium	70.1 mg
Saturated fat	2.9 g	Iron	2.1 mg
Carbohydrates	10.1 g	Vitamin C	5.0 mg

* Based on pasta containing rice and quinoa.

Parmesan Is Easy to Digest

Because of its digestibility, doctors in Italy recommend Parmesan cheese for babies. Its long aging process essentially predigests the proteins in milk, making them readily available for the body to use. Parmesan cheese does not have any lactose, which makes it a great choice if you suspect your baby can't tolerate lactose or is allergic to it.

Millet and Cauliflower with Fresh Oregano

If you and your child are not accustomed to eating millet, here's a great recipe to try. Millet is a particularly digestible "ancient" whole grain with a mild, nutty flavor. It is a nutritious and delicious addition to your baby's diet.

⚫ ⚫

Makes about 3 cups (750 mL)

Chef Jordan's Tip

After the millet is cooked, I prefer to use a potato masher rather than puréeing to achieve the desired texture. It resembles mashed potatoes — nice and fluffy.

Jill's Nutrition Tip

Oregano, like many herbs, is known for its medicinal properties. Fresh oregano actually has 42 times as much antioxidant activity as an apple — in fact, it has more antioxidant power than any other herb. Plus it is delicious!

- Potato masher

½ cup	millet, rinsed and drained	125 mL
2½ cups	filtered water or Vegetable Stock (page 154) or Roasted Chicken Stock (page 152)	625 mL
2¼ cups	chopped cauliflower florets	550 mL
1 tsp	chopped fresh oregano	5 mL

1. In a dry saucepan, toast millet over medium heat, stirring constantly, until golden brown, 2 to 3 minutes.

2. Add water and cauliflower and bring to a boil. Reduce heat to low and simmer until all the water has evaporated, about 25 minutes.

3. Transfer to a bowl and add oregano. Using a potato masher, mash until smooth (see Tips, left). Let cool until warm to the touch before serving or transfer to an airtight container and refrigerate for up to 3 days.

NUTRIENTS PER SERVING (½ cup/125 mL)

Calories 73	Dietary fiber. . . . . .2.4 g
Protein. . . . . .2.6 g	Sodium. . . . . 15.6 mg
Total fat . . . . .0.8 g	Calcium . . . . .14.0 mg
Saturated fat. . . . . 0.1 g	Iron. . . . . 0.7 mg
Carbohydrates . . . . . .14.2 g	Vitamin C . . . . .18.1 mg

Millet with Cheddar Cheese and Apple

Cheese and apples is a classic pairing. Your baby will absolutely love the gooey goodness of the melted Cheddar in this combo.

**Makes about
3 cups (750 mL)**

Chef Jordan's Tips

If you prefer a smoother consistency, use a potato masher to achieve the desired texture.

Fresh basil would be a wonderful substitute for the parsley.

Virtually any shredded cheese will work in this recipe. Feel free to use your favorites.

Jill's Nutrition Tip

Using real whole grains is an important component of a healthy diet. Millet and other whole grains are rich in the very important mineral magnesium, required in hundreds of chemical reactions in the body. Not only is it crucial for bone formation and strength, but sufficient magnesium ensures proper functioning of the entire body.

½ cup	millet, rinsed and drained	125 mL
2½ cups	water or Roasted Chicken Stock (page 152) or Vegetable Stock (page 154)	550 mL
¾ cup	shredded Cheddar cheese	175 mL
½ cup	finely diced apple	125 mL
1 tbsp	finely chopped parsley leaves	15 mL

1. In a saucepan, toast millet over medium heat, stirring constantly until golden brown, 2 to 3 minutes.
2. Add water and bring to a boil. Reduce heat to low and simmer until all the liquid has evaporated, about 25 minutes.
3. Transfer to a bowl and add cheese, apple and parsley. Let cool until warm to the touch before serving or transfer to an airtight container and refrigerate for up to 3 days.

NUTRIENTS PER SERVING (½ cup/125 mL)

Calories 129.2	Dietary fiber. . . . . .1.8 g
Protein. . . . . .5.3 g	Sodium. . . . . .92.3 mg
Total fat . . . . .5.5 g	Calcium . . . . .98.5 mg
Saturated fat. . . . . . . .2.9 g	Iron. . . . . .0.6 mg
Carbohydrates . . . . . .14.7 g	Vitamin C . . . . 1.6 mg

Savory Rice Pudding with Basil

This savory rice pudding will be a big hit with your children. The creamy texture mimics a traditional dessert rice pudding but it is infused with the flavor of fresh basil. Brown rice is far more nutritious than the white variety, which loses most of its nutrients in polishing. It is particularly rich in minerals, including magnesium, selenium, phosphorus and zinc, that help to keep your baby healthy in many ways.

● ●

**Makes about
1¼ cups (300 mL)**

Chef Jordan's Tip

If your baby prefers milder flavors, substitute 1 tbsp (15 mL) finely chopped parsley for the basil.

Jill's Nutrition Tip

Unlike white rice, brown rice has had only its outer hull removed, so it retains much of its original nutritional value. It is very high in the mineral manganese, which is important for producing energy in your baby's body. It also has about four times as much fiber as white rice, making it an important tool against constipation.

Always buy organic milk.

4 cups	organic whole milk	1 L
½ cup	long-grain brown rice	125 mL
2	fresh basil leaves (see Tips, left), finely chopped	2

1. In a saucepan, combine milk, rice and basil. Bring to a boil over medium heat. Reduce heat to low and simmer, stirring occasionally, until most of the milk has been absorbed and the rice becomes soft, about 2 hours. Let cool until warm to the touch before serving or transfer to an airtight container and refrigerate for up to 2 days.

NUTRIENTS PER SERVING (½ cup/125 mL)

Calories 278	Dietary fiber . . . . 0.7 g
Protein . . . . 13.5 g	Sodium . . . . 156.6 mg
Total fat . . . . 13.0 g	Calcium . . . . 445.7 mg
Saturated fat . . . . 7.4 g	Iron . . . . 0.3 mg
Carbohydrates . . . . . . 26.8 g	Vitamin C . . . . 0.1 mg

Soft Polenta with Cheddar Cheese and Broccoli

Your children will come to love this flavor combination of cornmeal, broccoli and cheese. It's wonderfully comforting, as well as nutritious. Whole-grain cornmeal, which, unlike refined versions, retains a wide range of nutrients, is particularly high in antioxidants.

**Makes about
3 1/2 cups (875 mL)**

Chef Jordan's Tips

I use the term "bloom" to describe the process in which the cornmeal opens up and absorbs the water, literally expanding.

I really love the flavor of this recipe when it's made with extra-old (sharp) Cheddar cheese.

Jill's Nutrition Tip

Cheddar cheese is a good source of calcium, which you know your baby needs for growing teeth. Even better is the fact that if you use aged cheese, the sharpness increases saliva flow, which washes away acids and sugars that contribute to tooth decay. It is never too soon to get a start on healthy teeth.

Always buy organic cornmeal and milk products.

- Ovenproof saucepan with lid
- Preheat oven to 350°F (180°C)

4 1/2 cups	water or Vegetable Stock (page 154) or Roasted Chicken Stock (page 152)	1.125 L
1 cup	organic coarse stone-ground cornmeal (see Tips, left)	250 mL
1/2 cup	finely chopped broccoli florets, blanched	125 mL
1/2 cup	shredded organic Cheddar cheese	125 mL

1. In a saucepan, bring water to a boil over medium heat. Slowly add cornmeal while whisking constantly to avoid lumps. Cook, whisking constantly, until cornmeal begins to "bloom" (see Tips, left) and mixture starts to thicken, 3 to 4 minutes. Cover and transfer pan to preheated oven. Bake, covered, until cornmeal is tender and creamy, about 40 minutes.

2. Remove from oven and stir in broccoli and cheese. (Remember: the pot handle will be very hot, so don't touch without oven mitts.) Cover and set aside until broccoli is fork-tender, about 10 minutes. Let cool until warm to the touch before serving or refrigerate for up to 3 days.

NUTRIENTS PER SERVING (1/2 cup/125 mL)

Calories	73	Dietary fiber	1.2 g
Protein	2.0 g	Sodium	260.2 mg
Total fat	1.0 g	Calcium	76.3 mg
Saturated fat	0.5 g	Iron	1.3 mg
Carbohydrates	14.7 g	Vitamin C	5.0 mg

Jasmine Rice with Butternut Squash and Saffron

Jasmine rice is one of the most aromatic grains on the planet, and it's a breeze to cook, too! I've always found the texture of jasmine rice to be child-friendly. It's soft and easy for kids to chew.

● ●

Makes about 2¼ cups (550 mL)

Chef Jordan's Tips

This is a great method for achieving perfect rice every time. Just be sure not to lift the lid until the 20 minutes are up. If you are using brown jasmine rice, increase the cooking time to about 40 minutes.

"Steep," in this case, refers to infusing the saffron cooking liquid into the rice. This combination is heavenly.

Jill's Nutrition Tip

Since ancient Egypt, saffron has been thought to have a calming effect on babies. It acts as an antispasmodic and cough suppressant, improves digestion and decreases gas. More recently, studies have demonstrated that this ancient spice may have anticancer and heart-protective properties.

1 tsp	organic unsalted butter	5 mL
1 cup	finely diced peeled butternut squash	250 mL
1¼ cups	filtered water or Vegetable Stock (page 154)	300 mL
⅔ cup	jasmine rice, rinsed and drained	150 mL
Pinch	saffron threads	Pinch

1. In a saucepan, melt butter over medium heat. Add squash and sauté until starting to soften, about 2 minutes. Stir in water, rice and saffron and bring to a boil. Cover, reduce heat to low and simmer for 5 minutes.

2. Remove from heat and let steep, covered, until liquid is absorbed and rice is tender, about 20 minutes (see Tips, left). Let cool until warm to the touch before serving or transfer to an airtight container and refrigerate for up to 2 days.

NUTRIENTS PER SERVING (½ cup/125 mL)

Calories 78	Dietary fiber . . . . 1.3 g
Protein . . . . 1.4 g	Sodium . . . . 4.4 mg
Total fat . . . . 0.9 g	Calcium . . . . 29.3 mg
Saturated fat . . . . 0.6 g	Iron . . . . 0.5 mg
Carbohydrates . . . . . . 16.7 g	Vitamin C . . . . 11.8 mg

Digestion Alert!

If your baby is recovering from stomach troubles and diarrhea, this is one time you should consider using white jasmine rice. Because it digests so much faster, it is easier on a recovering digestive tract. Once your toddler is well again, use brown jasmine rice in this recipe to add the extra nutrition and fiber he needs.

Oat Crêpes with Warm Bananas

This delicious dish is a cross between crêpes and pancakes. Either way, it is amazing, and good for your baby, too! Oats contain beta-glucans, a type of fiber associated with many health benefits. Not only do oats provide long-lasting, stable energy for your toddler, the beta-glucans support the body's immune action in response to bacterial infection. This recipe makes more crêpes than your baby will eat, because other family members will enjoy them, too.

• •

**Makes about
5 crêpes**

Chef Jordan's Tip

It is not necessary to add more butter to the pan in order to warm through the banana. Ample butter is used to make the crepes, so your pan should be well oiled and the banana shouldn't stick at all.

Jill's Nutrition Tip

Whole grains, such as rolled or steel-cut oats, are an important part of a healthy diet for you and your baby. Because they are minimally processed, they contain significant amounts of fiber, protein, essential oils, vitamins and minerals. Read labels carefully to make sure you are actually getting whole grains. Most of the nutrients are lost when grains are refined.

Always buy organic milk products.

1 cup	organic whole milk	250 mL
3	eggs	3
1/2 cup	old-fashioned rolled oats	125 mL
2 tsp	coconut sugar	10 mL
6 tbsp	sorghum flour	90 mL
1 tsp	baking powder	5 mL
1 tbsp	organic unsalted butter, divided	15 mL
1	large banana, sliced	1

1. In a bowl, whisk together milk, eggs, oats and sugar. Whisk in flour and baking powder until moistened. Cover and refrigerate for at least 1 hour or overnight.

2. In a nonstick skillet, melt 1 tsp (5 mL) butter over medium heat. Ladle 1/2 cup (125 mL) batter into the pan, swirling around to evenly coat the bottom of the pan. Cook until bottom is golden brown, 2 to 3 minutes. Flip and cook other side until light golden, about 1 minute. Transfer to a plate and repeat with remaining batter, adding more butter to the pan as necessary. Let cool until warm to the touch.

3. In the same skillet, cook sliced banana over low heat until warm, about 2 minutes. Spoon over crêpes and let cool until warm to the touch before serving.

NUTRIENTS PER SERVING (1 crêpe)

Calories 187	Dietary fiber . . . . 3.5 g
Protein . . . . 7.5 g	Sodium . . . . 66.2 mg
Total fat . . . . 8.3 g	Calcium . . . . 125.3 mg
Saturated fat . . . . 3.6 g	Iron . . . . 2.0 mg
Carbohydrates . . . . . . 39.4 g	Vitamin C . . . . 6.5 mg

Halibut in a Wrapper

The delicate flavor of the halibut shines through in this recipe and complements the fennel and sweet peppers. Kids love opening their little package of dinner. To ensure maximum nutritional value and make a contribution to the environment, always purchase sustainably wild-caught or responsibly farmed fish.

• •

**Makes
2 servings**

Chef Jordan's Tips

For a unique serving idea, bring the package to the table, cut with scissors to open the paper and allow the kids to eat from the wrapper. It adds an element of fun to their dinner.

Remember: before serving fish to a child, examine it closely for bones and remove any you find.

Try to purchase Alaskan halibut, which is sustainably caught.

Always buy organic bell peppers.

- 2 sheets parchment paper
- Baking sheet
- Preheat oven to 300°F (150°C)

½ cup	sliced fennel	125 mL
⅓ cup	coarsely chopped peeled asparagus	75 mL
⅓ cup	thin strips organic red bell pepper	75 mL
⅓ cup	thin strips organic yellow bell pepper	75 mL
1 tbsp	chopped fresh chives	15 mL
1 tbsp	freshly squeezed lemon juice	15 mL
8 oz	halibut fillet, cut into 2 pieces	250 g
1 tbsp	organic unsalted butter, divided	15 mL
1	egg white	1
1 tsp	water	5 mL

1. In a bowl, combine fennel, asparagus, red and yellow peppers, chives and lemon juice.

2. Fold in half 2 pieces of parchment paper, each about 12 by 8 inches (30 x 20 cm); set one aside. Place half of the vegetables on one side of one piece of parchment. Place one piece of fish on top of the vegetables. Top with half the butter. Fold the other side of the paper over to enclose the filling, and twist the two ends like a candy wrapper to create a seal. Repeat with remaining parchment, vegetables, fish and butter.

3. In a small bowl, whisk egg white with water. Brush the unsealed edges of the packages with the mixture, gluing them together.

4. Place packages on baking sheet and bake in preheated oven until paper turns golden brown, about 25 minutes. Let cool for 5 to 10 minutes before opening package (see Tips, left). If necessary, let cool until warm to the touch before serving.

Jill's Nutrition Tip

Halibut is the highest animal source of magnesium, a mineral that supports every function in your baby's body. Magnesium partners with calcium to keep your baby's muscles and organs relaxed and healthy, helping to alleviate muscle cramps and sleeplessness. This mineral also helps relieve constipation.

NUTRIENTS PER SERVING (1 package)

Calories	209	Dietary fiber	1.9 g
Protein	26.5 g	Sodium	131.4 mg
Total fat	9.3 g	Calcium	47.6 mg
Saturated fat	4.5 g	Iron	1.2 mg
Carbohydrates	6.2 g	Vitamin C	81.7 mg

Know Your Suppliers

In my world, both Mom and Dad work full time. With some planning, Tamar, Jonah, Jamie and I manage to eat nutritious, delicious food Monday through Sunday. Sure, it's a little easier for me because of my culinary background, but my wife has no training as a chef. However, she is a wonderful cook in her own right, and one of the reasons is that she lets knowledgeable people guide the way she cooks. She became acquainted with the staff at our local markets and questions them about what they are selling. They tell her what ingredients are the freshest and/or the best, and she takes their advice when making decisions. If you get to know your local shop owners, they'll look out for you and make sure you are getting their very best products.

I always try to develop relationships with my suppliers. Take my fishmonger, Gus. Once, when I was shopping for fish to use in this recipe, Gus suggested turbot because it was the best fish he had. I tried it and the results were superb. If halibut isn't available on the day you're trying this, ask your supplier the same question. You may end up with something else, but if he knows his stuff, with a little love, your dish will be great!

Best-Ever Salmon Cakes

I remember the salmon patties my mom used to make, which consisted of canned salmon with mayonnaise. Now I prefer to use fresh salmon, especially if it's wild. (Wild salmon has more nutrients, especially beneficial omega-3 fats.) Make extra when you're cooking salmon and save the leftovers to make this recipe. This is really an all-in-one dinner. The salmon provides great protein and healthy fat, the corn brings slow-release carbohydrates, and the pepper and onion round it out with antioxidants, minerals and vitamins.

● ●

Makes 6 cakes

Chef Jordan's Tips

This recipe can easily be halved if you aren't joining your baby for dinner.

These salmon cakes freeze well for up to 4 weeks, so feel free to make the whole batch and freeze the rest in an airtight container.

Remember: before serving fish to a child, examine it closely for bones and remove any you find.

Jill's Nutrition Tip

Salmon is one of the richest and best utilized sources of omega-3 fatty acids. These fats have many benefits, among which are their anti-inflammatory properties. An overview of dozens of omega-3 studies reviewed by the University of Maryland Medical Center suggests that consuming good amounts of omega-3 fats throughout childhood and as an adult may decrease the risk of inflammatory and autoimmune diseases such as rheumatoid arthritis, Crohn's disease and multiple sclerosis.

Always buy organic peppers and corn.

1 lb	cooked Pacific salmon fillet, skin removed, flaked	500 g
⅓ cup	diced red onion	75 mL
⅓ cup	organic corn kernels, thawed if frozen	75 mL
⅓ cup	diced organic red bell pepper	75 mL
1 tbsp	organic unsalted butter	15 mL

1. In a bowl, combine salmon, onion, corn and red pepper and mix well. Form into six cakes, each about 1½ inches (4 cm) thick. Place on a plate, cover and refrigerate until set, at least 1 hour or for up to 12 hours.

2. In a nonstick skillet, melt butter over medium-low heat. Add the cakes and cook until golden brown, about 5 minutes. Flip and cook until other side is golden brown, about 5 minutes. Transfer to a plate and let cool until warm to the touch before serving or cover and refrigerate for up to 3 days.

Variation

This dish will also appeal to older children and adults. For a tasty grown-up lunch, serve them on a bed of Boston or butter lettuce with a simple dressing of fresh lemon juice, olive oil and minced garlic.

NUTRIENTS PER SERVING (1 cake)

Calories	182	Dietary fiber	0.5 g
Protein	17.0 g	Sodium	51.3 mg
Total fat	11.1 g	Calcium	13.4 mg
Saturated fat	3.0 g	Iron	0.4 mg
Carbohydrates	2.9 g	Vitamin C	15.0 mg

Salmon, Potato and Cauliflower

Salmon and potato is a classic combination. The cauliflower adds textural contrast. It's a great way to introduce your toddler to this flavorful fish and nutritious cauliflower.

Makes about
2 ¼ cups (550 mL)

Chef Jordan's Tip

Before serving fish to a child, examine it closely for bones and remove any you find.

Jill's Nutrition Tip

Serving fatty fish such as salmon is one of the best ways to get important omega-3 fats into your baby's diet. A healthy brain contains high amounts of one of these omega-3 fats, called docosahexaenoic acid (DHA). DHA helps repair and make new brain cells and allows them to communicate with one another efficiently. Recent studies, including one done by U.K. researchers and published in the journal *PLOS One* in June 2013, suggest the importance of DHA and omega-3 fats and show that conditions such as attention deficit disorder and depression have improved with the consumption of fish oils. Is it any wonder they call them brain food?

Always buy organic potatoes.

3 cups	filtered water	750 mL
1½ cups	coarsely chopped peeled organic potatoes	375 mL
1	piece (about 6 oz/175 g) skinless salmon fillet	1
⅔ cup	chopped cauliflower florets	150 mL

1. In a saucepan, combine water, potatoes, salmon and cauliflower. Bring to a boil over medium heat. Reduce heat to low and simmer until potatoes are fork-tender, about 7 minutes.

2. In a colander set over a bowl, strain mixture, reserving cooking liquid. Transfer solids to a bowl. Add 2 cups (500 mL) reserved cooking liquid. Using a potato masher, mash until smooth. Let cool until warm to the touch before serving or transfer to an airtight container and refrigerate for up to 3 days or freeze for up to 1 month.

Variation

You can quickly transform leftovers into salmon cauliflower patties. Using the refrigerated mixture, form small patties. Bread with cornflake crumbs. In a nonstick skillet over medium heat, cook, turning once, until golden, about 2 minutes per side.

NUTRIENTS PER SERVING (½ cup/125 mL)

Calories 138	Dietary fiber. . . . . .2.3 g
Protein. . . . . .10.7 g	Sodium. . . . . .36.7 mg
Total fat . . . . .4.8 g	Calcium . . . . .33.3 mg
Saturated fat. . . . . . . .0.8 g	Iron. . . . . 1.0 mg
Carbohydrates . . . . . .12.8 g	Vitamin C . . . . .35.5 mg

World's Best Fish Sticks

The first time I tested this recipe for my children, Jonah and Jamie, I ate the whole thing myself. So I have made extra for you and your baby to enjoy together.

● ●

Makes about 4 servings

Chef Jordan's Tips

Halibut, sole and turbot are examples of firm white fish. Ask your fishmonger for advice if those aren't available.

Before serving fish to a child, examine it closely for bones and remove any you find.

If you prefer, use half almond flour and half gluten-free breadcrumbs or cornflake crumbs.

Caper and Lemon Remoulade: Combine ½ cup (125 mL) prepared mayonnaise and 1 tsp (5 mL) each minced capers, freshly grated lemon zest and freshly squeezed lemon juice. Mix well. Serve immediately or cover and refrigerate for up to 1 week.

Jill's Nutrition Tip

Although your baby has not yet developed a taste for salt, if you do decide to use salt, make sure you use it for taste and nutrition. We recommend using sea salt, which contains a smattering of many minerals, unlike refined table salt, which is pure sodium chloride. Refined table salt also contains additives to prevent clumping.

1 cup	almond flour (see Tips, left)	250 mL
⅓ cup	freshly grated organic Parmesan cheese	75 mL
1	egg white	1
1 tsp	water	5 mL
1	firm white fish fillet (about 8 oz/250 g)	1
2 tbsp	extra virgin olive oil	30 mL
½ cup	Caper and Lemon Remoulade (see Tips, left)	125 mL

1. In a bowl, combine almond flour and cheese. Set aside.

2. In another bowl, whisk together egg white and water. Set aside.

3. Cut fillet into 10 fingers and toss into egg mixture to fully coat. One finger at a time, drain off most of the egg wash and toss into almond flour mixture, pressing to adhere. Transfer to a plate. Repeat until all fingers are coated.

4. In a nonstick skillet, heat oil over medium heat. Cook fish, in batches as necessary, until golden brown on the bottom, about 2 minutes. Flip and cook until other side is golden brown and fish flakes easily with a fork, about 2 minutes. Let cool until warm to the touch. Serve with remoulade.

NUTRIENTS PER SERVING (½ cup/125 mL)*

Calories 517.5	Dietary fiber . . . . .0.9 g
Protein . . . . .20.1 g	Sodium . . . . 436.5 mg
Total fat . . . . 45.8 g	Calcium . . . . 142.2 mg
Saturated fat . . . . .5.6 g	Iron . . . . .1.1 mg
Carbohydrates . . . . . . 4.0 g	Vitamin C . . . . 1.3 mg

* Based on using all almond flour and serving with remoulade.

Beef Stew

There's nothing better than the classics! These dishes become classics because they have universal appeal. Once your children taste this, I guarantee it will become a family favorite.

	Makes about 5 cups (1.25 L)	

Chef Jordan's Tip

For added flavor, use vegetable stock instead of water.

Jill's Nutrition Tip

Red meat is one of the richest sources of vitamin B_{12}, which is found only in animal products and fermented foods. This vitamin affects the workings of your baby's nervous system and is essential for the production of red blood cells. If your baby is deficient in B_{12}, she may develop megaloblastic anemia, which can lead to neurological damage.

2 tbsp	extra virgin olive oil	30 mL
1¼ cups	diced stewing beef	300 mL
¾ cup	brown rice	175 mL
¼ cup	diced sweet onion, such as Vidalia	60 mL
5 cups	water or Vegetable Stock (page 154)	1.25 L
2	sprigs fresh thyme	2

1. In a saucepan, heat oil over medium heat. Add beef and sauté until golden brown, about 3 minutes. Add rice and onion and cook, stirring often, until onion is softened, about 5 minutes.

2. Add water and thyme and bring to a boil. Reduce heat to low and simmer until beef is tender and most of the water has evaporated, about $1\frac{1}{2}$ hours. Cut up or mash to desired consistency. Let cool until warm to the touch before serving or transfer to an airtight container and refrigerate for up to 3 days or freeze for up to 1 month.

NUTRIENTS PER SERVING (½ cup/125 mL)

Calories	116	Dietary fiber	0.6 g
Protein	7.0 g	Sodium	25.0 mg
Total fat	4.8 g	Calcium	11.0 mg
Saturated fat	1.2 g	Iron	0.9 mg
Carbohydrates	11.2 g	Vitamin C	0.5 mg

Pork with Red Cabbage

This is a perfect flavor combination. I'm certain your baby will love it. Cabbage belongs to the cruciferous family, which includes broccoli, Brussels sprouts and cauliflower. All these vegetables are potent cancer fighters, so it's worth the effort to familiarize your baby with their pungent flavors.

Makes about 1¼ cups (300 mL)

Chef Jordan's Tip

I have a real affinity for the combination of dried cherries with pork, but in the absence of dried cherries, most dried fruits would work well: currants, raisins, even apricots.

Jill's Nutrition Tip

Adequate amounts of vitamin A in your baby's body will ensure that her delicate skin has the best ability to rejuvenate and heal itself. Red cabbage is loaded with this vitamin and can help protect the skin from eczema and other rashes.

- Ovenproof skillet
- Instant-read thermometer
- Preheat oven to 350°F (180°C)

1 tbsp	extra virgin olive oil	15 mL
8 oz	pork tenderloin or loin	250 g
¾ cup	sliced red cabbage	175 mL
⅓ cup	unsweetened dried cherries	75 mL
2	sprigs fresh thyme	2
¼ cup	filtered water	60 mL

1. In ovenproof skillet, heat oil over medium-high heat. Add pork and brown, about 4 minutes per side. Turn pork over. Add cabbage, cherries, thyme and water.

2. Roast in preheated oven until internal temperature of pork is 160°F (71°C), about 15 minutes. Cut up or mash your baby's portion to desired consistency. Let cool until warm to the touch before serving or transfer to an airtight container and refrigerate for up to 3 days.

NUTRIENTS PER SERVING (½ cup/125 mL)

Calories 236	Dietary fiber. . . . . .5.0 g
Protein. . . . . .21.8 g	Sodium. . . . . 57.8 mg
Total fat. . . . . 9.1 g	Calcium . . . . 25.7 mg
Saturated fat. . . . . 2.0 g	Iron. . . . . .1.9 mg
Carbohydrates . . . . . . 15.3 g	Vitamin C . . . . .16.1 mg

Chicken with Caramelized Apples

Your toddler will absolutely adore the combination of chicken and butter with the sweetness of apples. This dish provides a winning combination of muscle- and bone-building protein from the chicken and slow-releasing carbohydrates from the apple. Can't beat good nutrition and great taste.

• •

Makes about 1 cup (250 mL)

Chef Jordan's Tip

Do not wash apples before storing, but remove any that are soft or spoiled. Keep the remainder loose and unbagged. Fruit gives off ethylene gas, which can take apples from crispy and fresh to soggy and old if they are stored in a bag.

Jill's Nutrition Tip

We think butter is better than margarine. It is high in vitamins A, E and D and the antioxidant selenium. Butter contains butyric acid and lauric acid, both of which contribute to a healthy immune system. It also contains cholesterol, which is present in large amounts in breast milk. Cholesterol is crucial for your baby's brain and nervous system development and is a precursor to the important fat-soluble vitamin D, which is needed for proper growth, healthy bones and strong immune function.

Always buy organic apples.

1 tsp	organic unsalted butter	5 mL
2	diced boneless, skinless chicken thighs, chopped (about 5 oz/150 g)	2
½ cup	chopped cored organic apple	125 mL
1⅓ cups	filtered water	325 mL

1. In a saucepan, melt butter over medium heat. Add chicken and apple and sauté until apple is soft, about 5 minutes. Add water and bring to a boil. Reduce heat to low and simmer until juices run clear when chicken is pierced, 5 to 7 minutes (see box, below). Cut up or mash to desired consistency.

2. Let cool until warm to the touch before serving or transfer to an airtight container and refrigerate for up to 3 days or freeze for up to 1 month.

NUTRIENTS PER SERVING (½ cup/125 mL)

Calories	139	Dietary fiber	1.5 g
Protein	14.9 g	Sodium	70.3 mg
Total fat	5.0 g	Calcium	16.7 mg
Saturated fat	2.0 g	Iron	0.9 mg
Carbohydrates	8.6 g	Vitamin C	2.9 mg

Is the Chicken Cooked?

To determine whether a piece of chicken is cooked, remove the meat from the pan and cut it in half. No hint of pink should remain. When feeding babies and toddlers, it's best to take no chances, because any food-borne illness can have serious consequences.

Oven-Roasted Duck with Red Cabbage

This recipe is so easy to make, yet it produces one of the most deliciously decadent dishes you'll ever eat. It is an excellent way to introduce your baby to sophisticated flavors and a wide range of nutrients, which will serve him well throughout life.

Makes about 1¼ cups (300 mL)

Chef Jordan's Tip

Many gourmet food shops sell vacuum-sealed individually wrapped cooked duck legs. The work is already done for you, so there are no excuses.

Jill's Nutrition Tips

This recipe makes a great dinner. The duck provides a rich protein source and the cabbage adds vitamins and minerals. Round it off with a nice single or mixed fruit purée.

If you make enough to have leftovers, this dish would be a good lunch the next day, paired with some soft-cooked and chopped green beans or cauliflower florets.

- Ovenproof skillet
- Preheat oven to 250°F (120°C)

1	skin-on, bone-in duck leg (about 8 oz/250 g)	1
1	sprig fresh thyme	1
1 tsp	organic unsalted butter	5 mL
2½ cups	sliced red cabbage	625 mL
1 cup	filtered water	250 mL
1 tsp	red wine vinegar	5 mL

1. In ovenproof skillet over medium heat, sear duck leg on all sides until caramelized, about 10 minutes. Flip duck over and stir in thyme.

2. Bake in preheated oven until meat is falling off the bone, about 2 hours. Let cool until warm to the touch. Pull meat off the bone, discarding skin and bones and shredding meat.

3. In a saucepan, melt butter over medium heat. Add cabbage and sauté until wilted, about 2 minutes. Add water, duck meat and vinegar and bring to a boil. Reduce heat to low and simmer until cooking liquid has reduced by about three-quarters, about 6 minutes. Cut up or mash to desired consistency. Let cool until warm to the touch before serving or transfer to an airtight container and refrigerate for up to 3 days.

NUTRIENTS PER SERVING (½ cup/125 mL)

Calories	92	Dietary fiber	1.5 g
Protein	7.6 g	Sodium	40.3 mg
Total fat	4.8 g	Calcium	38.3 mg
Saturated fat	2.2 g	Iron	1.3 mg
Carbohydrates	5.2 g	Vitamin C	40 mg

Gramma Jean's Turkey Meatloaf

I lived with my Gramma Jean while attending culinary school in Fort Lauderdale, Florida. I owe this fan favorite to her (many of my customers throughout the years have raved about this recipe). I'm certain your baby will love it. You are doing her a favor by introducing her to turkey at an early age. Not only is turkey one of the best sources of lean protein, it also provides valuable nutrients such as selenium, zinc and a range of B vitamins to provide support for her immune system and metabolism.

● ●

**Makes about
8 servings**

Chef Jordan's Tips

A few gentle taps of the loaf pan on the countertop will pack the meat tightly into the pan.

Brie, a soft cow's-milk cheese covered in a white rind, is one of my family's favorite cheeses. It makes a perfect addition to this meatloaf. The cheese seems to weave its way through the meat as it melts, and it's a wonderful pairing with the mushrooms and sweet pepper.

This recipe makes a relatively large quantity because other family members will enjoy it, too. You can also freeze leftovers in an airtight container for up to 4 weeks.

Always buy organic milk products.

- 9- by 5-inch (2 L) loaf pan
- Instant-read thermometer
- Preheat oven to 300°F (150°C)

½ cup	diced whole-grain gluten-free bread	125 mL
¼ cup	organic whole milk	60 mL
1 tsp	organic unsalted butter	5 mL
1½ cups	sliced mushrooms	375 mL
½ cup	finely diced organic red bell pepper	125 mL
1 lb	ground turkey	500 g
¼ cup	finely diced organic Brie cheese (rind on)	60 mL
1 tbsp	chopped fresh basil or parsley leaves	15 mL

1. In a large bowl, combine bread and milk; set aside until all of the milk has soaked into the bread, 5 to 7 minutes.

2. In a skillet, melt butter over medium heat. Add mushrooms and red pepper and sauté until all of the liquid from the mushrooms has evaporated, about 7 minutes. Transfer to bowl with bread and let cool to room temperature.

3. Add turkey, Brie and basil to vegetable mixture and stir until combined. Pack into loaf pan, ensuring that there are no air pockets (see Tips, left).

4. Bake in preheated oven until thermometer inserted into center registers 165°F (75°C), about 45 minutes. Cut into desired portions. Let cool until warm to the touch before serving or wrap in plastic wrap and refrigerate for up to 3 days.

Jill's Nutrition Tip

Why do we want to sleep after a turkey dinner? Turkey has high levels of tryptophan. This amino acid is the precursor to serotonin and melatonin, neurotransmitters that regulate vital functions of the central nervous system. Serotonin helps to keep you in a good mood, while melatonin calms the brain, settling your baby in to a peaceful night's sleep.

NUTRIENTS PER SERVING

Calories	132	Dietary fiber	0.9 g
Protein	13.1 g	Sodium	107.7 mg
Total fat	7.3 g	Calcium	44.2 mg
Saturated fat	2.6 g	Iron	1.0 mg
Carbohydrates	3.1 g	Vitamin C	12.9 mg

Snacking

When your child becomes a toddler, snacks (pages 178 to 205) become important, as they provide him with energy between meals and may help to prevent him from becoming overly hungry or too cranky to eat a proper meal. Choose wisely and don't rely on snacks that contain sugar and/ or processed grains. Avoiding such foods from the start will help to prevent your child from becoming dependent on them and developing a dislike of more healthy options. We are all naturally predisposed to sweet tastes, and if we aren't careful from an early age, this preference can pave the way for food habits that lead to unbalanced and dysfunctional blood sugar, which is at the root of major chronic diseases. Prepare soft fruits and vegetables in advance so your toddler gets healthy whole foods even when you're out and about. Our delicious smoothies aren't just for breakfast — they can provide quick, balanced nutrition.

When you're on the go, it's particularly easy to succumb to the temptation of prepared foods because they are so convenient. Soft fruits, vegetables or strips of truly whole-grain bread or pita, balanced with something that contains protein (such as small cubes of cheese) can be prepared in advance and stored in small containers that you can take with you.

Snacks and Desserts

Nutritious Bites 178

Snacks

Sour Cream "Latkes" 179

Frozen Grape Snacks 180

Parmesan Cheese Crisps
with Plum Salsa 181

Oven-Roasted Red Peppers 182

Roasted Red Pepper Vinaigrette . . 183

Chunky Pineapple Ice Pops 184

Mango Mint Ice Pops 185

Coconut Papaya Ice Pops 186

Apple Pie Ice Pops 187

Very Berry Ice Pops 189

Mini Sweet Potato Muffins 190

Cheddar Cheese Dip 192

Guacamole 194

Blueberry Banana Smoothie 196

Apple, Avocado and Grape
Smoothie 197

Coconut Mango Smoothie 198

Beet Strawberry Smoothie 199

Mango Lassi 200

Roasted Banana Lassi 201

Roasted Summer Fruit
Smoothie 202

Orange Yogurt Smoothie 204

Pineapple Yogurt Smoothie 205

Desserts

Frozen Blueberry Sorbet 206

Frozen Strawberries and
Coconut Cream 208

My Mom's Applesauce 209

Frozen Mango Mousse 210

Chocolate Macaroons 211

Maple Syrup–Glazed
Pineapple 212

Pomegranate and Kiwi
Purée 214

Nutritious Bites

Healthy Snacks for Long-Term Health

Study after study show that people who eat 5 or more servings of vegetables per day are less likely to become overweight or obese than those who consume less than 3 servings a day. Additional evidence is found in research review articles and summaries posted on the Harvard School of Public Health website, as well as those of Cancer Research UK and the World Health Organization, that support the link between high vegetable consumption (with the exception of french fries!) and decreased cancer, heart disease and diabetes rates. Ensuring that your child eats vegetables and fruit (with the emphasis on vegetables) at every meal and as snacks is the right way to lay the foundation for long-term health.

Snacks are important for your toddler. They provide the added energy these busy little people need. Snacking can expand the types of foods your child eats and can provide a way to ensure that he gets the nutrients he needs if he hasn't eaten particularly well at mealtime. In fact, snacking, or "grazing," as some like to call it, is really the natural rhythm for toddlers.

Snacking becomes a problem only when we reach for foods that are heavy on sugar or full of processed grains, which don't have much to offer from a nutritional perspective. Worse still, there is reason to believe that these foods may even contribute to childhood obesity. To keep your child on track, provide snacks that are nutrient-dense (see page 9). Choose cooked whole grains, small pieces of cooked or soft raw vegetables, soft fruits or protein such as cubes of cheese or thin slices of chicken.

In this chapter, we provide many recipes for healthy snacks that you can easily prepare for your child. Consider offering pieces of soft sliced fruit with Vanilla Bean Yogurt (page 93) for dipping, or cooked vegetables or small pieces of whole-grain bread served with Edamame Hummus (page 118) or even slices of cold Crispy Potato Galette (page 140).

All the recipes in this book are made from fresh whole foods, without refined sugar. Making dessert is no different. You can choose the juiciest, most perfectly ripened fruit and you can determine how sweet you want the result to be.

We have used a variety of sweeteners, from dates to maple syrup to coconut or cane sugar, and have eliminated the use of granulated sugar. Sweet treats may be a bit of an indulgence, but they have a place in a well-balanced diet as long as they don't crowd out more healthful offerings, such as fresh vegetables, fruits, lean proteins and whole grains.

Sour Cream "Latkes"

This recipe evolved from my gramma's loaded-with-sugar cheese latkes. It is a much healthier version that still provides all the satisfaction of a sweet snack. Latkes are easy to make and, better still, you can prepare a large batch and freeze the extra.

• •

Makes about 25 cakes

Chef Jordan's Tips

This recipe demonstrates how, with a little thought and preparation, keeping your family on track for healthy eating is not all that difficult. These latkes freeze well and are simple to reheat: in a nonstick skillet, melt a little butter and sear the frozen cakes until warm, about 2 minutes.

In this recipe I prefer to use alcohol-free organic vanilla extract. However, be aware that some alcohol-free vanilla extract may contain unwanted additives. Read the label carefully.

Jill's Nutrition Tip

Using whole grains and their flours, such as buckwheat (which bears no relation to wheat and is actually a gluten-free seed), in your cooking dramatically increases the nutritional value of the finished dish. Refined grains can be stripped of as much as 90 percent of their B vitamins, 70 percent of their fiber, 70 percent of their essential fatty acids and 60 percent of their calcium. Refining does provide extra shelf life, but at the sacrifice of a great deal of nutrition.

Always buy organic milk products.

¾ cup	organic full-fat sour cream	175 mL
¼ cup	raw cane or coconut sugar	60 mL
2	eggs, beaten	2
1 tsp	pure vanilla extract (see Tips, left)	5 mL
⅓ cup	buckwheat flour, sifted	75 mL
1 tbsp	organic unsalted butter, divided	15 mL

1. In a bowl, whisk together sour cream, sugar, eggs and vanilla. Gradually add flour, whisking until smooth.

2. In a nonstick skillet, melt ½ tsp (2 mL) of the butter over medium heat. Using 1 tbsp (15 mL) for each cake, drop in batter in batches, keeping cakes separate. Cook until edges are crisp, 2 to 3 minutes. Flip and cook until edges start to curl upward, about 1 minute. Transfer to a plate. Repeat with remaining batter, adding more butter to the pan as necessary. Let cool to room temperature before serving. Transfer leftovers to an airtight container and freeze for up to 6 months.

NUTRIENTS PER SERVING (1 cake)

Calories	34	Dietary fiber	0.2 g
Protein	0.9 g	Sodium	13.3 mg
Total fat	2.0 g	Calcium	7.3 mg
Saturated fat	1.1 g	Iron	0.3 mg
Carbohydrates	3.2 g	Vitamin C	0.0 mg

Frozen Grape Snacks

Small bits of frozen fruit make a great snack for kids and adults alike and are extremely simple to prepare. Here we've provided the basic instructions for freezing grapes, but you can use this same method to make frozen berries, peaches, bananas, pineapple, kiwi or mango. Choose your favorite fruits — if your toddler likes to eat them fresh, just wait until she tries them frozen!

**Makes about
1 lb (500 g)**

Chef Jordan's Tip

Frozen fruit is a snack adults can enjoy just as much as kids. For bigger folk, leave the fruit whole or cut it into larger pieces. Frozen fruit also makes a great addition to salads or a pretty garnish for dessert. Often I serve frozen grapes along with a bowl of warm chocolate sauce for dipping as a simple dessert.

Jill's Nutrition Tip

One of the most healthful components of red grapes is the flavonoid resveratrol, which is found in their skins. Scientists are actively engaged in studying this compound, which may have a wide range of health benefits, from helping your body to fight viruses to increasing stamina. Red wine is another good source of resveratrol, so enjoy a glass while treating your children to their own source with frozen grape snacks.

Always buy organic grapes.

• Rimmed baking sheet lined with parchment paper

| 1 lb | organic seedless grapes | 500 g |

1. In a colander, under cold running water, gently rinse grapes. Transfer to paper towels to dry.

2. Cut into halves or quarters, depending upon the age of your child. Place on prepared baking sheet and transfer to the freezer. Freeze until grapes are completely frozen, about 5 hours. Transfer to an airtight container. Enjoy immediately or keep frozen for up to 6 months.

NUTRIENTS PER SERVING (¼ cup/60 mL)

Calories	15	Dietary fiber	0.2 g
Protein	0.2 g	Sodium	0.0 mg
Total fat	0.2 g	Calcium	3.3 mg
Saturated fat	0.0 g	Iron	0.6 mg
Carbohydrates	4.0 g	Vitamin C	2.5 mg

Parmesan Cheese Crisps with Plum Salsa

This is a scrumptious, healthy spin-off of my favorite snack, tortilla chips and tomato salsa. It's also a great way to get your kids to eat fruit.

Makes about 5 servings

Chef Jordan's Tip

I've often served this to guests as an hors d'oeuvre. The saltiness of the cheese crisps combines with the sweetness of the fruit to create a delicious flavor contrast that adults enjoy as much as kids.

Jill's Nutrition Tip

Plums and their dried version, prunes, have been studied for their unique phytochemicals, specifically neochlorogenic and chlorogenic acids. These nutrients help prevent damage to the important fats in our brain cells and cell membranes. On a more practical level, these fruits also relieve constipation.

Always buy organic plums and cheese.

1½ cups	finely diced pitted organic plums	375 mL
1 tbsp	balsamic vinegar	15 mL
1 tbsp	liquid honey	15 mL
1 tsp	freshly grated lemon zest	5 mL
1 cup	freshly grated organic Parmesan cheese	250 mL

1. In a bowl, combine plums, vinegar, honey and lemon zest. Set aside.

2. In a nonstick skillet over medium heat, spoon 1 tsp (5 mL) cheese (per crisp) into the pan and cook until golden brown, about 3 minutes (be sure not to overload the pan or the cheese will run together). Using a spatula, carefully transfer to a plate to cool, keeping crisps in a single layer. Repeat until all of the cheese is cooked. Once cooled, serve crisps on a platter with the bowl of plum salsa.

NUTRIENTS PER SERVING

Calories	115	Dietary fiber	0.0 g
Protein	6.8 g	Sodium	265.5 mg
Total fat	4.9 g	Calcium	196.2 mg
Saturated fat	2.9 g	Iron	0.2 mg
Carbohydrates	11.3 g	Vitamin C	6.6 mg

Oven-Roasted Red Peppers

Roasted red peppers are a staple in my home because they are so versatile. If you have them on hand, you can simply chop them and toss with cooked noodles to create an excellent pasta dish for your baby (9 months +). They can also be served as a delicious, healthy snack along with some cooked broccoli or cauliflower florets and a small chunk of cheese.

Makes 6 servings

Chef Jordan's Tips

Use orange, red or yellow peppers for roasting, because they tend to be the sweetest.

If time is not of the essence, let roasted peppers cool overnight in the refrigerator before peeling, which makes them easier to peel.

Jill's Nutrition Tip

Sweet red peppers are actually green peppers that have been allowed to ripen on the vine. Because of this ripening process they have significantly higher levels of nutrients and phytochemicals than green peppers. To ensure that you are getting the freshest and therefore most nutritious peppers, select ones that are firm, heavy for their size and without wrinkles.

Always buy organic bell peppers.

• Large ovenproof skillet
• Preheat oven to 350°F (180°C)

3	organic red bell peppers	3
1 tbsp	extra virgin olive oil	15 mL
2	sprigs fresh thyme	2
2 tbsp	finely chopped fresh basil leaves, divided	30 mL
Pinch	kosher salt	Pinch
Pinch	freshly ground black pepper	Pinch

1. In large ovenproof skillet, combine red peppers, oil, thyme, 1 tbsp (15 mL) of the basil, salt and pepper. Toss until peppers are thoroughly coated. Roast in preheated oven, turning peppers every 10 minutes, until all sides are golden brown and soft, about 1 hour. Remove from oven and let cool to room temperature (see Tips, left).

2. Set a fine-mesh sieve over a bowl. Holding peppers over the sieve, remove skins and stems while catching all the residual cooking liquid in bowl. Cut peppers in half and gently scoop out seeds and membranes. Transfer to a clean bowl.

3. Add reserved liquid and remaining basil. Stir well. Cover and refrigerate for up to 3 days.

NUTRIENTS PER SERVING (½ pepper)

Calories 26	Dietary fiber. . . . . 1.2 g
Protein. . . . . .0.6 g	Sodium. . . . . .2.4 mg
Total fat . . . . 1.4 g	Calcium . . . . 4.9 mg
Saturated fat. . . . . .0.2 g	Iron. . . . . .0.3 mg
Carbohydrates . . . . . . .3.6 g	Vitamin C . . . . .76.1 mg

Roasted Red Pepper Vinaigrette

If your baby is old enough to tolerate peppers (9 months +), try adding this to plain yogurt and serving it as a dip for soft vegetables or gluten-free crackers or bread. A tiny amount also enhances the flavors of Roasted Beet Purée (page 50) and Diced Potato Gratin (page 98).

• •

Makes about 2 ¼ cups (550 mL)

Chef Jordan's Tip

If you don't have sherry vinegar, rice or champagne vinegar also works well in this recipe.

Jill's Nutrition Tip

Bell peppers can be a delicious tool for helping keep your baby's heart and eyes healthy. Among other beneficial compounds, peppers contain vitamin C, flavonoids and many different carotenoids. All these phytochemicals work synergistically as antioxidants to reduce inflammation and protect blood vessels.

Always buy organic bell peppers.

1 cup	puréed Oven-Roasted Red Peppers (page 182)	250 mL
½ cup	extra virgin olive oil	125 mL
¼ cup	sherry vinegar (see Tips, left)	60 mL
1 tbsp	liquid honey	15 mL
2 tsp	kosher salt	10 mL
2 tsp	freshly ground black pepper	10 mL

1. In a bowl, whisk together roasted red pepper purée, oil, vinegar, honey, salt and pepper. The vinaigrette will separate somewhat, so be sure to whisk it well immediately before using. Transfer to an airtight container and refrigerate for up to 1 month.

NUTRIENTS PER SERVING (¼ cup/60 mL)

Calories 132	Dietary fiber . . . . 0.4 g
Protein . . . . 0.2 g	Sodium . . . . 649.6 mg
Total fat . . . . 13.4 g	Calcium . . . . 3.2 mg
Saturated fat . . . . 1.9 g	Iron . . . . 0.1 mg
Carbohydrates . . . . 2.9 g	Vitamin C . . . . 11.0 mg

Chunky Pineapple Ice Pops

This is a very refreshing way to satisfy your child's cravings for sweets. And don't forget to have one yourself. In addition to having fabulous flavor, pineapple is loaded with vitamin C and provides a smattering of valuable minerals such as manganese. It also contains an enzyme called bromelain, which aids digestion (see Tips, page 130).

Makes about 14 ice pops

Chef Jordan's Tips

To make chunky pineapple purée, peel and core 1 medium pineapple. In a food processor, pulse until chunky (retaining some texture creates an excellent contrast between the smooth ice and the pineapple bits). If you prefer, place pineapple in a deep bowl and use an immersion blender to purée.

If you are using an ice pop kit, follow the manufacturer's instructions.

Jill's Nutrition Tip

Making puréed fruits into ice pops is a creative way to increase the fruit in your child's diet. All fruits contain healthful vitamins and phytonutrients, such as flavonoids, that provide antioxidant protection to every cell in your baby's body.

- Wooden sticks for ice pops

1¼ cups	chunky pineapple purée (see Tips, left)	300 mL
½ cup	filtered water	125 mL
1 tbsp	pure maple syrup	15 mL

1. In a bowl, combine pineapple, water and maple syrup. Stir thoroughly. Spoon into an ice-cube tray and freeze just until surface has frozen, about 1 hour.

2. Cover tray tightly with plastic wrap. Using the tip of a sharp knife, cut a small slit in the plastic directly over the middle of each cube. Insert sticks until submerged in purée. Freeze until completely solid, 2 to 3 hours. Although these will keep frozen for up to 1 month, I doubt they'll last that long.

Variations

Most fruits can be used to make these ice pops, although some may require a little more sweetener. Substitute an equal quantity of puréed berries, watermelon (or other variety of melon), peaches or nectarines. Trust your palate regarding the amount of sweetener to add.

NUTRIENTS PER SERVING (1 ice pop)

Calories	15	Dietary fiber	0.9 g
Protein	0.3 g	Sodium	0.9 mg
Total fat	0.2 g	Calcium	3.9 mg
Saturated fat	0.1 g	Iron	0.0 mg
Carbohydrates	3.5 g	Vitamin C	4.4 mg

Mango Mint Ice Pops

Mint complements the sweetness of mango beautifully. Not only do these ice pops provide valuable nutrients, they're a wonderful way to cool off on a warm summer day.

**Makes
12 to 14 ice pops**

Chef Jordan's Tips

Substitute an equal quantity of fresh basil leaves for the mint.

If you are using an ice pop kit, follow the manufacturer's instructions.

Jill's Nutrition Tip

Mangos are a delicious source of B vitamins, which play an important role in helping us to convert food into energy. The most abundant member of the vitamin B family in mangos is B_6, which is needed for melatonin production to help your baby set his internal sleep/wake clock.

- Blender
- Wooden sticks for ice pops

2	medium mangoes, peeled, pitted and roughly chopped	2
½ cup	filtered water	125 mL
3	fresh mint leaves	3

1. In blender, blend mangoes, water and mint leaves until smooth. (If you prefer, combine ingredients in a deep bowl and use an immersion blender to purée.) Spoon into an ice-cube tray and freeze just until surface has frozen, about 1 hour.

2. Cover tray tightly with plastic wrap. Using the tip of a sharp knife, cut a small slit in the plastic directly over the middle of each cube. Insert sticks until submerged in purée. Freeze until completely solid, 2 to 3 hours. Keep frozen for up to 1 month.

NUTRIENTS PER SERVING (1 ice pop)

Calories 22.5	Dietary fiber . . . . 0.7 g
Protein . . . . 0.2 g	Sodium . . . . 0.7 mg
Total fat . . . . 0.2 g	Calcium . . . . 3.5 mg
Saturated fat . . . . 0.0 g	Iron . . . . 0.1 mg
Carbohydrates . . . . . . 5.8 g	Vitamin C . . . . 9.6 mg

Coconut Papaya Ice Pops

This tropical sensation will be a hit with your children and their friends — and your friends, too! This recipe also has the best side effect: it will take you back to your last Caribbean vacation (you remember, the one without the kids).

● ●

Chef Jordan's Tips

If papaya can't be found, mango makes a perfect substitute.

If you are using an ice pop kit, follow the manufacturer's instructions.

Jill's Nutrition Tip

In the 1990s, a virus wiped out the papaya crop in Hawaii. Since then, genetically modified papayas (modified with a bit of the virus's DNA) have been grown on the island. In fact, over 80 percent of the papayas grown in Hawaii are genetically modified. If you are avoiding GMO food, be sure your papayas are from elsewhere or are certified organic.

- Blender
- Wooden sticks for ice pops

1	medium organic papaya, peeled, seeded and roughly chopped	1
½ cup	unsweetened coconut milk	125 mL
¼ cup	filtered water	60 mL
1 tsp	freshly grated lime zest	5 mL
¼ cup	freshly squeezed lime juice	60 mL
2 tbsp	coconut sugar	30 mL

1. In blender, combine papaya, coconut milk, water, lime zest, lime juice and coconut sugar and blend until smooth. (If you prefer, combine ingredients in a deep bowl and use an immersion blender to purée.) Spoon into an ice-cube tray and freeze just until surface has frozen, about 1 hour.

2. Cover tray tightly with plastic wrap. Using the tip of a sharp knife, cut a small slit in the plastic directly over the middle of each cube. Insert sticks until submerged in purée. Freeze until completely solid, 2 to 3 hours. Keep frozen for up to 1 month.

NUTRIENTS PER SERVING (1 ice pop)

Calories	37.2	Dietary fiber	0.4 g
Protein	0.4 g	Sodium	2.1 mg
Total fat	2.0 g	Calcium	8.5 mg
Saturated fat	1.8 g	Iron	0.4 mg
Carbohydrates	5.1 g	Vitamin C	17.3 mg

Apple Pie Ice Pops

Eating these ice pops is like eating a slice of apple pie topped with a scoop of vanilla ice cream. The difference is that these are much easier to make.

● ●

**Makes
12 to 14 ice pops**

Chef Jordan's Tips

To make cinnamon sugar, combine 5 tsp (25 mL) coconut sugar and 1 tsp (5 mL) ground cinnamon and stir well.

Reserve the vanilla pods to flavor sugar or salt. Simply place them in an airtight container along with the sugar or salt, cover and set aside for 1 to 2 weeks before using. Vanilla salt makes a great substitute for unflavored salt in most baking recipes.

Jill's Nutrition Tip

Apples and cinnamon make a terrific combination for steady and even blood sugar balance. Cinnamon is being studied for its effects on insulin, and the fiber in apples slows down the release of sugar into the bloodstream, leaving your baby free from sugar spikes and energy crashes.

- Wooden ice pop sticks
- Blender

2	medium organic apples, cored and roughly chopped	2
1	vanilla bean or 1 tsp (5 mL) pure vanilla extract (see Tips, page 179)	1
1 cup	filtered water	250 mL
2 tbsp	cinnamon sugar (see Tips, left)	30 mL

1. Using a paring knife, cut vanilla bean in half lengthwise, exposing the seeds. Scrape seeds into a saucepan. Add apples, water and cinnamon sugar. Bring to a simmer over medium heat and cook until apples are soft and begin to fall apart, about 10 minutes.

2. Transfer to blender and purée. (You can also do this in the saucepan, using an immersion blender.) Spoon into an ice-cube tray and freeze just until surface has frozen, about 1 hour.

3. Cover tray tightly with plastic wrap. Using the tip of a sharp knife, cut a small slit in the plastic directly over the middle of each cube. Insert sticks until submerged in purée. Freeze until completely solid, 2 to 3 hours. Keep frozen for up to 1 month.

NUTRIENTS PER SERVING (1 ice pop)

Calories 23.8	Dietary fiber. . . . . .0.8 g
Protein. . . . . 0.0 g	Sodium. . . . . .0.3 mg
Total fat . . . . 0.0 g	Calcium . . . . 3.9 mg
Saturated fat. . . . . 0.0 g	Iron. . . . . 0.1 mg
Carbohydrates . . . . . . .6.3 g	Vitamin C . . . . 1.4 mg

Very Berry Ice Pops

Berries, either fresh or frozen, are widely available year-round, just waiting to be transformed into delicious and nutritious ice pops.

● ●

**Makes
12 to 14 ice pops**

Chef Jordan's Tip

This is my favorite mixture, but any combination of berries will work well in this recipe.

Jill's Nutrition Tips

This ice pop is a powerhouse of vitamin C and other antioxidants. Vitamin C is responsible for the health of collagen, which helps your baby grow strong and flexible joints. As she grows, the other antioxidants join forces to prevent cell damage.

Although blackberries are not on the list of foods containing the most pesticides (likely because they are less common than many other berries), in an abundance of caution we advise buying organic fruit.

Always buy organic or wild berries.

- Fine-mesh sieve
- Wooden ice pop sticks

1 cup	hulled organic strawberries, roughly chopped	250 mL
½ cup	organic or wild blueberries	125 mL
½ cup	organic or wild blackberries	125 mL
½ cup	filtered water	125 mL
2 tbsp	coconut sugar	30 mL

1. In a saucepan, combine strawberries, blueberries, blackberries, water and sugar. Bring to a simmer over medium heat and cook until strawberries begin to fall apart, about 5 minutes.

2. Strain through fine-mesh sieve set over a bowl, using the back of a spoon to push the fruit through until only the seeds are left. Discard seeds.

3. Spoon into an ice-cube tray and freeze just until surface has frozen, about 1 hour.

4. Cover tray tightly with plastic wrap. Using the tip of a sharp knife, cut a small slit in the plastic directly over the middle of each cube. Insert sticks until submerged in purée. Freeze until completely solid, 2 to 3 hours. Keep frozen for up to 1 month.

Variation

As a fun, tasty treat, try using an ice pop as an ice cube in your child's water. It'll make their very own Very Berry water.

NUTRIENTS PER SERVING (1 ice pop)

Calories 18.3	Dietary fiber . . . . .0.8 g
Protein . . . . .0.2 g	Sodium . . . . .0.6 mg
Total fat . . . . 0.1 g	Calcium . . . . .4.8 mg
Saturated fat . . . . 0.0 g	Iron . . . . 0.1 mg
Carbohydrates . . . . . . 4.4 g	Vitamin C . . . . 10.5 mg

Mini Sweet Potato Muffins

Even though there is a minimal amount of sugar in these muffins, your children will be begging you to make them over and over again.

● ●

> ### Makes about 36 muffins

Chef Jordan's Tips

To make coconut icing sugar, in a blender, combine 1 cup (250 mL) coconut sugar and 1½ tsp (7 mL) organic cornstarch and blend until sugar is fine. Transfer to an airtight container and store at room temperature for up to 1 month.

What an excellent way to incorporate more vegetables into your children's diet! If you don't count the maple syrup, the muffins are sugar-free. If you prefer, omit the glaze.

Jill's Nutrition Tip

These mini muffins are a healthy snack for your baby once he is old enough to enjoy small finger foods. Even though they are a bit sweet, the ingredients help keep blood sugar levels stable. The roasted sweet potato purée and the sorghum flour provide insoluble fiber and complex carbohydrates to allow for a slow, steady release of energy for your baby.

Always buy organic milk products.

- 36-cup mini-muffin pan, greased
- Preheat oven to 300°F (150°C)

Muffins

1 cup	sweet sorghum flour	250 mL
1 tsp	baking powder	5 mL
Pinch	kosher salt	Pinch
¾ cup	Roasted Sweet Potato Purée (page 45)	175 mL
½ cup	pure maple syrup	125 mL
½ cup	organic whole milk	125 mL
1 tsp	melted organic unsalted butter	5 mL
1	egg	1
1 tsp	vanilla seeds (about 1 pod) or 1 tsp (5 mL) pure vanilla extract	5 mL

Glaze (optional)

½ cup	coconut icing sugar (see Tips, left)	125 mL
¼ cup	Roasted Sweet Potato Purée	60 mL
1 tbsp	pure maple syrup	15 mL
1 tsp	organic whole milk	5 mL

1. *Muffins:* In a bowl, whisk together flour, baking powder and salt. Set aside.

2. In a separate bowl, whisk together sweet potato, maple syrup, milk and melted butter. Add egg and vanilla and whisk until combined. Add to dry ingredients and stir just until incorporated (do not overmix).

3. Spoon batter into prepared muffin pan until cups are about two-thirds full. Bake in preheated oven until muffins have risen and a toothpick inserted into the center comes out clean, about 10 minutes. Remove from oven and let cool until warm to the touch.

4. *Glaze* (if using): In a bowl, whisk together coconut icing sugar, sweet potato purée, maple syrup and milk until glossy and thick. Cover and refrigerate until ready to use. When ready to serve, dip tops of the muffins into the glaze and set aside for 5 to 10 minutes at room temperature to let glaze set.

NUTRIENTS PER SERVING (1 muffin)

Calories	32.5	Dietary fiber	0.3 g
Protein	0.6 g	Sodium	6.0 mg
Total fat	0.5 g	Calcium	17.2 mg
Saturated fat	0.2 g	Iron	0.2 mg
Carbohydrates	6.6 g	Vitamin C	0.1 mg

Cheddar Cheese Dip

This is the greatest all-purpose cheese dip you and your children will ever taste. At the Wagman household, we use this dip with just about everything, from cut-up vegetables to pizza. It is an excellent source of calcium (see Tips, below) and, served with raw vegetable dippers, provides a nutritionally balanced snack.

	Makes about 1 cup (250 mL)

Chef Jordan's Tip

Vary this recipe to suit the ingredients you have on hand. Make a simple "ratatouille" dip by adding 1 tbsp (15 mL) each finely diced red bell pepper, yellow bell pepper, tomato and zucchini, immediately after you whisk together the milk and flour.

Jill's Nutrition Tips

This is a great way to help ensure that your child gets enough calcium. Not only is there ample calcium in the milk, cheese and yogurt, but the yogurt also contains intestine-friendly lactobacteria that help her body digest the calcium it contains, making it easier to absorb. This means even more calcium to build strong teeth and bones.

Always buy organic milk products.

½ cup	organic whole milk	125 mL
1 tsp	brown rice flour	5 mL
1 cup	shredded organic Cheddar cheese	250 mL
½ cup	plain full-fat organic yogurt or sour cream	125 mL

1. In a saucepan over medium-low heat, bring milk and flour to a simmer, whisking constantly to prevent lumps. Continue whisking until mixture thickens, about 5 minutes. Remove from heat.

2. Add cheese in small handfuls, whisking until fully melted and incorporated. Add yogurt and whisk to combine. Serve immediately or transfer to an airtight container and refrigerate for up to 3 days (serve chilled).

NUTRIENTS PER SERVING (¼ cup/60 mL)

Calories 152	Dietary fiber. . . . . 0.0 g
Protein. . . . . 10.1 g	Sodium. . . . . .218.1 mg
Total fat . . . . .10.4 g	Calcium . . . . .292.0 mg
Saturated fat. . . . . . . .6.5 g	Iron . . . . .0.2 mg
Carbohydrates . . . . . . .4.7 g	Vitamin C . . . . .0.0 mg

Most Fat Is Good for Your Baby

Fat has received a bad rap in the past, but current research is showing the benefits of different types of fat. Although it is higher in calories than carbohydrates or protein, fat is a critical component of a healthy diet. Without fat, for instance, your body would not be able to absorb the fat-soluble vitamins A, D, E and K or form the myelin sheath around your nerves.

Fat is made of building blocks called fatty acids, some of which are essential. This means you must obtain them from your diet because your body cannot make them. For instance, your body needs the essential omega-3 fats found predominantly in cold-water fatty fish such as salmon, cod, mackerel and herring, as well as some nuts and seeds and grass-fed meats. These fats have many benefits, such as reducing the risk of heart disease, contributing to good brain development and cognitive function, and decreasing inflammation associated with degenerative diseases such as type 2 diabetes. Unfortunately, these essential fats are in short supply in the typical North American diet because they have been eliminated from all packaged and processed foods in order to increase their shelf life.

Most of the polyunsaturated fats on the market, such as sunflower, safflower and canola oil, are predominantly omega-6 fats. Although we've been told for decades that these fats are good for us, nutritional science is now showing that too many omega-6 fats, in relation to omega-3 fats, can actually undermine our health.

We need both these fats, but in the right proportions. An imbalance may help explain the rise of asthma, heart disease, many forms of cancer, autoimmunity and neurodegenerative diseases, all of which are believed to stem from inappropriate inflammation in the body.

Then there is saturated fat. Although much vilified, saturated fats are part of the building blocks for cell membranes and a variety of hormones. They should be consumed in moderation, albeit with a watchful eye. Recent research is reshaping past ideas. As a study published in the *Annals of Internal Medicine* in 2014 states, "Current evidence does not clearly support cardiovascular guidelines that encourage high consumption of polyunsaturated fatty acids and low consumption of total saturated fats."

Trans fats that result from the process of partial hydrogenation of vegetable oils are the exception. Many researchers believe there are no safe levels of consumption for these fats. Processed foods and some baked goods, such as crackers, often contain trans fats, so be sure to read the ingredient listings and avoid products that contain hydrogenated oils, partially hydrogenated oils or shortening — these are all trans fats.

Just remember, though, that babies need proportionately more fat in their diet than adults to ensure proper brain and nervous system development. Avoid reduced-fat products when feeding your baby and ensure that her diet provides good quantities of health-promoting omega-3 fats.

Guacamole

Guacamole is a staple in our home, whether served at snack time with tortilla chips or with vegetables as a pre-dinner dip. On a piece of soft bread, it's perfect for older toddlers. For babies with some solid-food experience of stronger-tasting foods, this can be puréed and served on a spoon for a healthy delicious, creamy snack.

¼ cup	chopped tomato	60 mL
1	green onion, minced	1
1 tsp	freshly squeezed lemon juice	5 mL
2	avocados, peeled and pitted	2

Makes about 2 cups (500 mL)

1. In a bowl, combine tomato, green onion and lemon juice and stir well. Add avocado and, using a fork, mash and stir until it reaches desired consistency. Serve immediately or refrigerate for up to 3 days.

Chef Jordan's Tip

When refrigerating guacamole, be sure to place a layer of plastic wrap directly on top of the mixture to prevent air from getting in and turning your avocado brown.

Jill's Nutrition Tip

Avocados contain the carotenoids lutein and zeaxanthin, both of which may help keep your baby's eyes healthy. Avocados also contain a significant amount of healthy monounsaturated fat. Carotenoids are fat-soluble, meaning that fat must be present for them to be absorbed. A recent study in the *Journal of Nutrition* demonstrated a significant improvement in the body's ability to absorb carotenoids from other vegetables when avocados were eaten at the same time.

NUTRIENTS PER SERVING (¼ cup/60 mL)

Calories 82	Dietary fiber . . . . .3.5 g
Protein . . . . .1.1 g	Sodium . . . . 3.9 mg
Total fat . . . . .7.4 g	Calcium . . . . 7.6 mg
Saturated fat . . . . .1.1 g	Iron . . . . .0.3 mg
Carbohydrates . . . . . . .4.7 g	Vitamin C . . . . 6.7 mg

Blueberry Banana Smoothie

Smoothies make a wonderful, nutritious snack for your children and you! This is the perfect way to use overripe brown bananas that you typically throw away.

Makes about 5 cups (1.25 L)

Chef Jordan's Tip

Frozen blueberries make a great snack by themselves and also work wonderfully in smoothies. When wild blueberries are in season, take advantage of the harvest by freezing them: First gently rinse and dry the fruit, then spread in a single layer on a parchment-lined baking sheet. Freeze on sheet until completely frozen, about 5 hours, shaking the berries often to prevent their sticking together or to the parchment paper.

Jill's Nutrition Tip

Smoothies are a great snack or even a meal (when you add a protein) for the whole family. Once you have tried a few, the real fun begins when you start experimenting. Any vegetable or fruit can be used. Just start small when adding vegetables, to avoid changing the flavor too much until you get used to it. Everything you add will change the color — always a fun experiment!

Always buy organic or wild blueberries.

- Blender

2 cups	sliced ripe bananas (2 medium)	500 mL
1 cup	organic or wild blueberries	250 mL
2 cups	filtered water	500 mL
1 cup	ice	250 mL
2 tbsp	coconut sugar	30 mL

1. In blender, combine bananas, blueberries, water, ice and sugar and purée until smooth. Serve immediately.

NUTRIENTS PER SERVING (¼ cup/60 mL)

Calories	19.6	Dietary fiber	0.5 g
Protein	0.2 g	Sodium	0.6 mg
Total fat	0.1 g	Calcium	1.6 mg
Saturated fat	0.0 g	Iron	0.1 mg
Carbohydrates	4.8 g	Vitamin C	2.4 mg

Apple, Avocado and Grape Smoothie

The beautifully smooth texture of avocado paired with the sweetness of apples and grapes makes for a deliciously rich and creamy smoothie. Avocados are extremely healthful. They provide a smattering of beneficial nutrients, protein and an abundance of healthy monounsaturated fats. If your child hasn't tried spinach, this is a great way to introduce her to this nutritious leafy green.

Makes about 5 cups (1.25 L)

Chef Jordan's Tip

Avocados tend to discolor (oxidize) quite quickly. To prevent this, chop the avocado just before puréeing. Once blended, the acidity from the apples will maintain the avocado's lovely bright green color.

Jill's Nutrition Tip

This smoothie has a lovely green color and a wonderfully creamy texture. Adding vegetables to smoothies really increases the nutrient density (see page 9). Providing your baby with lots of vegetables over the course of a whole day is one of the healthiest things you can do for him.

Always buy organic apples, grapes and spinach.

- Blender

2 cups	roughly chopped organic apples	500 mL
1 cup	organic green seedless grapes	250 mL
2 cups	filtered water	500 mL
1 cup	ice	250 mL
1	medium avocado, peeled, pitted and roughly chopped	1
½ cup	organic spinach leaves	125 mL
2 tbsp	coconut sugar	30 mL

1. In blender, combine apples, grapes, water, ice, avocado and sugar and purée until smooth. Serve immediately.

NUTRIENTS PER SERVING (¼ cup/60 mL)

Calories 35.5	Dietary fiber . . . . 1.1 g
Protein . . . . 0.3 g	Sodium . . . . 1.6 mg
Total fat . . . . 1.5 g	Calcium . . . . 3.8 mg
Saturated fat . . . . 0.2 g	Iron . . . . 0.1 mg
Carbohydrates . . . . 5.9 g	Vitamin C . . . . 2.9 mg

Coconut Mango Smoothie

Turmeric gives this smoothie a magnificent yellow color — but just wait until you taste it! The texture is as smooth as silk. It's worth introducing your baby to turmeric early because this spice has been linked to numerous health benefits.

Makes about 5 cups (1.25 L)

Chef Jordan's Tip

You can transform this into a Coconut Peach Smoothie by substituting peaches, either fresh or canned (so long as they are not packed with sugar), for the mango in this recipe. If you like, you can also replace just some of the mango with peach. I sometimes use 1 cup (250 mL) each chopped mango and chopped peach. That ratio is equally delicious. Yum!

Jill's Nutrition Tip

Turmeric may be one of the most well-researched spices, for good reason. Ongoing studies are showing its beneficial properties in terms of cancer and Alzheimer's treatment and prevention. In terms of feeding it to your baby, long-term exposure seems to be one of the best ways to reap its health benefits. What could be more delicious than this glass of sunshine?

- Blender

2 cups	chopped mango	500 mL
2 cups	filtered water	500 mL
1 cup	unsweetened coconut milk	250 mL
1 cup	ice	250 mL
1	peach, pitted and chopped	1
2 tbsp	coconut sugar	30 mL
½ tsp	ground turmeric	2 mL

1. In blender, combine mango, water, coconut milk, ice, peach, sugar and turmeric and purée until smooth. Serve immediately.

NUTRIENTS PER SERVING (¼ cup/60 mL)

Calories	40.4	Dietary fiber	0.4 g
Protein	0.4 g	Sodium	1.8 mg
Total fat	2.4 g	Calcium	4.1 mg
Saturated fat	2.2 g	Iron	0.4 mg
Carbohydrates	5.0 g	Vitamin C	5.2 mg

Beet Strawberry Smoothie

Beets may not be on your children's radar now, but if you introduce them to their fantastic candy-like sweetness with this smoothie, they'll be hooked forever. Among other nutrients, beets are a good source of magnesium, a mineral that experts tell us is in short supply in our diets and that plays important roles in keeping your baby healthy.

● ●

**Makes about
5 cups (1.25 L)**

Chef Jordan's Tips

I love to use frozen berries for smoothies because they double as ice cubes. Not only do they chill, they also add intense flavor. When making smoothies, consider substituting frozen berries for some or all of the ice. Frozen organic berries are widely available. If you prefer, freeze berries in season yourself.

To freeze strawberries, gently rinse and dry the fruit. Spread in a single layer on a parchment-lined baking sheet. Freeze until frozen, about 5 hours, shaking the baking sheet often to prevent the berries from sticking together or to the parchment paper.

Jill's Nutrition Tip

Don't worry about using raw beets — they are delicious and sweet. When left raw, beets retain all of their folate (for a healthy heart) and potassium (for healthy nerve and muscle function). Remember that your baby's urine and bowel movements may be stained a bit red after beets, so don't be alarmed!

Always buy organic strawberries.

- Blender

1	vanilla bean or 1 tsp (5 mL) pure vanilla extract (see Tips, page 205)	1
2 cups	hulled organic strawberries	500 mL
2 cups	filtered water	500 mL
1 cup	beets, peeled and chopped	250 mL
1 cup	ice	250 mL
2 tbsp	coconut sugar	30 mL

1. Using a paring knife, cut vanilla bean in half lengthwise, exposing the seeds. Scrape seeds into blender. Add strawberries, water, beets, ice and sugar. Purée until smooth. Serve immediately.

NUTRIENTS PER SERVING (¼ cup/60 mL)

Calories	12.7	Dietary fiber	0.5 g
Protein	0.2 g	Sodium	5.5 mg
Total fat	0.0 g	Calcium	3.8 mg
Saturated fat	0.0 g	Iron	0.1 mg
Carbohydrates	3.1 g	Vitamin C	10.1 mg

Mango Lassi

This classic Indian treat will satisfy any sweet cravings your child might have. And it's good for her, too. In addition to being delicious, mangos provide a wide range of vitamins and minerals. They are particularly rich in beta-carotene, which your baby's body converts to vitamin A for healthy skin, and vitamin C, which among other benefits helps your baby to battle viruses such as the common cold. Both of these vitamins may also be helpful in reducing the risk for developing asthma.

● ●

**Makes about
5 cups (1.25 L)**

Chef Jordan's Tips

Native to India, cardamom is a wonderfully aromatic spice that has been used for thousands of years. Although freshly ground cardamom is best, good-quality ground cardamom is readily available and makes an acceptable substitute.

When making your mango purée, use an extra-large mango to achieve the quantity necessary for this drink.

Jill's Nutrition Tip

In addition to the antioxidant beta-carotene, mangos also contain zeaxanthin, which helps filter out blue light and protects your baby's eyes from damage from sunlight and the blue light emitted by computer, tablet and cellphone screens.

● Blender

2 cups	Mango Purée (page 41; see Tips, left)	500 mL
1 cup	filtered water	250 mL
1 cup	Jill's Homemade Yogurt (page 90)	250 mL
1 cup	ice	250 mL
¼ tsp	ground cardamom	1 mL

1. In blender, combine mango, water, yogurt, ice and cardamom and blend until smooth. Serve immediately.

NUTRIENTS PER SERVING (¼ cup/60 mL)

Calories 15.6	Dietary fiber. . . . . 0.1 g
Protein. . . . . 0.4 g	Sodium. . . . . 6.6 mg
Carbohydrates . . . . . . .2.6 g	Calcium . . . . 14.2 mg
Total fat . . . . 0.4 g	Iron. . . . . .0.0 mg
Saturated fat. . . . . . . .0.3 g	Vitamin C . . . . 1.0 mg

Roasted Banana Lassi

This very popular Indian drink is like a banana milkshake with significant health benefits. Enjoy it anytime, but especially on hot summer days.

**Makes about
5 cups (1.25 L)**

Chef Jordan's Tip

The recipe for Roasted Banana Purée can easily be doubled to achieve the quantity required for this recipe. Although roasting the bananas intensifies their flavor and sweetness, if you prefer, substitute 4 peeled bananas for the quantity of purée called for in this recipe.

Jill's Nutrition Tip

Mint is a very popular flavor, but in addition to being tasty, it can also improve digestion. Numerous studies have shown that by relaxing the gastrointestinal tract, peppermint can reduce symptoms such as stomachache and gas after a meal.

- Blender

2 cups	Roasted Banana Purée (page 36; see Tips, left)	500 mL
1 cup	filtered water	250 mL
1 cup	Jill's Homemade Yogurt (page 90)	250 mL
1 cup	ice	250 mL
5	fresh mint leaves	5

1. In blender, combine banana, water, yogurt, ice and mint and purée until smooth. Serve immediately.

NUTRIENTS PER SERVING (¼ cup/60 mL)

Calories 28.8	Dietary fiber . . . . 0.6 g
Protein . . . , , , , , , . . 0.7 g	Sodium . . . . 6.8 mg
Total fat . . . . 0.5 g	Calcium . . . . 15.4 mg
Saturated fat . . . . 0.3 g	Iron . . . . 0.1 mg
Carbohydrates . . . . 6.0 g	Vitamin C . . . . 2.0 mg

Roasted Summer Fruit Smoothie

What an excellent, healthy treat for your children and you — enjoy!

Makes about 2½ cups (625 mL)

Chef Jordan's Tip

When they are in season, I'll buy a surplus of my favorite fruits, roast them and freeze them. That way I don't even need ice. I just combine all the ingredients in a blender.

Jill's Nutrition Tip

To ensure optimum nutrition for your baby, supplement this recipe with a good protein powder and healthy oils. One scoop of protein powder (ask your local health food store to recommend a good one for your baby) and 1 teaspoon (5 mL) or so of hempseed or flaxseed oil, which provides essential omega-3 fats, will optimize the ratio among carbohydrates, proteins and fats — the three macronutrients your baby needs for growth.

- Blender

2 cups	Roasted Summer Fruit (page 132)	500 mL
½ cup	Jill's Homemade Yogurt (page 90) or organic plain full-fat yogurt	125 mL
½ cup	ice	125 mL
1 tbsp	chopped fresh mint	15 mL

1. In blender, combine fruit, yogurt, ice and mint. Purée until smooth. Serve immediately.

Variation

To make this smoothie even more delicious and nutritious, substitute an equal quantity of frozen fruit, such as berries, for the ice.

NUTRIENTS PER SERVING (½ cup/125 mL)

Calories	37	Dietary fiber	1.7 g
Protein	1.0 g	Sodium	7.8 mg
Total fat	0.4 g	Calcium	31.1 mg
Saturated fat	0.3 g	Iron	1.1 mg
Carbohydrates	7.2 g	Vitamin C	12.1 mg

The Nose Knows

In my part of the word, the beautiful robust local strawberries that appear at the markets are one of the first signs that summer is well and truly here. Unlike their impostor cousins (out-of-season strawberries imported from elsewhere), these berries are sweet, with a strong "nose" — a term you might have heard someone use when describing the aroma, or bouquet, of a fine wine. I think it also works for fruit.

In the absence of taste, the next best barometer is the nose of foods: literally, their smell. I can be found smelling fruits and vegetables, fish and even meats while I'm shopping. In most cases, the nose knows best.

Orange Yogurt Smoothie

My inspiration for this smoothie is one of my childhood loves, an orange cream frozen dessert. I'm sure this will become a favorite treat in your home!

Chef Jordan's Tip

Although I suggest making this smoothie using orange segments, I actually prefer the more labor-intensive version using "supremes." Just remove the peel, pith and membrane of a citrus fruit and separate its wedges. Supremes are much more delicate and yield a smoother texture.

Jill's Nutrition Tip

We tend to think of cinnamon as a treat — a delicious undercurrent of flavor, usually in sweet dishes. But cinnamon is currently one of the spices most actively studied by researchers. Among its many benefits, cinnamon appears to be a potent bacteria fighter and is even showing promise in battling antibiotic-resistant bacteria. Including small amounts of cinnamon in your baby's diet may help to keep him in optimal health.

- Blender

2 cups	orange segments (see Tips, left)	500 mL
1 cup	filtered water	250 mL
1 cup	Jill's Homemade Yogurt (page 90)	250 mL
1 cup	ice	250 mL
¼ tsp	ground cinnamon	1 mL

1. In blender, combine oranges, water, yogurt, ice and cinnamon and purée until smooth. Serve immediately.

NUTRIENTS PER SERVING (¼ cup/60 mL)

Calories	16.1	Dietary fiber	0.4 g
Protein	0.6 g	Sodium	6.2 mg
Total fat	0.4 g	Calcium	21.0 mg
Saturated fat	0.3 g	Iron	0.0 mg
Carbohydrates	2.7 g	Vitamin C	9.6 mg

Pineapple Yogurt Smoothie

Here's a tropical-flavored treat that can be enjoyed all year long. You will become quite good at making this recipe — your children will see to that. They will request it time and time again.

● ●

**Makes about
5 cups (1.25 L)**

Chef Jordan's Tips

I prefer to use alcohol-free organic vanilla extract. You cannot beat the flavor. However, be aware that some alcohol-free vanilla extract may contain unwanted additives. Read the label carefully.

If you can't find fresh pineapple, substitute an equal quantity of drained canned pineapple (packed in water).

Jill's Nutrition Tips

You can't go wrong adding pineapple to your baby's diet. For starters, it is an excellent source of manganese, which helps your baby to build strong bones. This fruit also provides an enzyme called bromelain that helps with digestion.

The nutrient analysis for most smoothie recipes was done on a very small quantity because we assumed your baby would be consuming a small amount with other foods. Feel free to serve more, as a stand-alone snack.

● **Blender**

2 cups	diced pineapple	500 mL
1 cup	filtered water	250 mL
1 cup	Jill's Homemade Yogurt (page 90)	250 mL
1 cup	ice	250 mL
½ tsp	pure vanilla extract	2 mL

1. In blender, combine pineapple, water, yogurt, ice and vanilla and purée until smooth. Serve immediately.

NUTRIENTS PER SERVING (¼ cup/60 mL)

Calories 15.8	Dietary fiber . . . . .0.2 g
Protein . . . . .0.5 g	Sodium . . . . .6.4 mg
Total fat . . . . 0.4 g	Calcium . . . . 16.0 mg
Saturated fat . . . . .0.3 g	Iron . . . . 0.1 mg
Carbohydrates . . . . . . .2.8 g	Vitamin C . . . . 7.9 mg

Frozen Blueberry Sorbet

Puréed frozen blueberries, with the addition of maple syrup, taste like sorbet. You can serve this to your children instead of ice cream — you'll actually get away with it! Not only do blueberries qualify as a superfood, maple syrup also contains minerals such as zinc and manganese that have many health benefits.

Makes about 2 cups (500 mL)

Chef Jordan's Tip

Double the quantity of frozen berries and keep half on hand for snacks.

Our family loves to eat frozen blueberries alone or added to morning cereal.

Jill's Nutrition Tip

Blueberries are called a superfood because they contain more antioxidants than virtually any other fruit or vegetable. If possible, feed them to your baby (and eat them yourself!) every day. Their high antioxidant level helps support your baby's immune system and, over time, reduces the risk of cancer and degenerative disease. Animal studies published in the *American Journal of Clinical Nutrition* in 2005 suggest that blueberries encourage the brain to grow new cells and to communicate better with the ones it already has. Brain food never tasted so good!

Always buy wild or organic blueberries.

- Baking sheet lined with parchment paper
- Blender

2 cups	organic or wild blueberries	500 mL
¼ cup	pure maple syrup	60 mL

1. Using a colander, gently rinse berries under cold running water. Drain well and transfer to paper towels to dry thoroughly.

2. Spread berries in a single layer on prepared baking sheet and place sheet in the freezer. Freeze until berries are completely frozen, about 5 hours.

3. Transfer half of the frozen berries to blender. Add half of the maple syrup and purée. Transfer to an airtight container. Repeat with remaining berries and maple syrup. Cover container and freeze for about 4 hours, until firm.

4. Before serving, remove sorbet from freezer. Scrape with the tines of a fork to loosen mixture, or transfer to blender and purée. Enjoy immediately or freeze for up to 6 months.

NUTRIENTS PER SERVING (¼ cup/60 mL)

Calories	51	Dietary fiber	1.1 g
Protein	0.4 g	Sodium	3.2 mg
Total fat	0.4 g	Calcium	16.3 mg
Saturated fat	0.0 g	Iron	0.2 mg
Carbohydrates	11.5 g	Vitamin C	6.9 mg

Better Than White Sugar

It can be tempting to focus on the apparent health benefits of "whole" sweeteners. This ignores the significant fact that they are all sugar. Despite their various nutrient components, they must be treated with caution. The authors of the maple syrup study mentioned below recognized this. They nicely summed up the benefit of using a whole-food sweetener by saying that "it is the complexity of the mixture rather than any one component that may serve to counter the unhealthful presence of the high concentrations of sugars in the syrup."

Raw Cane Sugar
When making desserts, we often like to use raw cane sugar, which is not as processed as granulated white sugar and retains some of the nutrients found in sugar cane. It is available in a number of forms such as Demerara, turbinado and muscovado, which vary in texture and flavor depending on the molasses content. Molasses contains some vitamins and more significant amounts of several minerals, including calcium, magnesium, potassium and iron.

Coconut Sugar
One of the newest members of the sugar family is coconut sugar. It is made from the sap of the coconut palm, which is boiled until the liquid evaporates and sugar crystals are left. Coconut sugar seems to contain some of the same minerals as maple syrup and molasses (magnesium, zinc, manganese and potassium), but there is not yet any official (USDA) data on this sweetener. Coconut sugar has gained a lot of attention because of claims that is has a lower glycemic index than regular table sugar. This would be due to the fiber it contains, called inulin, which may slow the sugar's absorption into the body's cells.

Maple Syrup
Pure maple syrup is another popular sweetener, but make sure to purchase real maple syrup and not maple-flavored syrup. There are two grades of maple syrup: grade A (broken down further into light amber, medium amber and dark amber) and grade B (the darkest). The darker syrups come from sap that has been extracted from the trees later in the harvesting season; they have a stronger maple flavor. Maple syrup contains a respectable amount of some minerals, especially zinc and manganese. According to a study published in 2011 in the *Journal of Functional Foods*, it also contains a novel compound, quebecol, as well as 23 other phenolic compounds with well-established antioxidant activity.

Frozen Strawberries and Coconut Cream

The contrast of textures — cold, hard strawberries and pillow-like whipped cream — make this a favorite anytime, but particularly on a warm summer day. Whipped cream is a delightful treat. Your baby needs a higher-fat diet for proper brain development, and this fits in perfectly.

**Makes
4 to 6 servings**

Chef Jordan's Tip

When freezing fruit, it's important not to stack it — you're looking for individually frozen pieces. To prevent pieces from sticking together or to the parchment paper, shake the baking sheet often while the berries are freezing.

Jill's Nutrition Tip

Strawberries are one of the foods most commonly associated with allergies, so introduce them at a meal when you are not introducing any other new foods. This way you will be able to tell if an adverse reaction is to the strawberries as opposed to any other new food. It used to be recommended that you wait until after the first year to introduce strawberries, but there is no evidence to suggest that is beneficial. Please see our section on allergies (page 25).

Always buy organic strawberries.

- Baking sheet lined with parchment paper

3 cups	hulled organic strawberries	750 mL
1 cup	heavy or whipping (35%) cream	250 mL
1 tbsp	unsweetened shredded coconut, toasted	15 mL

1. Using a colander, gently rinse berries under cold running water. Drain well and transfer to paper towels to dry.

2. Cut strawberries into quarters. Spread berries in a single layer on prepared baking sheet and place sheet in the freezer. Freeze until berries are completely frozen, about 5 hours. Transfer to an airtight container and freeze for up to 6 months.

3. In a bowl, whisk cream until stiff peaks form. (You can also do this using an electric mixer.) Add coconut and whisk until fully combined. The cream can be refrigerated for up to 24 hours.

4. Serve the strawberries and cream separately, with the cream as a dip.

NUTRIENTS PER SERVING

Calories	248	Dietary fiber	2.4 g
Protein	2.0 g	Sodium	24.1 mg
Total fat	23.1 g	Calcium	56.2 mg
Saturated fat	14.4 g	Iron	0.5 mg
Carbohydrates	10.2 g	Vitamin C	63.9 mg

My Mom's Applesauce

Applesauce is a nutritious treat that everyone loves. It's also the perfect baby food. This is a particularly delicious version that I have made in every kitchen I have ever worked in.

Makes about 3 cups (750 mL)

Chef Jordan's Tip

I prefer to use a food mill when making applesauce because it breaks down the skins, creating a wonderful texture that is difficult to achieve using a food processor.

Jill's Nutrition Tip

The pectin in apples helps keep your baby's bowels working well and is beneficial for her blood sugar level. Apples are also chock-full of immune-boosting vitamin C. Make sure you wash them well and leave the skins on, because the anti-inflammatory compound quercetin is found only in the apple skin.

Always buy organic apples and nectarines.

- Food mill or food processor

7 cups	chopped cored organic apples	1.75 L
2	nectarines, pitted and chopped	2
½ cup	freshly squeezed grapefruit juice	125 mL
½ cup	raw cane or coconut sugar	125 mL
1	2-inch (5 cm) stick cinnamon	1

1. In a saucepan, combine apples, nectarines, grapefruit juice, sugar and cinnamon. Bring to a boil over medium-low heat. Reduce heat to low and simmer, stirring occasionally, until apples are soft, about 1½ hours. Discard cinnamon stick.

2. Transfer to food mill (see Tips, left) or food processor and process to desired consistency. Let cool to room temperature before serving or transfer to an airtight container and refrigerate for up to 3 days or freeze up to 6 months.

Variation

If you have leftover figs, dates or even bananas and plums, this recipe is a great opportunity to use them up. Simply substitute an equal quantity for the nectarines.

NUTRIENTS PER SERVING (½ cup/125 mL)

Calories	185	Dietary fiber	3.9 g
Protein	1.0 g	Sodium	19.8 mg
Total fat	1.4 g	Calcium	13.3 mg
Saturated fat	0.2 g	Iron	1.4 mg
Carbohydrates	43.9 g	Vitamin C	8.9 mg

Frozen Mango Mousse

A cross between sorbet and granita (a granular Italian frozen ice dessert), this delicious dessert is good for your baby, too.

• •

¼ cup	pasteurized egg whites (see Tips, left)	60 mL
1 tsp	coconut sugar	5 mL
1¾ cups	Mango Purée (page 41)	425 mL
1 tsp	liquid honey	5 mL

Makes about 2 cups (500 mL)

Chef Jordan's Tips

We recommend the use of pasteurized egg whites rather than raw egg whites in an uncooked dish because of the possibility of salmonella.

Since this recipe contains honey, serve it only to babies aged 12 months or more.

Jill's Nutrition Tip

Along with its tropical cousins papayas and pineapples, mangos contain a group of enzymes that help digestion. Some of these are called proteolytic enzymes, which means they break down proteins. The presence of these powerful enzymes explains why mangos are often used in meat tenderizer in the countries where they grow.

1. In a bowl, vigorously whisk together egg whites and sugar until stiff peaks form.

2. In a freezer-safe bowl, combine mango purée and honey. Fold stiff egg whites into mango mixture until well combined.

3. Cover and freeze for at least 4 hours, removing 5 or 6 times to scrape mixture with the tines of a fork to create little "pebbles." Serve or cover tightly and freeze for up to 1 month. Let stand at room temperature for about 10 minutes before serving.

NUTRIENTS PER SERVING (¼ cup/60 mL)

Calories 26		Dietary fiber . . . . 0.3 g	
Protein . . . . 0.9 g		Sodium . . . . 14.8 mg	
Total fat . . . . 0.1 g		Calcium . . . . 1.5 mg	
Saturated fat . . . . 0.0 g		Iron . . . . 0.0 mg	
Carbohydrates . . . . 5.4 g		Vitamin C . . . . 2.3 mg	

Chocolate Macaroons

I prefer my macaroons on the smallish side, almost one-biters. When a recipe is this easy, can you really justify eating store-bought macaroons?

Makes about 18 macaroons

Chef Jordan's Tip

Whisking egg whites to "stiff peaks" means to whip them until they resemble a mountain range: stiff, with zero movement.

Jill's Nutrition Tip

When it comes to chocolate, from a health perspective the best choice is high-quality plain dark chocolate. The more the chocolate is processed, the more its polyphenols are lost. These polyphenols are potent antioxidants that help the body's cells resist damage. Dark chocolate retains much more of this antioxidant capability than milk chocolate does, plus it generally contains less sugar and butterfat. To reap the health benefits of chocolate, look for the first ingredient to be "cacao" or "cocoa" or for the chocolate bar to contain at least 70 percent cocoa solids. Even though this recipe calls for milk or semisweet chocolate, you can experiment by adding some dark chocolate chips, knowing that the macaroons will still taste great!

- 2 nonstick baking sheets
- Preheat oven to 350°F (180°C)

2	egg whites	2
2 tsp	coconut sugar	10 mL
1 cup	unsweetened shredded coconut	250 mL
½ cup	milk or semisweet chocolate chips	125 mL

1. In a bowl, whisk together egg whites and sugar until stiff peaks form (see Tips, left). Fold in coconut and chocolate chips.
2. By tablespoonfuls (15 mL), drop mixture onto baking sheets, spacing 2 inches (5 cm) apart.
3. Bake in preheated oven until golden brown, about 10 minutes. Transfer to a wire rack and let cool to room temperature before serving. Store in an airtight container at room temperature for up to 5 days.

NUTRIENTS PER SERVING (1 macaroon)

Calories	124.8	Dietary fiber	2.6 g
Protein	11.7 g	Sodium	10.9 mg
Total fat	11.1 g	Calcium	0.7 mg
Saturated fat	9.0 g	Iron	0.01 mg
Carbohydrates	7.0 g	Vitamin C	0.2 mg

Maple Syrup–Glazed Pineapple

This is the "northern" way of eating pineapple, coated with maple syrup and served while it's snowing outside. But it's so good you can enjoy it any time of the year. It used to be that foods like pineapple weren't introduced to babies until after the 12-month mark, but there is no reason to wait. Sometimes babies can get a bit of a rash from acidic foods, so if you know your baby is susceptible, start with small amounts.

**Makes about
2 cups (500 mL)**

Chef Jordan's Tips

Feel free to grill the pineapple slices on the barbecue prior to dicing. This adds a wonderful smoky dimension to the dessert.

If time is your enemy, by all means purchase a pineapple that has been peeled and cored and stored in its own juices. I do, however, recommend that you scrutinize the label to verify its freshness.

Jill's Nutrition Tip

Not only does pure maple syrup taste wonderful, it also provides the minerals manganese and zinc. Manganese is important for diminishing the harmful effects of free radicals in the body's cells, and zinc provides a nice boost for the immune system.

2 tbsp	organic unsalted butter	30 mL
2½ cups	diced pineapple	625 mL
1 tbsp	pure maple syrup	15 mL

1. In a saucepan, melt butter over medium heat. Add pineapple and cook, without stirring, until all liquid from the pineapple has evaporated and the chunks begin to caramelize, about 8 minutes. Stir in maple syrup, reduce heat to low and cook until pineapple is fully coated, about 1 minute. Cut up or mash to desired consistency. Let cool to room temperature before serving or transfer to an airtight container and refrigerate for up to 3 days.

NUTRIENTS PER SERVING (¼ cup/60 mL)

Calories	56	Dietary fiber	0.7 g
Protein	0.3 g	Sodium	1.1 mg
Total fat	2.9 g	Calcium	9.2 mg
Saturated fat	1.8 g	Iron	0.2 mg
Carbohydrates	8.1 g	Vitamin C	18.5 mg

Pomegranate and Kiwi Purée

The velvety texture of this recipe resembles a mousse or a pudding — either way, it's a hit!

**Makes about
1¾ cups (425 mL)**

Chef Jordan's Tips

You can use prepared pomegranate juice in this recipe so long as it is unsweetened, or you can make your own by pressing the seeds of a fresh pomegranate through a fine-mesh sieve. Discard the seeds and use the juicy pulp in this recipe.

I prefer to whip the cream at the last moment because it tends to deflate rather quickly.

Crème fraîche is available in specialty food shops. If you can't find it, an equal amount of sour cream works well, too.

Jill's Nutrition Tip

Move over, oranges — here comes the kiwifruit. Ounce for ounce, the kiwi contains more vitamin C than oranges, which have been a traditional source of this nutrient. The combination of the strong antioxidant properties of vitamin C and the polyphenols found in kiwis may be helpful in reducing respiratory-related issues in children, such as wheezing and night coughing.

- Blender

½ cup	unsweetened pomegranate juice (see Tips, left)	125 mL
1 cup	chopped peeled kiwifruit	250 mL
½ cup	pure maple syrup	125 mL
½ cup	organic crème fraîche or sour cream	125 mL
½ cup	organic heavy or whipping (35%) cream, whipped	125 mL

1. In blender, combine pomegranate juice, kiwi and syrup and purée until smooth. Transfer to a fine-mesh sieve set over a bowl and strain, allowing the juice to flow naturally; reserve solids. Fold crème fraîche and whipped cream into juice.

2. Transfer reserved solids to a saucepan and bring to a boil over medium heat. Cook until reduced by three-quarters, about 5 minutes. Set aside to cool until warm to the touch.

3. To serve, drizzle some of the reduction overtop of the mousse. Serve immediately.

NUTRIENTS PER SERVING (¼ cup/60 mL)

Calories	155	Dietary fiber	0.8 g
Protein	1.1 g	Sodium	14.3 mg
Total fat	6.4 g	Calcium	45.6 mg
Saturated fat	3.8 g	Iron	0.4 mg
Carbohydrates	23.6 g	Vitamin C	24.8 mg

Acknowlegments

Tamar, Jonah and Jamie, you have made me a winner at the game of life. I love you. Today, tomorrow and forever.

— Jordan Wagman

I'd like to thank my co-author, Chef Jordan Wagman, for asking me to contribute to this book. Helping parents start their children off with the best possible nutrition is close to my heart and I am delighted to have been a part of this book.

Many thanks to everyone at PageWave Graphics who worked on the design and styling of this book, especially Joseph Gisini. I'd also like to thank copy editor Tracy Bordian, recipe editor and tester Jennifer MacKenzie, photographer Colin Erricson, prop stylist Charlene Erricson, food stylist Kathryn Robertson, and Marian Jarkovich and Martine Quibell at Robert Rose for their publicity and marketing expertise.

Special thanks to Judith Finlayson for her gentle editorial guidance and to Bob Dees at Robert Rose for his vision and commitment to bringing this book to market.

Thanks also to Joey Shulman for her ongoing support and to Julia Rickert for her assistance and friendship.

Many thanks to Dr. Piché and Kim Zammit for their work on the nutrient analyses and for their patience as we tweaked recipes.

A final thank-you to my parents for starting me on the right nutritional path; to Stewart and Duncan for always agreeing to eat anything I put in front of them; and finally to Bob for his constant and profound support.

— Jill Hillhouse

Nutrient Analysis

The nutrient analyses for most of the recipes in this book were prepared by Kimberly Zammit in conjunction with Professor Leonard Piché, Ph.D., R.D., both of Brescia University College, University of Western Ontario, London, Ontario. These analyses were performed with the Food Processor SQL, version 10.1, from ESHA Research, Inc., Salem, Oregon. Additional nutritional analyses were prepared by Jill Hillhouse using the United States Department of Agriculture National Nutrient Database for Standard Reference, release 27.

The nutrient analyses were based on:

- imperial measures and weights
- the first ingredient listed when there was a choice
- the exclusion of "optional" ingredients
- the exclusion of ingredients with "non-specified" or "to taste" amounts

Library and Archives Canada Cataloguing in Publication

Wagman, Jordan, author
    The best baby food : 125 healthy & delicious recipes for babies & toddlers /
Jordan Wagman & Jill Hillhouse, BPHE, CNP.

Includes index.
ISBN 978-0-7788-0507-6 (pbk.)

    1. Baby foods. 2. Infants—Nutrition. 3. Cookbooks. I. Hillhouse, Jill, author II. Title.

RJ216.W34 2015   641.5'6222   C2015-900821-2

Index

A

Acorn Squash Purée, 46
ADHD, 22, 156
allergies, 25–26, 57, 148, 155
allium (onion) family, 99
alpha-linolenic acid (ALA), 21
amino acids, 52, 82, 149, 175
antibiotics
  for children, 93
  in foods, 14–15, 16
apples, 127, 187, 209
  Apple, Avocado and Grape
    Smoothie, 197
  Apple, Pear and Avocado
    Purée, 78
  Apple and Fig Brown Rice
    Cereal, 59
  Apple and Strawberry
    Compote, 129
  Apple Medley, 37
  Apple Pie Ice Pops, 187
  Applesauce, My Mom's, 209
  Chicken with Caramelized
    Apples, 172
  Millet with Cheddar Cheese
    and Apple, 159
  Red Cabbage, Fennel and
    Apple Purée, 108
  Red Lentil and Apple Purée,
    73
  Roasted Apple, Blueberry
    and Pear Purée, 61
  Roasted Summer Fruit
    (variation), 132
  Sautéed Chard with Apples,
    115
  Strawberries with Apple,
    127
applesauce, 12, 209
apricots, 10, 39, 119
  Apricot and Acorn Squash
    Purée, 63
  Beef and Dates (variation),
    122
  Fresh Apricot Purée, 39

  Oven-Roasted Chicken with
    Apricots, 119
Artichokes, Oven-Roasted,
  135
asparagus, 137, 249
  Asparagus and Roasted
    Tomato Purée, 136
  Asparagus Basil Soup, 149
  Grilled Asparagus with
    Three Cheeses, 142
  Halibut in a Wrapper, 164
avocado, 78, 83, 194
  Apple, Avocado and Grape
    Smoothie, 197
  Apple, Pear and Avocado
    Purée, 78
  Avocado, Carrot and
    Cucumber Purée, 76
  Grilled Chicken and
    Avocado Purée, 83
  Guacamole, 194

B

baby-feeders, 89
baby food, 9. *See also* foods
  for babies 6 to 9 months, 27,
    34–84
  for babies 9 to 12 months,
    87–123
  for toddlers, 125–74
  equipment for, 29, 31
  preparing, 29–30, 31, 73
  processed, 10
  storing and freezing, 30–31
bacon, 105
  Brussels Sprouts with Bacon,
    105
  Corn and Chickpea
    Chowder, 147
  Oven-Roasted Artichokes,
    135
bacteria
  allium family and, 99, 109
  chlorine and, 26
  cleanliness and, 29, 30, 31
  drug-resistant, 15

  healthy (intestinal), 26, 93,
    142, 147, 182
  herbs and, 65, 113
  protective foods, 67, 134,
    163, 204
  in raw foods, 19, 75
bananas, 36
  Applesauce, My Mom's
    (variation), 209
  Banana and Blueberry
    Purée, 71
  Blueberry Banana Smoothie,
    196
  Millet Cereal with Bananas
    and Sour Cream, 101
  Oat Crêpes with Warm
    Bananas, 163
  Quinoa and Banana Purée, 57
  Roasted Banana Lassi, 201
  Roasted Banana Purée, 36
  Tofu, Pear and Banana
    Purée, 60
Basic Quinoa, 52
basil, 65, 113. *See also* herbs
  Asparagus and Roasted
    Tomato Purée, 136
  Asparagus Basil Soup, 149
  Citrus Fruit Salad with
    Fresh Basil, 131
  Colorful Vegetable Medley,
    114
  Eggplant Parmesan, The
    Best, 95
  Green Bean Purée with
    Fresh Basil, 65
  Mediterranean Fried
    Eggplant, 97
  Oven-Roasted Cherry
    Tomato Purée, 106
  Oven-Roasted Red Peppers,
    182
  Peach, Chive and Basil
    Purée, 77
  Savory Rice Pudding with
    Basil, 160
  Zucchini and Basil Purée, 68

beans, 85, 117
Edamame Hummus, 118
Green Bean Purée with
Fresh Basil, 65
White Bean and Fennel
Purée, 116
White Navy Bean and Beef
Purée, 84
beef. *See also* meat
Beef and Dates, 122
Beef Stew, 170
White Navy Bean and Beef
Purée, 84
beets, 50, 199
Beet Strawberry Smoothie,
199
Roasted Beet Purée, 50
berries, 30. *See also specific types
of berries*
Lamb with Parsnips and
Cranberries, 123
Roasted Summer Fruit, 132
Roasted Summer Fruit
Smoothie, 202
Very Berry Ice Pops, 189
The Best Eggplant Parmesan,
95
Best-Ever Salmon Cakes, 166
beta-carotene, 41, 45, 46, 72.
See also vitamin A
beverages, 73, 89. *See also*
smoothies
blood sugar, 54, 59, 113, 187
blueberries, 40, 67, 206. *See
also* berries
Banana and Blueberry
Purée, 71
Blueberry Banana Smoothie,
196
Blueberry Purée, 40
Date and Blueberry Purée,
79
Frozen Blueberry Sorbet,
206
Honeydew, Blueberry and
Mint Purée, 66
Plum and Blueberry Purée,
67
Roasted Apple, Blueberry
and Pear Purée, 61

Watermelon, Peach and
Blueberry Purée, 74
Bok Choy with Ginger, 104
Bone Broth, 153
bottle feeding, 10, 21, 34. *See
also* formula
brassica (cruciferous)
vegetables, 96, 108, 145.
See also specific vegetables
breastfeeding, 21, 27, 34. *See
also* breast milk
breast milk, 20, 21, 35, 106,
155, 172
broccoli, 42
Broccoli, Potato and Spinach
Pie, 141
Broccoli Purée, 42
Soft Polenta with Cheddar
Cheese and Broccoli, 161
bromelain, 130
Brown Rice Cereal, 54
Brussels sprouts, 96
Brussels Sprout Gratin, 96
Brussels Sprouts with Bacon,
105
butter, 139, 172
butyric acid, 172

C

cabbage
Oven-Roasted Duck with
Red Cabbage, 173
Pork with Red Cabbage, 171
Red Cabbage, Fennel and
Apple Purée, 108
calcium, 141, 192
cane sugar, 207
Caper and Lemon Remoulade,
169
Caramelized Parsnip Purée, 51
carbohydrates (complex), 47,
70
carotenoids, 19, 72, 194. *See
also* beta-carotene; lutein;
lycopene
carrots, 48
Avocado, Carrot and
Cucumber Purée, 76
Carrot and Split Pea Purée,
72

Carrot and Sweet Potato
Soup, 150
Carrot Purée, 48
Nectarine and Carrot Purée,
62
Potato Salad with Cheddar
Cheese and Boiled Eggs,
143
Quick Mushroom Soup, 146
Roasted Chicken Stock, 152
Vegetable Stock, 154
White Navy Bean and Beef
Purée, 84
cauliflower, 69
Cauliflower and Chickpea
Chowder, 70
Cauliflower and Parsnip
Purée, 69
Millet and Cauliflower with
Fresh Oregano, 158
Oven-Roasted Cauliflower
with Fresh Herbs, 145
Salmon, Potato and
Cauliflower, 168
celery
Roasted Chicken Stock, 152
Vegetable Stock, 154
Celery Root and Chicken
Purée, 80
celiac disease, 24
cereals, 52–58, 100–101
Chard, Sautéed, with Apples,
115
cheese, 143. *See also specific types
of cheese (below)*
Grilled Asparagus with
Three Cheeses, 142
Pineapple with Cottage
Cheese, 130
Turkey Meatloaf, Gramma
Jean's, 174
cheese, Cheddar, 161
Cheddar Cheese Dip, 192
Millet with Cheddar Cheese
and Apple, 159
Potato Salad with Cheddar
Cheese and Boiled Eggs,
143
Soft Polenta with Cheddar
Cheese and Broccoli, 161

cheese, goat
  Millet Cereal with Bananas and Sour Cream (tip), 101
  Oven-Roasted Cauliflower with Fresh Herbs (tip), 145
  Plum and Blueberry Purée (tip), 67
cheese, Parmesan, 157
  Broccoli, Potato and Spinach Pie, 141
  Broccoli Purée (variation), 42
  Brussels Sprout Gratin, 96
  Diced Potato Gratin, 98
  Eggplant Parmesan, The Best, 95
  Fish Sticks, World's Best, 169
  "Mac and Cheese", Jonah's, 156
  Mediterranean Fried Eggplant, 97
  Oven-Roasted Artichokes, 135
  Parmesan Cheese Crisps with Plum Salsa, 181
  Pasta with Fresh Herbs and Parmesan Cheese, 157
  Sweet Potato Purée (variation), 44
cherries, 100
  Pork with Red Cabbage, 171
  Summer Cherry Quinoa, 100
chicken, 82, 172. See also poultry
  Celery Root and Chicken Purée, 80
  Chicken and Red Lentil Purée, 82
  Chicken with Caramelized Apples, 172
  Chicken with Roasted Butternut Squash and Leeks, 120
  Grilled Chicken and Avocado Purée, 83
  Onion Soup with Chicken, 151

Oven-Roasted Chicken with Apricots, 119
  Potato, Parsnip and Chicken Soup, 110
  Roasted Chicken Stock, 152
chickpeas, 70, 85
  Cauliflower and Chickpea Chowder, 70
  Corn and Chickpea Chowder, 147
  Edamame Hummus, 118
chives, 77
  Cauliflower and Chickpea Chowder (variation), 70
  Chive Parsley Pesto, 112
  Peach, Chive and Basil Purée, 77
chlorine, 26
chlorogenic acid, 132, 181
chlorophyll, 112
Chocolate Macaroons, 211
cholesterol, 59, 172
chromium, 54
Chunky Pineapple Ice Pops, 184
cinnamon, 113, 187, 204
  Apple Pie Ice Pops, 187
  Applesauce, My Mom's, 209
  Nectarine and Orange Compote, 128
citrus fruits, 131. See also oranges and orange juice
  Applesauce, My Mom's, 209
  Caper and Lemon Remoulade, 169
  Citrus Fruit Salad with Fresh Basil, 131
  Coconut Papaya Ice Pops, 186
"Clean Fifteen", 13
coconut. See also coconut milk
  Chocolate Macaroons, 211
  Frozen Strawberries and Coconut Cream, 208
coconut milk, 134
  Coconut Mango Smoothie, 198
  Coconut Papaya Ice Pops, 186

Papaya and Coconut Milk Purée, 134
coconut sugar, 207
Colorful Vegetable Medley, 114
corn, 17
  Best-Ever Salmon Cakes, 166
  Corn and Chickpea Chowder, 147
cream. See also milk
  Broccoli, Potato and Spinach Pie, 141
  Celery Root and Chicken Purée (variation), 80
  Frozen Strawberries and Coconut Cream, 208
  Pomegranate and Kiwi Purée, 214
Crispy Potato Galette, 140
cross-contamination, 29, 56
cruciferous (brassica) vegetables, 96, 108, 145
Cucumber Purée, Avocado, Carrot and, 76
curcumin, 113
cynarin, 135

D

dairy products, 14–15. See also specific dairy products
dates, 79, 122
  Applesauce, My Mom's (variation), 209
  Beef and Dates, 122
  Date and Blueberry Purée, 79
desserts, 206–14. See also fruit; snacks
DHA (docosahexaenoic acid), 21, 168
Diced Potato Gratin, 98
dips, 70, 72, 76, 116, 183, 192, 194
"Dirty Dozen", 12, 13
drinks, 73, 89. See also smoothies
Duck, Oven-Roasted, with Red Cabbage, 173

E

edamame, 20, 60
  Edamame Hummus, 118
eggplant, 97
  The Best Eggplant
    Parmesan, 95
  Colorful Vegetable Medley,
    114
  Mediterranean Fried
    Eggplant, 97
eggs, 14–15, 25, 89, 143
  Chocolate Macaroons, 211
  Egg and Sweet Pepper Fried
    Rice, 102
  Oat Crêpes with Warm
    Bananas, 163
  Potato Salad with Cheddar
    Cheese and Boiled Eggs,
    143
ellagic acid, 132
enzymes, 130, 210
EPA (eicosapentaenoic acid),
  21
essential fatty acids, 21–22,
  123, 168, 193
eye health, 48, 119, 194, 200

F

fats, 20–22, 83, 193
  butter, 139, 172
  essential fatty acids, 21–22,
    123, 168, 193
  oils, 17, 139, 202
fennel
  Fennel and Orange Sauté,
    138
  Halibut in a Wrapper, 164
  Red Cabbage, Fennel and
    Apple Purée, 108
  White Bean and Fennel
    Purée, 116
fiber, 37, 44, 109, 162. See also
  grains; legumes
figs, 58
  Apple and Fig Brown Rice
    Cereal, 58
  Applesauce, My Mom's
    (variation), 209
finger foods, 88–89, 126

fish, 22–23
  Halibut in a Wrapper, 164
  Salmon, Potato and
    Cauliflower, 168
  Salmon Cakes, Best-Ever,
    166
  World's Best Fish Sticks, 169
flavonoids, 98, 100. See also
  quercetin; resveratrol
flours (gluten-free), 55
  Fish Sticks, World's Best,
    169
  Mini Sweet Potato Muffins,
    190
  Oat Crêpes with Warm
    Bananas, 163
  Sour Cream "Latkes", 179
folate (folic acid), 68, 146
foods. See also baby food
  antibiotics in, 14–15
  freezing and thawing, 30–31
  introducing, 25, 26, 27,
    34–35, 88–89, 126
  label information, 15, 17
  organic, 11–14, 16, 91
  raw, 19, 75
  shopping for, 165, 202
  washing, 30, 138
formula, 10, 21, 34. See also
  breast milk
Fresh Apricot Purée, 39
Fresh Soybean Hummus, 118
Frozen Blueberry Sorbet, 206
Frozen Grape Snacks, 180
Frozen Mango Mousse, 210
Frozen Strawberries and
  Coconut Cream, 208
fruit, 11–14. See also berries;
  citrus fruits; specific fruits
  pesticides in, 11, 12–13
  washing, 30, 138

G

gai-lan (Chinese broccoli),
  104
garlic, 99
  Chive Parsley Pesto, 112
  Edamame Hummus, 118
  Oven-Roasted Artichokes,
    135

  Poached Garlic with Thyme
    and Sour Cream, 99
  Potato, Parsnip and Chicken
    Soup, 110
  Quick Mushroom Soup, 146
  Vegetable Stock, 154
ginger, 104, 113
  Bok Choy with Ginger, 104
  Egg and Sweet Pepper Fried
    Rice, 102
  Papaya and Coconut Milk
    Purée, 134
gluten, 24. See also flours
  sensitivity to, 24, 156
glycemic index, 157
GMOs (genetically modified
  organisms), 16–17
grains, 24, 59. See also gluten;
  specific grains
  washing, 30
  whole, 59, 159, 163, 179
Gramma Jean's Turkey
  Meatloaf, 174
grapefruit and grapefruit juice
  Applesauce, My Mom's, 209
  Citrus Fruit Salad with
    Fresh Basil, 131
grapes
  Apple, Avocado and Grape
    Smoothie, 197
  Frozen Grape Snacks, 180
  Whole-Grain Oat Cereal
    with Grapes, 56
Green Bean Purée with Fresh
  Basil, 65
Grilled Asparagus with Three
  Cheeses, 142
Grilled Chicken and Avocado
  Purée, 83
growth hormone, 15
Guacamole, 194

H

Halibut in a Wrapper, 164
herbs, 113, 130. See also specific
  herbs
  Oven-Roasted Cauliflower
    with Fresh Herbs, 145
  Pasta with Fresh Herbs and
    Parmesan Cheese, 157

Pineapple with Cottage Cheese, 130
Roasted Chicken Stock, 152
Turkey Meatloaf, Gramma Jean's, 174
histamine, 148
Honeydew, Blueberry and Mint Purée, 66
hormones, 15
Hummus, Edamame, 118
hyaluronic acid, 131

I

ice pops, 184–89
inulin, 142
iron, 23, 35, 60, 79, 155

J

Jasmine Rice with Butternut Squash and Saffron, 162
Jill's Homemade Yogurt, 90
Jonah's "Mac and Cheese", 156

K

Kiwi Purée, Pomegranate and, 214
kukoamine, 98

L

lamb, 81, 123. *See also* meat
Lamb with Parsnips and Cranberries, 123
Sweet Pea, Lamb and Parsnip Purée, 81
lauric acid, 134, 172
leeks, 94
Chicken with Roasted Butternut Squash and Leeks, 120
Stewed Leeks with Butter, 94
legumes, 116, 117. *See also* beans; lentils; peas
lentils, 155
Chicken and Red Lentil Purée, 82
Red Lentil and Apple Purée, 73
linoleic acid, 22
liver health, 50

lutein, 119, 194
lycopene, 74, 106

M

"Mac and Cheese", Jonah's, 156
magnesium, 159, 165
manganese, 101, 212
mangos, 41, 185
Coconut Mango Smoothie, 198
Frozen Mango Mousse, 210
Mango Lassi, 200
Mango Mint Ice Pops, 185
Mango Purée, 41
maple syrup, 207, 212
Citrus Fruit Salad with Fresh Basil, 131
Frozen Blueberry Sorbet, 206
Maple Syrup–Glazed Pineapple, 212
Mini Sweet Potato Muffins, 190
Pomegranate and Kiwi Purée, 214
mealtimes, 7, 27, 129
meat, 14–16, 105. *See also specific types of meat*
Mediterranean Fried Eggplant, 97
melatonin, 175
melon
Honeydew, Blueberry and Mint Purée, 66
Watermelon, Peach and Blueberry Purée, 74
methionine, 82
milk, 91. *See also* cream
Celery Root and Chicken Purée (variation), 80
Cheddar Cheese Dip, 192
Diced Potato Gratin, 98
Homemade Yogurt, Jill's, 90
Oat Crêpes with Warm Bananas, 163
Quick Mushroom Soup, 146
Savory Rice Pudding with Basil, 160
millet, 53, 101. *See also* millet flour

Millet and Cauliflower with Fresh Oregano, 158
Millet with Cheddar Cheese and Apple, 159
millet flour, 55
Millet Cereal with Bananas and Sour Cream, 101
Simple Millet Cereal, 53
Mini Sweet Potato Muffins, 190
mint, 66, 113, 201
Avocado, Carrot and Cucumber Purée, 76
Cauliflower and Chickpea Chowder, 70
Honeydew, Blueberry and Mint Purée, 66
Mango Mint Ice Pops, 185
Roasted Banana Lassi, 201
Roasted Summer Fruit Smoothie, 202
molasses, 207
mushrooms, 146
Quick Mushroom Soup, 146
Turkey Meatloaf, Gramma Jean's, 174
My Mom's Applesauce, 209

N

nectarines, 62
Applesauce, My Mom's, 209
Nectarine and Carrot Purée, 62
Nectarine and Orange Compote, 128
neochlorogenic acid, 181
nitrates, 105
noodles. *See* pasta
nutrient density, 9
nutrients. *See also specific nutrients*
in raw food, 19
in vegetarian diet, 27
nuts and seeds, 155

O

oat flour, 55
Whole-Grain Oat Cereal with Grapes, 56

oats, 56
Oat Crêpes with Warm Bananas, 163
oils, 17, 139, 202
omega-3 fats, 21–22, 123, 168, 193
omega-6 fats, 22, 193
onions, 109
Colorful Vegetable Medley, 114
Egg and Sweet Pepper Fried Rice, 102
Onion Soup with Chicken, 151
Pork with Peaches, 121
Quick Mushroom Soup, 146
Roasted Chicken Stock, 152
Roasted Sweet Onion Purée, 109
Sautéed Chard with Apples, 115
Vegetable Stock, 154
oranges and orange juice, 138
Citrus Fruit Salad with Fresh Basil, 131
Fennel and Orange Sauté, 138
Nectarine and Orange Compote, 128
Orange Yogurt Smoothie, 204
oregano, 113, 158
Millet and Cauliflower with Fresh Oregano, 158
organic foods, 11–14, 16
nutrition content, 14, 91
pesticides in, 11

P

papaya, 186
Coconut Papaya Ice Pops, 186
Papaya and Coconut Milk Purée, 134
Parmesan Cheese Crisps with Plum Salsa, 181
parsley, 113. See also herbs
Chive Parsley Pesto, 112
parsnips, 51

Caramelized Parsnip Purée, 51
Cauliflower and Parsnip Purée, 69
Lamb with Parsnips and Cranberries, 123
Potato, Parsnip and Chicken Soup, 110
Roasted Chicken Stock, 152
Sweet Pea, Lamb and Parsnip Purée, 81
Turnip and Parsnip Smash, 107
Vegetable Stock, 154
pasta, 156, 157
"Mac and Cheese," Jonah's, 156
Pasta with Fresh Herbs and Parmesan Cheese, 157
peaches
Beef and Dates (variation), 122
Coconut Mango Smoothie, 198
Peach, Chive and Basil Purée, 77
Pork with Peaches, 121
Roasted Summer Fruit, 132
Roasted Summer Fruit Smoothie, 202
Watermelon, Peach and Blueberry Purée, 74
pears, 38
Apple, Pear and Avocado Purée, 78
Pear Purée, 38
Roasted Apple, Blueberry and Pear Purée, 61
Tofu, Pear and Banana Purée, 60
peas, 47. See also chickpeas
Carrot and Split Pea Purée, 72
Sweet Pea, Lamb and Parsnip Purée, 81
Sweet Pea Purée, 47
peppers (bell), 102, 182, 183
Cheddar Cheese Dip (tip), 192

Colorful Vegetable Medley, 114
Corn and Chickpea Chowder, 147
Egg and Sweet Pepper Fried Rice, 102
Halibut in a Wrapper, 164
Oven-Roasted Red Peppers, 182
Roasted Red Pepper Vinaigrette, 183
Salmon Cakes, Best-Ever, 166
Turkey Meatloaf, Gramma Jean's, 174
pesticides, 10–13
phenylalanine, 82
phosphorus, 80
phytochemicals, 9. See also specific phytonutrients
pineapple, 130, 205
Chunky Pineapple Ice Pops, 184
Maple Syrup–Glazed Pineapple, 212
Pineapple with Cottage Cheese, 130
Pineapple Yogurt Smoothie, 205
pizza, 94
plums, 132, 181
Applesauce, My Mom's (variation), 209
Parmesan Cheese Crisps with Plum Salsa, 181
Plum and Blueberry Purée, 67
Roasted Summer Fruit, 132
Roasted Summer Fruit Smoothie, 202
Polenta, Soft, with Cheddar Cheese and Broccoli, 161
Pomegranate and Kiwi Purée, 214
POPs (persistent organic pollutants), 11
pork, 121. See also bacon; meat
Pork with Peaches, 121
Pork with Red Cabbage, 171
potassium, 136

potatoes, 98, 140
    Broccoli, Potato and Spinach Pie, 141
    Crispy Potato Galette, 140
    Diced Potato Gratin, 98
    Potato, Parsnip and Chicken Soup, 110
    Potato Salad with Cheddar Cheese and Boiled Eggs, 143
    Salmon, Potato and Cauliflower, 168
    Smashed New Potatoes, 139
poultry, 16. *See also* Bone Broth; chicken
    Oven-Roasted Artichokes, 135
    Oven-Roasted Duck with Red Cabbage, 173
    Turkey Meatloaf, Gramma Jean's, 174
prebiotics, 109
proanthocyanidins, 67
probiotics, 93
protein powder, 202
prunes, 181
    Beef and Dates (variation), 122
purées, 35, 88

Q

quercetin, 14, 127, 209
Quick Mushroom Soup, 146
quinoa, 52. *See also* pasta
    Basic Quinoa, 52
    Quinoa and Banana Purée, 57
    Quinoa Minestrone, 148
    Summer Cherry Quinoa, 100
quinoa flour, 55

R

ramps, 94
raspberries, 14. *See also* berries
    Roasted Summer Fruit, 132
    Roasted Summer Fruit Smoothie, 202
Red Cabbage, Fennel and Apple Purée, 108

Red Lentil and Apple Purée, 73
Red Potato Salad with Cheddar Cheese and Boiled Eggs, 143
resveratrol, 132, 180
rice, 160. *See also* rice flour
    Beef Stew, 170
    Egg and Sweet Pepper Fried Rice, 102
    Jasmine Rice with Butternut Squash and Saffron, 162
    Savory Rice Pudding with Basil, 160
rice flour (brown), 55
    Apple and Fig Brown Rice Cereal, 58
    Brown Rice Cereal, 54

S

Saffron, Jasmine Rice with Butternut Squash and, 162
sage, 113
    Quick Mushroom Soup, 146
salicylates, 148
salmon, 166
    Best-Ever Salmon Cakes, 166
    Salmon, Potato and Cauliflower, 168
salt, 154, 169
    vanilla-flavored, 187
saturated fat, 193
Savory Rice Pudding with Basil, 160
seaweed, 117
serotonin, 175
Simple Millet Cereal, 53
Smashed New Potatoes, 139
smoothies, 196–205
snacks, 175, 178–205
sodium, 117. *See also* salt
soups and stocks, 146–54
sour cream
    Cauliflower and Chickpea Chowder (variation), 70
    Cheddar Cheese Dip, 192
    "Mac and Cheese", Jonah's, 156

Millet Cereal with Bananas and Sour Cream, 101
    Poached Garlic with Thyme and Sour Cream, 99
    Pomegranate and Kiwi Purée, 214
    Sour Cream "Latkes", 179
Soybean Hummus, Fresh, 118
soy products, 17, 20, 104, 155. *See also* edamame; tofu
spices, 113. *See also* cinnamon; ginger; turmeric
spinach, 141
    Apple, Avocado and Grape Smoothie, 197
    Broccoli, Potato and Spinach Pie, 141
spreads, 67, 77, 97, 106, 118
squash, 46. *See also* zucchini
    Acorn Squash Purée, 46
    Apricot and Acorn Squash Purée, 63
    Chicken with Roasted Butternut Squash and Leeks, 120
    Jasmine Rice with Butternut Squash and Saffron, 162
    Roasted Sweet Potato Purée (variation), 45
stocks, 152–54
strawberries, 208. *See also* berries
    Apple and Strawberry Compote, 129
    Beet Strawberry Smoothie, 199
    Frozen Strawberries and Coconut Cream, 208
    Roasted Summer Fruit, 132
    Roasted Summer Fruit Smoothie, 202
    Strawberries with Apple, 127
sugars, 17, 207. *See also* maple syrup
sulforaphane, 96, 145
sulfur, 82, 94, 149
Summer Cherry Quinoa, 100
sweeteners, 17, 178, 207
Sweet Pea, Lamb and Parsnip Purée, 81

Sweet Pea Purée, 47
sweet potatoes, 44, 45
    Carrot and Sweet Potato
        Soup, 150
    "Mac and Cheese", Jonah's,
        156
    Mini Sweet Potato Muffins,
        190
    Roasted Sweet Potato Purée,
        45
    Sweet Potato Purée, 44

T

teething-feeders, 89
teething pain, 71
thiamin (vitamin B$_3$), 59, 121
thyme, 113. *See also* herbs
    Beef Stew, 170
    Colorful Vegetable Medley,
        114
    Onion Soup with Chicken,
        151
    Oven-Roasted Artichokes,
        135
    Oven-Roasted Cherry
        Tomato Purée, 106
    Oven-Roasted Duck with
        Red Cabbage, 172
    Oven-Roasted Red Peppers,
        182
    Poached Garlic with Thyme
        and Sour Cream, 99
    Pork with Red Cabbage,
        171
toddlers, 126
Tofu, Pear and Banana Purée,
    60
tomatoes, 148
    Asparagus and Roasted
        Tomato Purée, 136
    Cheddar Cheese Dip (tip),
        192
    Eggplant Parmesan, The
        Best, 95

Guacamole, 194
    Oven-Roasted Cherry
        Tomato Purée, 106
    Quinoa Minestrone,
        148
trans fats, 20–21, 193
tryptophan, 175
turkey
    Oven-Roasted Artichokes,
        135
    Turkey Meatloaf, Gramma
        Jean's, 174
turmeric, 113, 198
    Coconut Mango Smoothie,
        198
    Turnip and Parsnip Smash,
        107

V

vanilla bean
    Apple Pie Ice Pops, 187
    Beet Strawberry Smoothie,
        199
    Mini Sweet Potato Muffins,
        190
    Vanilla Bean Yogurt, 93
vegetables, 11–14. *See also*
    specific vegetables
    pesticides in, 12–13
    skins of, 44
    washing, 30
vegetarian diet, 27, 116, 155
Very Berry Ice Pops, 189
vitamin A, 41, 48, 171. *See also*
    beta-carotene
vitamin B$_1$, 59
vitamin B$_3$ (thiamin), 59,
    121
vitamin B$_6$, 59, 139, 185
vitamin B$_{12}$, 155, 170
vitamin C, 19, 61, 102, 128,
    189
vitamin D, 27, 155, 172
vitamin K, 69

W

water, 26, 189
Watermelon, Peach and
    Blueberry Purée, 74
White Bean and Fennel Purée,
    116
White Navy Bean and Beef
    Purée, 84
Whole-Grain Oat Cereal with
    Grapes, 56
World's Best Fish Sticks, 169

Y

yogurt, 93
    Carrot and Split Pea Purée
        (tip), 72
    Cheddar Cheese Dip, 192
    Homemade Yogurt, Jill's,
        90
    Mango Lassi, 200
    Nectarine and Carrot Purée
        (variation), 62
    Orange Yogurt Smoothie,
        204
    Pineapple Yogurt Smoothie,
        205
    Roasted Apple, Blueberry
        and Pear Purée (variation),
        61
    Roasted Banana Lassi, 201
    Roasted Summer Fruit
        Smoothie, 202
    Vanilla Bean Yogurt, 93

Z

zeaxanthin, 194, 200
zinc, 84, 212
zucchini, 68
    Cheddar Cheese Dip (tip),
        192
    Colorful Vegetable Medley,
        114
    Zucchini and Basil Purée, 68